Journey to Truth

Why Celebrities Convert to Islam

Khalid Al Sayed

Katara
دار كتارا للنشر
Katara Publishing House

Number of Pages: 426 pages Legal Deposit:
2022/901 ISBN: 9789927160233
First Edition: 2022

"Katara" Cultural Village

Building No. 15, P. O. Box: 16214
Telephone: +974-444080045 | Email: info@kataraph.com Doha, Qatar

Executive Editor
Khalid Al Sayed

Coordinating Editor
Hussain Ahmad

Contributing Writers

Fakhriya Muhammad Suleiman
Doha

Roshan M Salih
London

Rob Hyde
Hamburg

Sonya Schoeman
Cape Town

Hanan Al-Nufaie
Doha

Marta Maroto
Madrid

Feyza Gumusluoglu
Istanbul

So Jeong Lee
Seoul

Copy Editor
Dawn Lewis

CONTENTS

A journey into a journey

Recently, a friend told me about a Westerner converting to Islam. Conversion is no unearthly affair that should surprise us. Throughout the history of this religion, its ranks have swelled through conversions in varying degrees. This age is no different; there are often stories of people embracing Islam, and some of them create headlines due to their celebrity status. Social media, especially YouTube, has a steady stream of videos of people narrating their stories of conversion or reversion, depending on how we choose to describe it, and platforms like Twitter are home to people announcing their conversions.

But said conversion, I was told, was triggered by the person listening to *adhan,* the call to prayer from mosques, which touched off a spiritual nerve. That's indeed interesting. Living in Qatar, an Islamic country, *adhan* is stitched into our daily existence; its sonorous sounds emanating from mosques five times a day are not only woven into our social and religious fabric, they govern our daily routine, serving as an invisible and invaluable clock – a gentle, piety-laden reminder of the passage of time.

So, what's in it that triggers enough curiosity in a person to embrace Islam? Is it the beauty of the adhan or its meaning that struck them most?

These questions set off a chain of other questions in my mind. Why do so many people become interested in Islam, when religion in general is being looked down upon? What is it that they discover during their exploration? Do they discover something different that hasn't caught my attention as a born Muslim? What are the challenges they face on their road to truth? What impact has the negative stereotyping of Islam had on their journey?

These questions, though relevant at all times, acquire poignancy and a special significance in an age that has seen Islam being singled out for attacks from multiple quarters.

No other religion has been maligned so maliciously in the past few decades and painted with the darkest, dirtiest brush, as a breeding ground of terrorism, a promoter of misogyny and oppression of women, and an ideology completely at odds with the modern Western values of freedom and liberalism. What Islam and Muslims have suffered in the wake of 9/11 is unimaginable. In a sense, the attacks on the Twin Towers were as much an attack on the image of Islam as on America.

Conversion is as old as religion itself. People have switched, abandoned and embraced religions with equal zeal. But if Islam is found to be an apt abode to park one's soul in in these turbulent, Islamophobic times, and if anyone feels lured by the beauty of this religion when it's constantly portrayed as ugly, that's worth some curiosity and even enquiry. It's this curiosity that set me on a journey of enquiry that resulted in this book.

Today, conversion is far more difficult, complex, and complicated. People of this world are mostly born into their respective faiths or faithlessness, and that's how the world's current religions are populated and replenished. The embracing of a new religion is frowned upon, and has severe consequences if it's into Islam - a much vilified faith - at least for some.

So, what prods a person to convert should be of interest to all.

Is there more to it than we comprehend? And how come some of Islam's bitterest enemies and visceral haters are ending up in its fold? Did they find all the answers they were seeking? What were the questions they asked? It's a long and arduous journey they are embarking upon and worth talking about. Several of them have written books explaining their experiences in exciting, even excruciating, detail.

This book is an attempt to look at the conversion stories of some celebrities – a look at their collective experiences through a holistic and wholesome approach. This will give readers a deeper and all- encompassing perspective and purview of all aspects of their journey – its myriad threads and nuances, complexities and challenges. What makes this book unique is that it's the first of its kind in terms of the number of celebrities in contemporary society it covers, offering a wealth of diverse perspectives and information, enabling readers to learn, compare and thus derive their own conclusions.

This brings us to the key question: Why celebrities? The conversion process is the same for all – for the average citizen and public figures alike. It has a beginning, a middle and an end – at first some doubts, a few questions or a simple curiosity, leading to a prolonged and complex investigation and study that could run into years, which sees the person grappling with intense ideological and theological uncertainties and psychological dilemmas and, finally, the joy of discovery and conversion. All of this is mostly a personal process, undertaken in secrecy, hidden from family and the gaze of the public eye. But conversion is a social and public phenomenon; it requires an announcement, and all the challenges tumble out. It's immensely upsetting – the renunciation of one faith for another, the migration from one order to another, one lifestyle to another, and one society to another. Conversion is both a breakup and a union rolled into one.

Celebrity conversion is arguably more difficult because celebrities have far more at stake; they are watched by a community of followers who may not approve of their idol switching to another faith, and also by an ever-vigilant media keen to stoke controversies. Conversion into Islam, a negatively stereotyped religion, is doubly difficult. No one has spoken of this more eloquently and succinctly than Kareem Abdul Jabbar, American former professional basketball player, who converted when he was just 24. He said: "For most people, converting from one religion to another is a private matter requiring intense scrutiny of one's conscience. But when you're famous, it becomes a public spectacle for one and all to debate. And when you convert to an unfamiliar or unpopular religion, it invites criticism of one's intelligence, patriotism and sanity. I should know. Even though I became a Muslim more than 40 years ago, I'm still defending that choice." (This excerpt is from an opinion piece of his written for *Al Jazeera* America on March 29, 2015.)

If a celebrity still converts against such heavy odds, that deserves a special study and it speaks volumes about the truthfulness and irresistibility of a faith that is under constant scrutiny. The factors that led them on this path, the enormity and intensity of their experiences and turmoil, the new findings on their ideological journey, the abandonment of their prejudices and existing beliefs, and the answers they found must all be examined in detail, not to discredit their previous faiths but to dispel the misunderstanding about a faith that has been unfairly targeted since 9/11.

This book features the experiences of 24 public figures, who have made a mark in their respective fields that include music, sports, academia, media and entertainment, etc. This is also the first book to encapsulate the transformative experiences of so many celebrities, which revolves around a single, seminal question posed to them, which has pestered many minds: *'WHY DID YOU CONVERT?'*

The answers, with all their diversity, depth and nuances, take us on an exciting and inspiring journey of our own. A journey into a journey.

As shall be revealed in this book, there are many lessons to be drawn, and messages to take home. What emerges from these stories are thought-provoking, even stunning, revelations that sharpen our understanding of what we already know about Islam, both as Muslims and non-Muslims, and they throw light on what we don't know, and turn into black and white what we have considered grey.

First, this book straightens a record, making the glass shine in its true colour after the muck has been erased. One of the dominant themes of this book, and an experience that all celebrity converts shared unanimously, is how they had harboured misconceptions about Islam. The gulf between reality and propaganda was so wide some found it unbelievable that truth could be disfigured so badly, which, according to them, explains the rampant Islamophobia that has gripped the world. Disbelief at the media portrayal of Islam led many of them to study the religion on their own to check if all this could be true.

For instance, American former rapper Mutah 'Napolean' Beale's reaction, before his conversion, shows the real-life consequences of Islamophobic rhetoric. During his first visit to a mosque, aged 24, he went armed with a loaded gun and an entourage of 20 people because, he says, "My whole life up until that point, I was prejudiced against Muslims. So I wasn't gonna take no chances [sic]." Alfred Wondratsch, an Austrian politician, spoke of the media fostering such abhorrence and fear of Islam in him that he thought it necessary to ask his own Muslim friends and colleagues why they were so gracious and polite while the media projected a completely different image, to which they told him - 'go and read' about Islam. Dr Yvonne Ridley, British journalist, first read the Quran "to try and find out why this religion oppressed women and promoted violence."

The negative stereotyping did not pertain to any specific aspect, but involved the entirety of Islamic faith and its tenets. Converts spoke of their immense surprise as one after the other of their misconceptions were dismantled, be it about the teachings of the Quran, the life of the Prophet Muhammad (peace be upon him), the treatment of women, or the attitude towards people of other religions.

However, this negative stereotyping had a beneficial impact, too, as was seen in a huge rise in interest in Islam after 9/11, resulting in mass conversions. According to the non-governmental US Religion Census, between 2000-2010, Muslims in the US grew from an estimated one million to 2.6 million, a 160 percent increase, making it the fastest growing religion in the United States.

The fact that many converts initially approached Islam from a position of hostility and hatred is unsurprising in the post 9/11 milieu, but their attitude was a continuation of a pattern in Islamic history where some of its famous adherents were previously its most vociferous and vicious critics. The same people in Makkah, who first expelled the Prophet, later embraced Islam en masse, and one remarkable example is that of Caliph Omar, who had set out to murder the Prophet but instead headed home with an unsheathed sword after hearing that his own sister and brother-in- law had embraced Islam. Omar hit his sister so hard she fell to the ground, bleeding from her mouth, but later accepted Islam after listening to a verse from the Quran. Omar's unsheathed sword was a symbol frozen for posterity, of Islam's fiercest critics joining its ranks later, which we have witnessed throughout its more than 1400-year history. Islam has always thrived in adversity; the present is a reenactment of the past and a foreshadowing of the future.

So, the most important message which this book gives readers is: Do not fall prey to disinformation, prejudices and propaganda, and make at least feeble steps to find out the truth on your own.

In this age of technology and information explosion, it's not the lack of information that creates prejudices, but a deliberate unwillingness and reluctance to ask questions. All converts were driven by a genuine desire to find out the truth and, when they did, the pull of truth was so irresistible they couldn't but take refuge in its embrace. Secondly, this book is meant to be an open discussion with the celebrities and a peep into their psyche during their transformative phase – a transformation of mind, heart and soul. There is no attempt to prove anything, no taking of positions and setting of agendas and promotion of any sect or idea, and no attempt to promote one religion against the other – the entire focus is on the journey as it was undertaken, and as was told by them, without drawing borders and fitting them into a pre-planned narrative. That these celebrities hail from different geographical areas lends a special significance, diversity and depth to their stories; it also proves the universality of truth and that truth doesn't recognise borders. It is also for this reason that I chose to make this book a collective effort, with writers from other parts of the world chipping in. It allows for approaching the subject from multiple perspectives and permits an impartiality and independence that lets the reverts just
narrate their stories.

Another message this book conveys is that conversion isn't linear and doesn't follow a specific path. People have entered this religion through multiple doors, attracted by different aspects and examples of Islam in a testimony to its completeness and comprehensiveness. However, the Quran has been mentioned as the most powerful attraction. Different verses have appealed to different converts, and many say they felt like the holy book was speaking directly to them, both as an answer to a burning question they had in mind and as guidance on the future. Joram van Klaveren, former far-right Dutch MP, felt an arrow pierce his heart when he read: *It's not the eyes that are blind, but the hearts.* (Quran 22:46).

The sonorous recitation of the Quran has touched millions of hearts, and is precisely what moved American singer Jennifer Grout to explore Islam. Her own recitation of the Quran now mesmerises millions with her melodious voice. Alfred Wondratsch said: "Quran stirs and moves me to this day and it's such a powerful experience!"

Muslims believe the Quran is the word of God and it's interesting when non-Muslims, too, attest to this fact, as in the case of Mutah, who said, upon his first reading of the holy book, and long before his conversion: "As a rap artist, I knew that these words could never be inspired by man. The stories within the Quran – although some were also told to me by my grandmother – the way Islam explained it, I just knew it had to be from my Creator."

The Quran is liked for its enunciation of *tawhid*, the concept of oneness of God. The simplicity and straightforwardness of the concept of God in Islam is its main allure; there is no scope for confusion or doubt, and all of the religious precepts of Islam have this simplicity.

Further, the life of Prophet Muhammad (PBUH) also had immense appeal for many converts, as in the case of Spanish journalist Amanda Figueras. The Prophet's forgiveness, nobility of character, mercy, integrity, resolute faith, love of animals and care for environment were all cited by them with specific examples to show how he influenced them in their journey, and how the Prophet is being misrepresented in today's hate-filled world. Joram was particularly struck by the Prophet's act of forgiving his uncle's assassin, which represents an apotheosis of kindness and mercy, while British writer and actor Lauren Booth, as a cat lover, remembered how she was moved when she heard of the Prophet's love of cats and other animals, going to great lengths not only to ensure their safety but even not to disturb their lives.

This book also sheds light on the futility of fame, an intensely pursued and vigorously cherished dream of modern life and its failure to provide happiness, self-fulfilment and spiritual satisfaction. Many spoke about the fickleness and vacuity of fame and why it couldn't give meaning and purpose to their lives, and how their sense of spiritual void deepened after worldly achievement, leading to disappointment and despair. "Where do you go from there?" Amir 'Loon' Muhadith, American former rapper, asked after reaching the pinnacle of success, while Kristiane Backer, a former presenter for MTV Europe, wrote in her diary, *It's work, work, work and then I'm alone again.* For the world at the time, she was a celebrity who had it all. Islam ultimately filled her inner void, leading to a permanent *fulfillment*.

These celebrities have shown the world that it's inner fulfilment that brings lasting peace and happiness; the rest is transitory, fleeting and worldly.

Also, the experiences of reverts have been widely different. While most of them understood Islam through an intense study and comparison, for others, it has been through lived experiences and emotions. For the intellectually and philosophically inclined, the quest has been long, strenuous and meticulous; they pored through the holy book and history books, studied the life of the Prophet, compared religious texts, and asked questions and sought answers. British vlogger and former civil servant Paul Williams didn't consider his conversion interesting and, according to him, his journey was slow and winding, scholarly and rational. Italian author and philosopher, Dr Sabrina Lei, too, embraced Islam after rigorous study; she waded through volumes of text before arriving at her ultimate destination.

It's truly amazing how diverse the paths to Islam are. There isn't a common pattern. When you approach some converts expecting an intellectual depth and vigour to their journey, there is a disappointment because they didn't traverse the same road; but the disappointment turns to excitement as we learn their journey was through their heart rather than their brain. They spoke about their emotional experiences, like Prof. Paul Keeler at Cambridge University, who said he entered Islam through 'food, friendship and beauty', while Ayana Moon, a South Korean celebrity, was influenced by her interactions with Korean Muslim sisters. Every convert sees and studies Islam through his/her own prism, and for each, there is something that attracted them. In the case of American playwright and poet Dr Kari Ann Owen, the scientific truths in Islam were enough to convince her of the truthfulness of this religion.

It's also astounding how all-encompassing their knowledge of Islam is. They start their journey with little or no knowledge but, by the time they convert, they have learned almost everything about all aspects of the faith. If you ask them questions, they have convincing, crystal-clear and ready answers – answers we may not get from many born Muslims.

In all cases, the journey doesn't end after arriving at the destination. They continue to learn more, engaging in debates and discussions and clarifying doubts. Many said their faith remained unwavering and grew stronger, even decades after conversion, never doubting their decision even once. After trading the unlimited freedom of unbelief for the limited freedom of faith, they now find joy in the restricted, regimented life of a believer. It's both inspiring and moving when Wayne Parnell, a South African cricketer, says Islam has enabled him to accept the ups and downs of life and the pressures it brings. As a Muslim, he now understands that even if something bad happens, "trust in your Creator helps you overcome it".

All converts talk about the peace and contentment they feel after embracing Islam. There is something mysteriously appealing about this peace because it springs from within, and never dries up, and is divine in its origin and gives them an inexplicable sense of belonging, care and love that cools their otherwise turbulent minds, which non-believers are unable to fathom.

All these are beautiful, spiritual rewards, but at what cost? What Kareem Abdul Jabbar calls the perils of converting to 'an unfamiliar or unpopular religion', the most excruciating part of it for him being still having to defend his choice, even 40 years or more later, is a reality shared by most converts. The reactions from families, friends and society, in most cases, were hostile. The most heart-rending experience in this book is that of Abdulrahman Afia, a British business consultant and verified TikTok user, who was given a painful ultimatum by his father, who bluntly told him one night: 'You have a choice to make tonight, Joel. Either, you go back to normal, stop praying and come back home with us tonight, or consider yourself no longer my son.' César Kaab Abdul, Brazilian former rapper, speaks of seeing graffiti every day calling him and his family terrorists after a report in a famous magazine linked him to terrorism, a baseless accusation for which he was never charged. On the other hand, women converts had to contend with another unique problem – hijab. A piece of cloth worn for rules of modesty and to cover one's head, which has been turned into a symbol of hate in today's world. They spoke of the taunts, the slurs, and the insults they faced because of that harmless piece of cloth perching on their heads, suddenly making them second- class citizens from a position of privilege they had enjoyed until then, making them aware of what ordinary Muslim women are going through on a daily basis, which they now could feel in all its ugliness and bigotry. Ayana Moon boldly talks about the challenges of being a hijab-wearing Muslimah in South Korea where Muslims are a miniscule minority.

Franco-Irish journalist Dr Myriam François immediately became aware of the strain many French Muslim women endure, in the hostile atmosphere induced by France's laïcité doctrine, when she found herself being refused service at Parisian restaurants and cafés once she started donning the veil.

The unjustness and unfairness of all this is heart-wrenching – the suffering converts of both sexes had to go through just for choosing a faith they liked. A question inevitably springs to mind: How are they coping with it? Or, more straightforwardly, did they ever regret their decision in the face of these challenges? This question was posed to all of them and the answers were heart-warming – they said that, although the negative reactions pained them, they didn't even for a moment doubt their decision. As explained earlier, they drew strength and courage from an inner spring – their faith. It's a tough sail through the turbulent waters of life; if their boats didn't capsize, it was due to their calm minds and steady hearts. With every trial and tribulation, their faith strengthened because they believe that Allah tests those whom He loves.

At the same time, there have been moments of discomfort and disillusionment at the attitude of Muslims towards converts. Western converts, and those from countries where Muslims are a minority, face challenges in fitting into a new society and lifestyle having abandoned the ones they were born into, and they suffer mild cultural shocks. The attitude of some Muslims, too, hasn't been helpful; they are too eager to take up the moral guardianship of new Muslims, offering free religious advice and even dictating how they should behave, and what to accept and what to eschew, and how to conduct themselves. No one explains this more aptly than Jennifer Grout who said: "It was as though I became an infant once again. The only difference was, instead of having just two parents telling me what to do, I now had millions of people telling me, 'do this', 'don't do that', 'you have to do this', 'you can't do this anymore!' What a lot of people don't understand is that this puts the convert under immense strain."

Also, this isn't the story of all celebrity converts, but of enough of them to provide a pattern of the process. In fact, there are several of them who aren't on these pages, like Mike Tyson, Kareem Abdul Jabbar, Yusuf Islam, Clarence Seedorf, Jermaine Jackson, and A R Rahman, to name a few, and those who are in the forefront of spreading the message of truth like Abdul Hakim Murad, Yusuf Estes and Bilal Philips. Also, there are no Arab converts on these pages, though their journeys aren't less exciting. Arabs, both Muslims and non-Muslims, share a common culture, heritage and ethos and therefore their conversions aren't considered as challenging as the ones in other societies.

I would like to end this introduction on a personal note. What started out as a curiosity for me grew and morphed into a journey that was as intense and exciting as the ones I was trying to track. This journey into a journey has been immensely transformative for me, too, as I was ushered into an amazing new world of their experiences and knowledge. I stand in awe of their intelligence, the depth of their erudition, the strength of their conviction, the intensity of their faith, the extent of their honesty and their indomitable spirit.

My journey has shattered some of my own notions of faith and practice; I now consider these reverts to be the real Muslims compared to those of us born into the faith. This book is a fitting tribute to their courage, conviction and determination – all 24 of them and everyone else who has trod the same path, whose sacrifice, commitment, honesty, hard work and, finally, their resolve to stand for what they believe in, deserves applause. Their experiences should serve as a wake-up call to all Muslims who inherited the faith from their parents without any efforts of their own.

Most of these chapters I couldn't read in one go. Emotions got in the way; I had to pause to digest the weighty words, the enormity of their experiences, the depth of their wisdom, and the extent of their sacrifices. The knowledge of Islam they have gleaned within a short time is much more than what an average Muslim does in a lifetime. They have found new meanings to what we have taken for granted, and are able to provide a scientific and logical explanation to tenets of our faith which many born Muslims cannot.

Finally, if this book conveys any message, it's this: Self-fulfillment and happiness are not to be found in the success and fame that so many of us hanker after, which are just worldly embellishments that bring us adulation and adoration, but there is an emptiness inside that needs to be filled, which can only be filled with true faith. And once this void is filled, everything else falls into place, or just becomes irrelevant.

Khalid Al Sayed

1

Faith and fame: Connecting with the inner self

———•◆◆◆•———

Waleed Wayne Dillon Parnell – South African and international cricketer

———•◆◆◆•———

Wayne's first, deep interaction with Islam happened at the Cricket Academy. Training there was rigorous, Monday through to Friday, but on this last day of the week, Muslim players were excused to attend the mosque. One day Wayne asked two Muslim boys he was friendly with if he could tag along. They said yes and instructed him, "just follow what we do". So, for the first time ever in his life, he stepped into a mosque.

WHEN South African cricketer Wayne Parnell converted to Islam in 2011, it made national and international headlines. At the time, he was 21 and playing for the Proteas, South Africa's national team, and there was some intimation that his Muslim teammates, Hashim Amla and Imran Tahir, had 'influenced his conversion from Christianity', a suggestion that cast doubt over whether the young cricketer had taken that decision on his own initiative.

In Wayne's telling of the story, it is clear the decision was his alone. Becoming Muslim was a gentle, exploratory and deeply emotional journey that took place over the course of two or three years. There were other people involved, friends who passed on books or CDs, but no one person in particular and not in any proselytising way. None of them were the men mentioned above. Rather, the interest came from him and people gave him leads, and it was up to him to explore them.

The way he describes it, discovering Islam was like finding a new friend with whom you click and your values sync, and then growing the natural friendship, the kind that you know will last forever and give your life greater richness. Getting to know Islam was a growing curiosity, and it was matched by Islam seeking him out over the years, he feels, moving him to delve deeper, until he finally decided to give himself over to it fully.

Wayne Dillon Parnell was born on 30 July, 1989, in the small seaside city of Port Elizabeth, the capital of the Eastern Cape Province, in South Africa. Port Elizabeth was renamed Gqeberha in 2019, but it is known colloquially by the initials of its old name, P.E. It has a small population of around one million, but despite its small size, it has produced many talents across many fields, including world-class cricketers Graham and Shaun Pollock, Alviro and Robin Petersen as well as national rugby stars Siya Kolisi and Schalk Burger. South Africa's world-renowned playwright Athol Fugard comes from there, as do many more famous artists, singers, authors, poets and entrepreneurs. Some people joke that there is something in P.E.'s water that gives rise to brilliance. Wayne definitely drank a lot of that; he is one of its most celebrated sons.

Boys of Booysen Park: Ardent cricketers

The international cricketer grew up in a suburb called Booysen Park with his mother, father and two siblings, who all still live there. He grew up in a Christian community, but was not particularly religious. There were very few Muslims in the area, he says – in fact, he only remembers one person, a man his mother used to work with. There was one mosque, a small house that had been converted, and plenty of churches, four or five within a small radius of where he lived, which was wonderful for him – churches had large grounds that were perfect for playing cricket. "My mom used to go to church every Sunday, and as kids
we were expected to go that way as well," remembers Wayne. "At Sunday school, we were involved with things like choir and youth group. We were all encouraged to take part in church activities." As his older brother and sister began growing up, they began making up their own minds about attending church, he says. But for him, who was younger by seven years, he was still expected to go, something he sometimes resented deeply and bickered with his mother about.

The boys of Booysen Park were ardent cricketers. Each section of about four or five streets would gather up the boys in the area and set up little teams, which would compete and organise to meet at this church or that school at a pre-arranged time. "We used to jump the fence and play cricket in the church yard. We'd either play there or in the school grounds, but they had security, and if the guards were patrolling they would kick us out," he remembers.

In Wayne's section of Booysen Park, the boys were closer to his brother's age. From the age of seven or eight, he played on his brother's team with boys around seven years older than him, something he thinks probably contributed to his success. "I was probably fearless. I didn't really see age," he says, which is remarkable considering how from a child's perspective the difference of one year can seem like a whole, new social universe. Footballwasactually Wayne's first love, butmoreopportunities came with cricket. He won a cricket scholarship to Grey High School, and began playing club cricket when he was just 11 years old and provincial cricket at 12, which was incredibly exciting for him. "As a youngster playing with men, it was nice to mix with

names that you've heard of," he says.

It was at Grey that he came into closer contact with people from other religions. He had "obviously" heard some negative things about Islam from television news, he says, but he didn't take much notice – he takes most things with a pinch of salt and likes to form his own opinions once he's done some investigation on a matter, he says. Plus, he adds, "I've always been of the opinion that in a whole batch of people there are obviously some bad apples, but not everyone is bad."

South Africa is a multi-cultural society and pluralistic in terms of religion. Numerous faiths are practised here, a large percentage of them Christian-based. Others are based in African traditions, and in smaller percentages there's Islam, Hinduism, Judaism, Buddhism and Bahaism; many people are secular. He hasn't really come across anti-Muslim sentiment on home ground, Wayne says; South Africans are generally tolerant of other religions. However, having travelled to many countries over the last decade, he's seen first-hand how people from different races and religions are treated, particularly in the West, and especially at airports.

But back then in the early 2000s at Grey High School, what most aroused

Wayne's curiosity about Islam is that Muslim kids were allowed to skip class on Friday afternoons. "I was fascinated and curious. Like, what is this mosque thing that they go to on a Friday?" He was also intrigued about the fasting, and Eid. It was a passing curiosity, though, because by that time he was already on the fast-track to an international cricket career, having been noticed as one of the country's most promising young players.

He had just turned 17 and was still in school when he made his first-class debut for the national provincial team Eastern Province in 2006. In only his fifth first-class match, he took a hat-trick against competing national provincial team Western Province, and that got people's attention. In 2008, he was recognised twice and awarded the Coca-Cola Khaya Majola U19 Player of the Tournament, and the CSA U19 Cricketer of the Year. That same year he was selected to play in the U/19 Cricket World Cup, and was chosen to attend the South Africa Cricket Academy in Pretoria, South Africa's capital. By then he was 19.

Training at Cricket Academy

Wayne's first, deep interaction with Islam happened at the Cricket Academy. Training there was rigorous, Monday through to Friday, but on this last day of the week, the Islamic players could get off to attend mosque. One day Wayne asked two Muslim boys he was friendly with if he could tag along. They said yes and instructed him, "just follow what we do". So, for the first time ever in his life, he stepped into a mosque.

"The first thing that stood out for me was the fact that in the downstairs area there were only males sitting there – boys, young men and grown men. Then the actual prayers began and everyone stood and moved shoulder to shoulder. It took me off-guard, that experience, because it was something different from what I had expected," he recalls.

Pressed to describe what that difference was, he explains that in a Christian church, everyone sits in different places. Parents, uncles, brother and sister, all may be spread out and, he's quick to add, in that individuality one may also experience a oneness with your Creator. "But with this," he says, referring to the mosque experience, "it felt like unity to me and that's what stood out for me." He felt unity, calmness and a sense of community. He was overwhelmed by emotion, in awe of that moment. That day, a seed was planted.

One of the two young men he was with picked up that something was in motion. He gave Wayne a small book, a basic introduction to Islam, with simple sketches that illustrated how to perform *wudu* (ablution) and pray. During the days following the mosque visit, scenes and emotions from that experience kept playing over and over in Wayne's head. In the evenings at the academy, when he was bored, he would dip into the book and read a couple of lines.

At the end of 2008, Wayne returned to P.E. and began to connect more with Muslim friends. He and a schoolmate, Faizel Smith, began hanging out more and became close. He also made a new friend, Zane Abrahams, who was a bit older than him, a hockey player and manager of a clothing store. They would often meet in a group at the store Zane managed, hang out and spend time chatting about life in general.

Early in 2009, Wayne made his international debut for South Africa against Australia. The season went well, and he was the youngest player to be given a national contract by Cricket South Africa. He shone at the 2009 World T20, too, taking nine wickets, which included a remarkable 4 for 13 against the West Indies. He was named Man of the Match. He went on to play three Tests that year and earned a lucrative deal – the figure surprised even him – with the Indian Premier League team Delhi Daredevils.

His career was ramping up.

With this, though, came pressure. Wayne had been earmarked for success very early, and while it might have been exciting to play serious cricket amongst "names you've heard of" when he was just a boy of 12, that must have brought its own pressure.

"In terms of sport, I've always been … insecure," he says, with a pause before naming the word and drawing quotation marks in the air. "I don't see myself as other people see me. Apparently I was a young prodigy and going places, and I never really saw myself like that. So even when I started playing internationally, I didn't think I was this hot shot, and I always thought I'm not good enough."

Also, some issues were beginning to arise that year. He had a recurring groin injury, leading to some inconsistent performances. The press had things to say and he hints at the difficulty of navigating the public gaze and the loss of autonomy over your self-image that comes with that. It is clear that he found the intense public gaze and expectations increasingly challenging, and he hints at the fact that the possibility of failure was a very present worry.

Mosque experience

In October, 2010, Wayne had another significant mosque experience. He was back in P.E. and decided, again on an impulse, to join his friend Faizel at Maghrib prayers. As he was walking into mosque, lagging behind Faizel, a friend of Faizel's father smiled at him and said, "Hey Parny, howzit going? Good to see you. Ah, you have a lot of *noor* in your face." Wayne thanked him and said, "Thanks. I've been growing it for a while." The man responded with a curious look, so Wayne checked in with Faizel: "Is noor the Arabic word for beard?" *Noor* means light, explained Faizel, and they both laughed, but the compliment moved Wayne.

He thought it was a really nice thing to say to another person.

Inside the mosque the two young men sat down, somewhere in the middle of the crowd, towards the back. Three Malaysian scholars were in attendance, and after prayers the men began to talk about Islam and tell stories. Although Faizel didn't normally attend these sessions – he usually wanted to get home for dinner, says Wayne – on this day he decided to sit down. One of the men began talking about how people go through life on this earth chasing worldly things that give us validation through our peers when what we should be striving for is better relationships with the people around us and our Creator. This is where the real validation is, he said; this is what will define you as a person and your time on this earth. This resonated with Wayne.

"[It] kind of hit home for me, being in the public eye and also trying to fit in and trying to do things that is [sic] accepted by society because you're in this role. You need to walk like this, you need to talk like this, you need have this haircut, you need to dress like this, you need to behave in this manner because you're now this athlete, you know?" says Wayne. "And that was quite a thing that sat with me … the battle between worldly validation and the validation from within, the relationship that you have with your creator."

The scholars then began asking people who would consider doing missionary work. At one point, one of the men fixed his gaze on Wayne and asked him, "Brother, will you commit to jamaat?" but Wayne didn't understand the term. "I'm not Muslim," he answered. "I'm just here with my friend." The scholar was taken aback and began walking through the crowd towards him. "What's your name?" he asked. When Wayne told him, the scholar responded, "No, brother, your name is Waleed." He began telling the story of Khalid ibn-al Walid, the powerful warrior and Muslim commander in the service of Prophet Muhammad, peace be upon him, during the early stages of Islam, who never lost a battle. Then he said to Wayne, "You are Muslim; everyone is born a Muslim." Wayne 'thought the story was cool', about Khalid and his father Walid, who always had God on their side, but he was beginning to feel self-conscious and uncomfortable as he thought people recognised him, and so he just nodded and agreed and he and Faizel headed out of the mosque.

Over dinner at Faizel's home, his friend told his mother what the scholar had said. Curious, she got out a book of Arabic names. Waleed, she read, means 'new-born son'.

Wayne felt this was significant somehow. He describes how the scholar had also explained another fundamental concept of Islam, that one is born into the same religion as one's parents, because babies don't have free will. However, one of the major differences between human beings and animals is that Allah has given us free will, so when you reach a certain age, you can comprehend this and make your own decision. This kept playing over and over in his mind all night.

Moved by these teachings, Wayne made up his mind to explore further. He began reading up about Islam and going through the concepts. He listened to videos by Indian Islamic televangelist Dr Zakir Naik, founder of the Peace TV Network and Islamic Research Foundation, who talked about the similarities and differences between religions and focused on the Islamic point of view. He also listened to many debates about the differences between the various major world religions. Zane's brother gave him a number of books and CDs on Islam, and told him to listen to them when he had time. He did, and started falling in love with the simplicity of the religion.

"It just kind of spoke to me," says Wayne. He loved the concept of oneness, that there is only one creator and no-one is equal to Him, and that Prophet

Muhammad, peace be upon him, is the last and final prophet (he had always found the Christian concept of the holy trinity confusing, he says — are the Father, Son and Holy Spirit all Gods?). With Allah, there is only Him, no wife, no son, no other children. He loved the fact that the Quran is still in its original Arabic form and, although there are translations of it, there are no other versions, unlike with the Bible and Torah. He loved the sense of brotherhood and unity that Islam brought him.

'Paradise lies at the feet of your mother'

Another concept that resonated with him really deeply was that paradise lies at the feet of your mother. He had not always been close to his mother, he says. Some of that he attributes to the resentment he felt about having to go to church on Sunday when he'd played sport all Saturday and all he wanted to do was chill and sleep in. That had led to arguments. But now he understood that your entry into heaven rests on how you treat your mother, and your mother's *duas* (prayers) are the most powerful *duas* that can be said for you.

As he studied more, he grew a new and deep appreciation for his mother and father. He understood that if he was serious about Islam — and now he was certain that he was — he had to include them on his journey by asking for their blessing on his choice. "The final step was speaking to them and saying, this is what I want to do and this is what I want to follow. This is where my heart lies," recounts Wayne. "It really resonates with me and speaks to me and I feel like this is not something I'm choosing, it feels like this is choosing me," he told them. The Parnells told their son the choice was his, it was his life, and they gave their blessing wholeheartedly.

That was early 2011. After getting their blessing, Wayne threw himself into a period of study. In March, a month later, he felt ready and went to P.E. to say his *shahadah* with Mufti Desai. Only Zane was present. Wayne finds it difficult to remember exactly how he felt at the time. Joy, he thinks, but really his focus was deeply personal. This had nothing to do with what the outside world thought, he says, this was between him and his Creator and was about solidifying his relationship and committing to Allah absolutely. "It was more about delving into the feeling of having to be accountable for my actions," he says.

A few weeks later he left with the Proteas to play India in the 2011 Cricket World Cup, a tour that took place over eight or nine weeks. "That was actually a really interesting time," he says, "because now I'm on my own and having to practice Islam." It was a self-reflective period where he spent a lot more time by himself and grew to understand himself a little bit better, he says. The most challenging thing was finding the time to say his *salaahs* in between travelling and training, although he appreciated these times of prayer because it allowed him to reset and feel grounded again. Besides that, transitioning into the Islamic faith wasn't difficult, he says.

"When you want to do something and when you set your mind to something, there are ways to fall in line with that," he says. "Drinking wasn't hard to give up at all, because I was a social drinker anyway. Even fasting for the first time. At first I thought I'd never be able to do it for 12 or 13 hours, and then you do it and you realise it's actually kind of easy. You just kind of do it, because you understand that it has greater meaning and you understand what it represents as well."

For the most part, he kept the knowledge of his conversion to friends and family, who were happy for him and wished him well. He felt he wasn't ready to share it with the outside world yet. The time was not right. He was worried that even if he "told people straight", they were still going to misinterpret his spiritual journey and purpose, and think he might be "doing it for a headline." He was concerned they might think others had influenced him and he didn't want to put anyone else in the spotlight. He has a healthy scepticism for journalists' tendency to opt for, at best, the instrumental positioning of events, or at worst, sensationalism, and he didn't want to fuel the media fire in any way. But even without him saying anything, there were already rumours and conflicting stories floating about.

Wayne becomes Waleed

The news was picked up around July that year and reported as widely as India. South African online news channel IOL ran the headline *"Wayne becomes Whallid [sic] Parnell"*, with a picture of the young cricketer with a scarf around his head. The article stated "an SMS doing the rounds on Monday attributed his conversion to the influence of fellow Protea players Hashim Amla and Imraan Tahir". It had exactly the kind of speculation Wayne wanted to avoid. The SMS, which was not attributed to any source by IOL, went on to claim Whallid means 'the great one'. Someone wrote he should not get ahead of himself, he says. Wayne decided to put out a statement saying he was approaching his first period of fasting and asked for privacy around his choice of faith, and declined any further interviews. He explains that he didn't want to engage about something that was so fresh for him and speak about a religion he was just starting to know on a public platform. Islam is a subject matter that people spend lifetimes on and he was not a scholar, he said. "I haven't studied Islam; I'm going to tell you the things I know and have heard from others." Although he understands why people would find this an interesting story – he has had many private, deep conversations about it with people he trust within and outside of cricket circles, he says – he also has experience of how things can be misinterpreted.

However, for the most part, he says, people responded positively and were respectful of his space, including his fans. "It's like anything, where some people will be happy for you and others will curse you or be not so happy." His father's advice kept him steady. "My dad said whenever you step into a group of people, there will always be people who like you and people who dislike you based on what they see. And that's so true," says Wayne. "I've come to terms with the fact that, with everything I do, there will be people who like it, and people who don't."

He has no concerns that being a Muslim, and particularly not drinking, will create a barrier between himself and friends or fans. "With drinking there was already a barrier and now that I'm Muslim there are still barriers. There always will be," he says, and repeats that "…there will always be people who like you for who you are, and those that don't. It goes back to validation: it's not about what people say, it's about your relationship with your Creator."

It's been 11 years since his conversion. He is now 33 and married to fashion blogger Aisha Baker, also Muslim, who has a bigger Instagram following than him (143k). She has slayed being in the public eye. They have two adorable, tousle-haired children, a boy (Khalid, of course) and a girl (Salma). Life has changed. "I still go out with friends, and I live in a Western society and I still go out for dinners," he says. His clubbing days are in the past, though. "I can't remember the last time when I went out to a nightclub. These days I enjoy going out with a couple of friends more. I interact with Muslim and non-Muslim people, and also, now I have kids."

He has had over a decade of living as a Muslim and getting to know Islam and its tenets intimately. He is no longer the young man discovering a new faith, hesitant to speak about it. Today he is a considered, steady presence, and is ready to open up about his journey. The time is right.

The years have only made his love for his faith stronger, he says. The discipline of prayer and following the five pillars of Islam have brought a constancy to his life he appreciates deeply. This is clearly something that he needs. In a television interview, his wife Aisha describes how different they are, she impulsive and spontaneous, he firmly based in routine – after all, he is a professional sportsman whose life revolves around training schedules.

His relationship with his Creator is still his central focus, he says. "Probably one of the most important things that I like about the religion is the remembrance of your Creator in everything that you do. For example, when you start any task or activity, you say *Bismillah* (in the name of God), and I think that's something that's a really, really special concept."

He tries to complete the Quran every Ramadan, although he still reads it in English. His goal is to learn Arabic, but he's struggling with it, he says. He is still learning to know the Quran, but he has his favourite verses. "I love the opening verse of the Quran," he explains. "It's the verse you read every single time you pray *salah* – naturally, because it's important. But because of this, it's become one of my favourites." Surah Ikhlaas, he says, "…is beautiful, because it goes hand-in-hand with 'Allah has no companions and he's the most powerful being'. It's back to the concept of only one God, so even if Prophet Muhammad, (PBUH), is really important, you'd still never compare him to God."

His other favourite verse speaks about the concepts of unity, community and brotherhood that so moved him in the beginning of his journey. It's the Surah Al Asr. He reads it in Arabic first, and then translates it:

"By the declining day, lo man is at a state of loss, save those who believe and do good works, and exhort one another to truth and exhort one another to endurance."

"This is about believers trying to do good deeds and works, and to hold one another to the truth," he explains. "Even in the difficult times you can come back and stay steadfast in your religion, despite the fact that there are a lot of distractions in today's world, this can help you stay focused."

He turns to Quran when anxious

Wayne has an app on his phone that he can tap into when he's travelling, and when he's feeling anxious, he goes to the Quran for guidance and reassurance. Fear of failure is one of the ultimate human traits we all have in common, and it must be especially intense as a sportsman where every match has winners and losers. His faith has made Wayne more at ease with the possibility of either.

"In the last few years, I've accepted what's happening. I don't have such a fear of failure now, because if it's part of my journey, then it's part of my journey. You just go and do what you have to do. Respect your team and respect the game and do your best," he says.

Islam has enabled him to accept the ups and downs of life, the pressures it brings, and understand that even if something bad happens, if you trust in your Creator, there is a good lesson to be learnt. He adds that the same goes if something good happens, the Creator may also be testing you to see if you can avoid the temptation to become arrogant. This is another thing he loves about the Quran; it exhorts believers to treat one another as equal, and he's always felt this was a strong part of him, to treat others with respect and dignity.

It was the sense of affinity Wayne felt towards the values of Islam that drew him to Islam. He sometimes wonders what he would have done if his parents had not given their blessing. But believing, as he does, that the Creator's journey for you is meant to be, then their blessing was never going to be denied. Islam had always intended to make him a Muslim again.

2

'I became Muslim while writing an anti-Islam book'

⸺⸺ ◆◆◆◆◆ ⸺⸺

Joram van Klaveren, former far-right Dutch MP for the Freedom Party

⸺⸺ ◆◆◆◆◆ ⸺⸺

As he started writing the book, something weird, and eerily unexpected, happened: not only did not he get facts to support his arguments, he actually came across information that was at odds with his ideas. He learned that many of his ideas were stated by orientalists, far-right politicians and even by Islamic extremists and had little or no basis in historical Islam.

"It's not the eyes that are blind, but the hearts."
Quran 22:46

I T IS AN uninspiring scene from the the Dutch parliament in 2013. In a grainy video, Joram van Klaveren, a far-right MP for the Freedom Party, walks to the lectern with a clutch of papers and holds forth fiercely on a subject that is close to his heart.

"I request the government that Islam be banned from the Netherlands as much as possible," he proclaims, his voice oozing with the eloquent enthusiasm and confidence of a man whose determination knows no bounds.

The ban Joram sought on Islam was all-inclusive. He notoriously called the holy Quran a poison, wanted to ban minarets and hijab, and any mention of Islam was enough to inject an insidious, eerie sense of unease, anger and hatred into his whole being. Joram symbolised the virulent strain of Islamophobia that his far-right party, and by extension Dutch politics, is still notorious for.

Why would such a man end up in Islam, exactly the faith he wanted banished? What forces conspired to bring about a complete change in his belief? What was the cataclysmic, catalytic process that tore through his mind before conversion?

Joram's ideological journey and transformation is a roller- coaster that stretches credulity. It doesn't read like a conversion story, but like a thriller that is suffused with an abundance of stress and suspense and has a remarkable denouement that makes it essential reading for every student of religion, philosophy and what not.

Twin Tower attacks

It was September 11, 2001. At first glance, a very ordinary Tuesday.

For Joram, however, it was not a day like any other. It was his first day as a student of religious studies at the Free University in Amsterdam.

That this day would also be special for a very different reason would soon become apparent. In the afternoon, rush hour, he learned via text message (WhatsApp did not yet exist) that an attack with airplanes was underway on the Twin Towers in New York. It would be the beginning of a political and social roller- coaster. For society as a whole, but certainly also for him as a person.

Everything that had anything to do with Islam would become the subject of a fierce debate within a short period of time. A debate in which he already had somewhat negative feelings. The basis for those negative feelings, by the way, had been laid long before 9/11.

In 1979, he was born into a Protestant-Christian family in Amsterdam. Especially in light of the geographical context - Amsterdam is, of course, known for being very liberal - having a religious background was not the social norm.

However, his brothers, sister and he were all baptized, given religious names, read from the Bible and prayed both before and after dinner. Furthermore, his grandfather was an 'elder on duty' in the church, his aunt married the son of the minister and, in   a distant past, his great-great-grandfather - minister Van Raalte
- fled to America because of a religious dispute (to found the capital of the American state of Michigan, Holland, by the way). So, the Christian faith had left its (positive) mark on the family and, since the father of his best friend was also a minister (and he regularly went along to services, lectures and listened a lot to the best man), he got a double dose of religion, as it were.

Joram first became aware of Islam as an 'alternative' philosophy of life, and apart from the information from the denomination, when he read a controversial book *The Downfall of The Netherlands: Land of Naive Fools,* written under the pseudonym Mohammed Rasoel. It must have been in the early 1990s (he was around 14 at the time) that he found a copy of this on the 'book table' at a friend's house. "The book spoke about the growing influence of Islam and its dangers and negative consequences for freedom in our country. The work made an instant impression on me," he says. He would later meet at the office of the Freedom Party (in Dutch: de PVV) the eccentric (and later convicted) figure behind the pseudonym Mohammed Rasoel, who was an ex-Muslim.

Interest in Christianity and nice Muslims

In later teen years, he began to read more and more and was particularly interested in the foundations of broader Christianity. Books by and about Martin Luther, and on Calvin, Erasmus, and great names in the Christian tradition. Through their works, he was first introduced to the polemic between Christianity and Islam. The theological differences were firmly emphasized. The rejection of the Trinity, the divinity of Christ, the atonement and original sin were reasons mentioned for seeing Islam as a heresy, an evil cult and even as the religion of the antichrist.

According to Joram, inquiries in minister circles reveal that many still hold this opinion today. It was stated that individual Muslims can, of course, be very nice people; however, this was not because of, but in spite of the religion. Islam was essentially a false religion.

There were indeed nice Muslims he knew because, as a youngster, he used to play soccer with Walid, his friend from the neighborhood. Walid once told him that his Muslim father had left him and his Christian mother alone and now lived back in Egypt.

"A very distant land. Because of his young age and the fact that Walid was

Muslim but otherwise grew up in a totally non-Islamic environment, Islam played no further role. In my student days, one of my best friends was also a Muslim. We also talked about religion but, subconsciously, I was still convinced that it was not thanks to but in spite of his religion that he was such a good friend," Joram reminisces about his past links with Muslims.

"The fact that both Christianity and Islam are, at their core, and have been from the beginning, transmitting religions that claim to hold the truth, obviously also plays a role in the historically tense relationship. They are competing giants," he adds.

Joram probes the historical context that shapes the negative view in Europe of Islam, which also has to do with the conflict and war between, among others, Europe and the Ottoman Empire. The traditional aversion against Islam can sometimes still be seen culturally in Europe. Consider, for example, the croissant, which was baked for the first time in the year 1683 after the Europeans defeated the Ottoman Empire in the battle of Vienna. The Christian Europeans took dough, shaped it into a crescent moon (that's why it's called croissant) and ate it to celebrate the defeat of the invading Muslim enemy.

Almost nobody knows this anymore or thinks about this story when they buy a croissant (and he loves its taste by the way), but it is related to this tensed past. In addition to this cultural aversion and the theological objections that shaped his views on Islam, there were also the fears and worries that he experienced during the years of his study.

"In addition to 9/11, in my student days, the famous Dutch filmmaker Theo Van Gogh was murdered by a man who called himself a jihadist (not too far from my old home in Amsterdam) and very deadly attacks followed in cities such as Madrid, London and Beslan.

"Also, the overrepresentation in crime of youngsters with a Muslim background (apparently - I thought - their value system, Islam, is unable to correct them or teaches them to behave like this in a non-Muslim country) and of course the negative media coverage (having to do with the secular-liberal signature that sees religion as something alien) confirmed and deepened my negative feelings about Islam in such a way that I felt the need to protect my country against this evil ideology called Islam," he chuckles.

And what better way to achieve his goal than to become politically active? He thought he could change the law and have the biggest impact, and so joined the newly founded PVV, the most anti-Islam political party of Europe. This party was a fertile breeding ground of Islamophobia, not only for him then, but for a considerable part of societies in the West even now. The PVV considered its noble mission to rid the entirety of Europe of Islam, not just the Netherlands, and started an international tour to unite all similar parties. These organisations use the same rhetoric and got the same responses and support of the people – from Belgium to Austria and from France to Italy.

A book to demolish Islam

From 2006 until 2017, he was actively involved in politics. In 2010, he became an MP. The leader of the Freedom Party, Geert Wilders, asked him to be the spokesperson on Islam-related topics in parliament. And that became the core of his work.

During his parliament tenure, he did everything he could to fight Islam. He tried to make legislation to shut down all Islamic schools in the Netherlands, attempted to close every mosque in the country and even tried to ban the holy Quran.

He used his position and charisma as a very active member of parliament to warn people against the dangers of Islam. He did not even consider Islam a real religion, employing the choicest, ugliest epithets to describe it, calling it the most deadly political ideology in the world. Not only in parliament, but also in discussions on TV shows, on the radio, at schools, universities and wherever he had an opportunity, he unleashed his fiery rhetoric against Islam. "I believed Islam should be fought wherever possible," he remembers.

In 2014, Joram became an independent MP because the Freedom Party shifted its focus temporarily from Islam to Moroccan immigrants. "That was not my cup of tea. I was in politics to fight Islam, not a specific ethnic group. Many supporters of the PVV don't know that there are ex-Muslims with a Moroccan and Turkish background working for the Freedom Party. It felt like a betrayal towards these partners in our fight against Islam, when Geert Wilders asked his supporters during a rally if they wanted more or less Moroccans in the Netherlands," he explains.

Although he left the party, he was still in parliament until 2017 and a staunch critic of Islam. So, after leaving the PVV, he thought he finally had the time to fulfill a long-held desire: to write an anti-Islam book - a book that would provide conclusive theoretical groundings for all of the objections he held against Islam. A book that would brilliantly demolish Islam with his brainy, sizzling arguments!

Also, this book would settle the dispute once and for all and make it absolutely clear: Islam is a danger for The Netherlands, for Europe and, actually, for the whole world.

He was convinced that Islam was, above all, a false religion, very violent too, and anti-women, anti-Christian, anti-Jew and, of course, pro-terrorism.

As he started writing the book, something weird, and eerily unexpected, happened: not only didn't he get facts to support his arguments, he actually came across information that was at odds with his ideas. He learned that many of his ideas were stated by orientalists, far-right politicians and even by Islamic extremists and had little or no basis in historical Islam.

His research often presented him with contexts and interpretations that were very different from those he had propagated for years.

'My views started to change'

"My views slowly started to change. Seeking more information, I wrote to various academic authorities on Islam, including Professor Abdul Hakim Murad of Cambridge Uni v ersity. In the e-mail I sent him, I had put the English link of my Wikipedia page, so that he would know who I was. I did n 't want him to think I was tricking him," Joram says, his face brightening at the new discovery he was making.

"For weeks, I didn't hear anything and, to be honest, I didn't even expect him to answer me. After all, why would a Muslim professor from the UK help a person who was known as an anti-Islam politician from another country (although genuinely interested and already somewhat moderate)?"

But one Saturday evening, after several weeks, he answered. And he did that quite extensively. He pointed out various scholars, books and facts and advised him to read again and more deeply this time. "And that's what I did. One by one, my objections to Islam vanished. With such strong knowledge and my negative emotions towards the *deen* (Islam) broken down, Islam was no longer a religion that promoted hatred and division. It was no longer anti-women, anti-Christian, anti-Jew and calling for violence. By the way, these are the topics I get the most questions about from non-Muslims to this day. It is partly why I covered these points in my book *The Apostate*," he says.

For example, there is a perception in the West, and it also appears with some regularity in Orientalist literature, that Islam sees women as less than men, legitimises violence against them, and we see this explicitly reflected in an unloving example of Prophet Muhammad (peace be upon him). Studying the Islamic sources, however, taught him something quite different.

To illustrate, he stumbled upon *surah* (chapter) 3:195 of the holy Quran, and the *tafsir* (exegesis) was given as, "And their Lord responded to them, 'Never will I allow to be lost the work of (any) worker among you, whether male or female, you are of one another'." Thus, in the eyes of the Creator, there is no distinction in deeds between men and women. In sura 49:13, he further read who is most prominent with God: "Verily, the most noble of you in the sight of Allah is the most righteous of you." So it is about deeds, about intentions, about righteousness, not about the gender of the servant.

Also, the beautiful Quranic description of marriage is mostly unheard of in the West: *And of His signs is that He created for you from yourselves spouses, that you may find tranquility in them: and He placed between you love and mercy. Verily, in this are signs for a people who give thought.* (Quran 30:21)

It can even be said – based on several Prophetic narrations – that women, in their role as mothers, are above that of men: "Abu Hurayra said: 'O Messenger of Allah, who amongst the people is deserving most of my good treatment? He (the Prophet) said: 'Your mother, again your mother, again your mother, then your father, then your nearest relatives according to the order (of nearness)' " (Sahih Muslim, no. 2548b.) During his entire life, Muhammad (PBUH) emphasized: "The best of you are those who are the best to their wives" (Jami' al-Tirmidhi, no. 1162) and in a hadith of Muslim he read: "The Messenger of Allah never hit anyone with his hand, neither a woman nor a servant..." These findings shook his image of the Prophet (PBUH) to its foundations.

"That, with respect to the treatment of women, there are sometimes problems no one will deny. That is a global issue. However, the Man (PBUH) whom I saw as evil and the source of female misery, turned out to be an enlightened example and to proclaim a message which should not be characterized as a problem but as an absolute solution," he says.

Similarly, with regard to the issue of violence, upon closer examination, it was the context and background that turned his perception. He revisited Surah 9:5 (the so-called sword verse) often cited by critics of Islam as 'proof' that the Quran is a 'licence to kill', and which he, too, considered back then as very telling of Islam:

And when the sacred months have passed, then kill the polytheists wherever you find them and capture them and besiege them and sit in wait for them at every place of ambush. But if they should repent, establish prayer, and give alms, let them (go) on their way. Verily, Allah is Forgiving and Merciful.

The first thing he remarkably noticed when rereading surah 9:5 (while he was writing the book), was surah 9:6: "And if any one of the polytheists seeks your protection, then grant him protection so that he may hear the words of Allah. Then deliver him to his place of safety. That is because they are a people who do not know."

Astonishing facts

He discovered more astonishing facts. Quranic verses 9:5-6 were revealed in their entirety at the end of the Medina period and have a limited context. The hostilities that were ongoing at that moment had been 'paused' for a period of several months — an ancient Arab custom with regard to escalating conflicts — in which the various groups pledged not to engage in battle. Muhammad (PBUH) used this period to call various forces to join the Muslims, or, if they preferred, to leave the area that had initially been under Islamic rule. However, if these groups would resume their hostilities after the 'sacred months' passed, the Muslims would fight back.

He found it quite remarkable, especially considering the ancient law of war, that even in this setting of battles and quarrels, revelation ends with emphasising the principles of forgiveness and mercy. In order to minimise hostilities, Muslims were commanded to offer refuge, aid and shelter to anyone who sought it, even to those who belonged to the enemy forces, as can be read in verse 9:6. This idea took shape in a more or less chivalrous fashion: the person who sought refuge would receive the message of the Quran, but was not forced to accept it. Then, he or she, regardless of his or her religion, would be led to safety. "'Incredible' was the only thing I thought after reading this for the first time," Joram exclaims.

Furthermore, upon deeper investigation, he understood that the battle the Muslims were involved in at that time was a battle against the community that had robbed Muhammad (PBUH) and his companions of their homes and their possessions and had driven them out of their birthplace of Makkah, and in this way forcing them to go to the 'unknown' Yathrib.

The call in verse 9:5 concerned a defensive situation; it was with an already existing enemy and was directed at groups that were set on resuming the conflict even after the 'pause'. It also became clear to him that the aforementioned commandments with regard to fighting were not applicable at an individual level, but were for the sake of preservation and defence of a new society and community, which was striving to bloom and thrive as a nation.

Although he really wanted to feel the opposite about this verse, it was the context that made it more than just in his eyes and completely logical.

"A last example of an objection I held against Islam that vanished after I studied the life of the Prophet (PBUH) is about Islam being inherently antisemitic. And I'm not talking about politics or the state of Israel here. I'm only and explicitly talking about the Jewish religion and its followers. Jew-hate legitimised by Islam is an argument used in the West quite often to discredit the deen (the religion). I used it myself numerous times during debates in parliament or in media shows. A very sad example I used to show 'how true this argument' was an incident in Paris a couple of years ago, where an 85-year-old lady — a holocaust survivor — was killed and burned by her Muslim neighbour for 'being a wealthy Jew'. Another incident that I mentioned a lot was a demonstration in the Hague, the residence city of The Netherlands, in which 'death to the Jews' was chanted by groups of young Muslim men."

While writing the book and looking at the history of Jews in Europe, which is a very bloody history, he asked himself why he saw the religion of Islam as inherently antisemitic, while most of the killing and persecution of Europe's Jews was done in Europe by Christians. But he didn't see the Christian religion as antisemitic.

"I didn't really want to ask this question, but my curiosity and desire to know the truth was stronger. Like with the previous topics, I thought it would be best to look at the example of the Prophet to see what Islam teaches about Jews as a people. And although I found several occasions in history where there were clashes between Muslims, Jewish tribes and Jewish individuals, I found not one that specifically had to do with the Jewish religion of that tribe or person."

No hatred of Jews

He didn't find even a single sign of any hatred of Jews that was intrinsic and instructed by Muhammad (PBUH). Often times, practically as well as theologically, a 'common ground' was sought. First, the Quran states that kosher food (i.e. prepared by Jews) is permitted for Muslims to consume. Naturally, Islam also proclaims to bring a message that is rooted in the Jewish tradition and refers to Jewish Prophets such as Moses, David and Solomon. Then there is the oldest constitution in the world, that of Medina. In this constitution, or charter, three remarkable articles are specifically about the Jews and their status in the new community back then:

- Jews that followed the believers would be assisted and treated equally;
- No Jew would be treated unjustly on account of his religion;
- The enemies of those Jews who followed the believers would not be assisted.

"Equality and justice is what I bumped into while studying this topic. A very phenomenal attitude, especially when one considers the brutal and violent times in which people lived then."

The following Prophet's saying similarly shows no trace of the hatred of Jews. Once, one of Muhammad's (PBUH) companions asked him why he stood up for a funeral procession of a deceased Jewish man. In this context, it was unusual to stand up for anyone outside of one's own clan or group. The Prophet (PBUH) responded that "we were all equal in death. The Hadith of Muslim (961) is as follows: '...While Qays b. Sa'd and Sahl bin Hunayf were both in Qadisiyya, a funeral procession passed by them and they both stood up. They were told that it was the funeral procession of one of the people of the land (who were non-Muslim). They said that a funeral procession passed before the Prophet and he stood up. He was told that he (the dead man) was a Jew. Upon hearing this, he remarked: 'Was he not a human being, or did he not have a soul?'"

That Muhammad (PBUH) explicitly expressed his appreciation towards the Jewish tradition and its Prophets —

and that Jews ought to be proud of this — becomes clear in the following Hadith (about two of the Prophet's wives): "It reached Safiyya that Hafsa said: 'The daughter of a Jew', so she wept. Then the Prophet went to her while she was crying, and he said: 'What makes you cry?' She said: 'Hafsa said to me that I am the daughter of a Jew.' So the Prophet said: 'You are the daughter of a Prophet, your uncle is a Prophet and you are married to a Prophet, so what is she boasting to you about?' Then he said: 'Fear Allah, O Hafsa'" (Jami'al-Tirmidhi, book 46, no. 3894).

The aforementioned issues - the position of women in Islam, the violent nature of the faith, and the inherent anti-Semitism - that Islam critics bring up against the religion did not hold up in any way upon closer examination. On the contrary, what he discovered attracted and surprised him in the most positive sense of the word.

"During my research, I also received surprisingly satisfying Islamic answers to my existing Christian questions about specific dogmas, such as the Trinity, the sacrifice of Christ and original sin. From a young age on, I was wrestling with these subjects."

A phalanx of questions about Christianity perturbed him. How can God, for example, exist out of three persons? Christianity teaches that God the Father, the Son and the Holy Spirit are three separate persons but one in being. But in the Bible, Jesus asks God for strength; Jesus says he doesn't know everything and in the end Jesus even dies. If he is God, though, why does he ask himself for strength? How can an all-knowing God (and that's what the Bible teaches) not know everything? And how can an infinite God die? You cannot be eternal and mortal at the same time.

"That's something like a square circle. As a child, I often didn't know who to pray to: Jesus or God the Father? It was confusing." Another Christian dogma troubling to him was the belief in the crucifixion and resurrection of Christ as the only way to salvation. How was that possible? The ministers he knew told him that prophets such as Adam, Noah, Abraham and Moses were in heaven. But they, of course, didn't believe in the resurrection. Jesus was not even born yet. They couldn't provide a satisfying answer.

And, why is God unable to forgive sins without the death of a man anyway? The Bible says God forgives who he wants and explicitly puts forward that the sons, the children, are not to be punished for the sins of their fathers. But that's exactly what happens if someone has to die for the sins of Adam, the original sin, as Christianity teaches.

Questions like these were always in the back of his mind. But he put them away for a long time and accepted, as a teenager, that there were certain aspects of Christianity that he just didn't understand. When he was writing the book though, these questions popped up again. But now he was asking them not as a child but as a grown man.

Comparing Bible and Quran

Rereading the Bible - the Old and the New Testament - in the light of the Quran was like completing a puzzle. Especially when it came to the Oneness of the Creator. The Islamic concept was so clear: one God, all powerful, all knowing and we, as humans, have a direct relationship with Him. It made sense. Of course, he knew the basics of the Islamic theology, and had read the Quran several times before, during his studies, but never considered it to be the Truth with a capital T.

So, with great discomfort, he noticed that he was veering towards Islam at this point. Finally, Surah Al Ikhlaas captured his imagination so much that it cast a spell. He had read the Surah many times before, but now it stuck in his head:

*"Say, He is Allah, the One, Allah, the
Eternal Refuge,
He neither begets nor was begotten, Nor is there
to Him any equivalent,"*

It reminded him of the Old Testament text in Deuteronomy 6:4: "Hear Israel, the Lord is our God, the Lord is One" and of the words of Jesus himself (in the New Testament): "The first of all the commandments is, Hear, O Israel; The Lord our God is one Lord" (Mark 12:29). Jesus didn't speak about a trinity, didn't speak about a God being born or about something outside the total Oneness of the Creator. He realized that Jesus spoke about God in the way the Quran does.

The first time he read Surah Al Ikhlaas it felt like an attack on Christianity and its core beliefs, but now it was different. It felt like an objective and consistent reference to the words of all the Prophets. It was a necessary correction, but personally worrying for him.

Despite this discomfort, he searched on, and wanted to know the truth. The 'new' information he read in Islamic sources and the 'roller-coaster' of conflicting feelings (blossoming admiration for something you hate), affected his work on the book in such a way that it began to take on the character of a personal search for God. During this search, the person of Prophet Muhammad, (PBUH), raised the most questions. Who was this man? A deceiver, an antichrist, or was he truly - as Muslims believe - the last prophet of God? He started to read again about his life, but now without any previous biases. And he saw a more than special man. A man with almost supernatural patience, care, love, guidance, and, above all, dedication to his God and to his mission
for justice.

The arguments against his person disappeared as he made a comparison with Old Testament prophets. Why did he, for examples, believe in Moses but not in Muhammad (PBUH)? After all, there were a lot of similarities. Like Moses, the Prophet preached the belief in one God: Allah. Like Moses, the Prophet was given a law. Like Moses, the Prophet had to start a community. Like Moses, the Prophet lived an earthly life with a wife and children and, like Moses, the Prophet was operating in a very hostile and dangerous context.

He was intrigued and wanted to know more. He started reading more about the Prophet's life from the earliest Islamic sources. For the first time, he saw what Muslims see when reading and learning about Muhammad (PBUH) – he saw a teacher, a general, a diplomat, a merchant, an administrator, a husband and a father. All combined in one person. All combined in one life. A unique and universal example – a true Prophet of God.

One of the stories that led him to these conclusions was that of Hind, which affected him deeply. Forgiving a person who got your uncle killed and mutilated. The first time he read it, he
thought: "Wow, that's not an evil man. On the contrary, it shows a deep character of love and strength to act the way he did." It shook his image of the Prophet (PBUH).

This Prophet was more than a King. He was a hero. He was fighting for a higher cause of God and justice for all mankind.

Joram says that since he had never lost faith in God, by writing this book he could no longer refute the prophethood of Muhammad. "I was led to Islam in a very natural and rational way," he says like a punchline that evocatively sums up his turbulent journey.

But, that was something he really didn't want.

"It was late one evening that I realized that, in accepting the Prophethood of Muhammad, combined with my revised view of God (His Oneness), I had become a de facto Muslim in my heart."

Sitting at the dinner table, surrounded by piles of books on the life of the Prophet but looking at the Bible in the cabinet next to him, a lot went through his mind:

So is the God of Abraham, Isaac and Jacob the same God as the God of Ishmael's descendants? Do I consider myself a Muslim? Is that at all possible as a former anti-Islam politician? What would my wife, mother, brothers, sister and the rest of my family and friends say? And how would my former colleagues in politics, the media and the rest of the people who knew me take it? What would it mean in practice? And then, of course, all the rituals of that (then seemingly) 'difficult' Muslim life that would come with it.

"I had so many questions in my head. So many 'unpleasant' scenarios. I actually didn't want to think about it anymore when something remarkable happened."

While putting the books at the table away, some of them fell off the shelf because it was way too full. One of these books was the Quran.

It was on the floor, open, with its cover up. When he picked it up and turned it around, his thumb was on a page where he read ayat (verse) 46 of Surah Al Hajj:

"It's not the eyes that are blind, but the hearts."

The Book spoke to him

It was as if The Book spoke to him. It explained exactly what was holding him back, and he could literally see what he had written down about the truth of Tawheed and the life of the Prophet but still couldn't accept it because his heart was closed. When he read that passage, it was as if someone turned the key and opened the door… What seemed totally impossible only a few years before, took place: he became a Muslim.

It was a few days after this event that he took *shahada*. This happened after an excellent dinner in a cozy, homey setting and in a small company of three Muslims, two of whom were imams. After the pronouncement of the *shahada*, it was not raining gold and he did not see the stars twinkling extra loudly, he says, jokingly.

What he did notice was a personal joy and a great deal of inner peace. He was convinced in his head, and he felt it in his heart. Pronouncing the simple testimony of faith was the moment that the tension he always felt as a Christian - a tension between his heart and his mind - disappeared. Religiously, he was home now. Looking back at the whole process, which took over three years (he began writing and researching in 2014 and took shahada at the end of 2018), it was almost as if his heart was so closed, so blind to feel the truth that God took the other door. The door of reason, the door of the mind. "And, of course, I know that Islam is a religion of both heart and mind, but for a lot of non-Muslims, especially in the West, it is the mind, it is knowledge, that opens doors," he says.

Joram's conversion to Islam undoubtedly created a storm. For all those who still revel in painting Islam and Muslims with the ugliest brush – and these include right-wing politicians, mainstream media and willing and unwilling Islamophobes of all ilks – he stands like a beacon on a shore of darkness that has been buffeted by an unceasing array of anti-Islamic waves.

You may or may not agree with Joram – but you can't ignore him. When he speaks, everybody listens, because he has seen it all. He has appeared on countless TV shows and given countless speeches explaining his roller-coaster journey. But his most eloquent testimony is that book he wrote - *Apostate: From Christianity to Islam in times of secularisation and terror* – which describes in stunning and evocative detail his personal and theological journey and the development he has undergone. A book which achieves exactly the opposite of what he intended, but which achieves exactly what he intends now.

Joram has answers on how to restore the image of Islam. "That's why good religious education and stable Muslim communities, who practice what they preach, are so important. Especially in the West where the culture slightly became hostile towards religion in general and Islam in particular. We need scholars, who know both the Islamic tradition and the Western context we live in. People of knowledge, who can train the next generation to teach, and lead, but above all, to explain Islam in the correct and historic way," he says.

"From the many messages I receive, I gather that my personal experience has helped many others in their search for Islam. Since I am not a scholar, I try to do this by simply showing the beauty, the power and the answer that Islam can be in the personal lives of people. In this case, mine.

"Of course, I was somewhat reluctant to do this because, first of all, it is not pleasant for the ego. Admitting your deepest injustice, publicly, is difficult. Having to say that the hard battle you fought for years was in fact the wrong battle is not easy. Especially in a political context where everything is always extra charged. And then also on the subject of religion.

"But secondly, it was also a dangerous step to take. Among the supporters of my former party, but also outside it, there is sometimes a rough crowd. This was evident from the flood of insults, invective and death threats. Both in my direction and in the direction of my family. There were some pretty extreme slurs and 'promises' among them - from torture to public execution with a sword. I was also asked if, in that context, I would not be better off keeping it to myself and practising Islam in silence."

Joram says the answer to that question was a firm 'no'. For one thing, it would be practically impossible because of who he was as a public figure. "Suppose I had not told anyone about my conversion and I walked into a mosque on a random Friday to follow the *kuhtbah* (Friday sermon) and start praying. People might be startled, the police might be called in, there might be a threatening situation - even for myself. Furthermore, a praying Joram van Klaveren in a mosque would be leaked via social media in no time anyway."

Besides, he found it his personal duty, and that was the least he could do, after all those years of Islam and Muslim-bashing, to publicly explain why he was wrong. With this he could perhaps prevent others from making the same mistakes and inform those who are already in the same corner as he was. "And how better to do that than through a book where you can share all your ideas and experiences in your own words with the outside world?"

"Finally, I was and am very proud to be a Muslim and to be part of the most beautiful religion on earth. It's not something I wanted to hide. There has not been a second after my *shahada* that I have doubted the decision to become a Muslim. It has been the most deliberate and best decision I have ever made. Every prayer, every moment during Ramadan, eating halal consciously, reading the Quran, and trying to act in the proper Islamic way, has been a deepening of my faith. Where some think it is a burden, I experience it as a liberation."

Frequently asked question

Of course, he is often asked about his experience of not consuming alcohol or pork after conversion. "From my early teenage years, I had already stopped eating pork because it gave me juvenile pimples. Stopping consuming alcohol was related to the birth of my first daughter. I didn't want to be in a situation where you are under the influence next to your baby's crib. From that moment on, Diet Coke made its appearance."

To a frequently asked question what the essence of his conversion is and why people should embrace Islam in the first place, he has a brief answer: "God is real and Islam is the way to the Truth. And the Truth, deep down in our hearts, we all want to follow. It attracts and welcomes. Therefore, free yourself from the lies, superficiality, flat materialism and selfishness of this world (in all its manifestations). Become Muslim."

"The *deen* (religion) has brought me inner peace and has also softened my character. I also notice that I get angry less easily and have become more patient. And others notice it, too. Even though my mother still hasn't read my book and prefers not to talk about Islam, she told me at one point that she prefers me as a Muslim than a Christian. However, she immediately added that she still doesn't like the fact that I became a Muslim. But apparently action speaks louder than words."

At the same time, he has remained very much the same as a person. Although some converts think they have to forget their cultural and ethnic background, Joram understood from the Islamic tradition that "'our faith was revealed for all peoples, for all times and for all places'. *Urf,* the concept that you retain and adopt from the culture what does not conflict with the foundations of the religion, I have taken to heart. Islam is not just Arab. It is also Indonesian, Mauritanian, Moroccan, Turkish, Pakistani but also Dutch, Mexican and Japanese. After all, the whole world created by Allah is our masjid. And Islam fits everywhere. That is precisely the beauty and power of the religion."

He also says the much-cited contradiction between Islam and the West is a fable. For example, every historian knows that the Renaissance in Europe could never have taken place without Islam, many laws introduced by Napoleon in Europe were based on Shariah law which he learned in Egypt, the greatest German writer of all time - Johann Wolfgang Goethe - was more than fond of Islam and to this day the American Library of Congress shows that the founding fathers of that country saw Islam as one the foundations of Western civilisation. A beautiful painting accompanied by the words 'Islam' and 'science' adorns the ceiling of this central library, at the heart of American democracy.

Joram wants to conclude his long story with a personal anecdote, which also shows, at its core, the merging of Islam and the West.

"Before it was made public, I had to tell those close to me: my wife, mother, brothers, sister, friends and my grandfather. Telling my grandfather was the hardest.

"My grandfather was a very Christian man and kind of the head of the family. He was 93 years old and dying. He was lying on his bed at home when I told him. At that specific moment, he stopped talking, closed his eyes and I even thought he stopped breathing. But suddenly he looked at me and said:

'Well, at least you didn't become a Catholic.'"

"And this may sound a little strange to an outsider, but it was kind of an approval and has to do with the history of the country. The Netherlands once was a Colony of Spain. "I am talking about the end of the 16th century. The Spanish were Catholic Christians and the north of The Netherlands were protestant Christians."

The Spanish imperialist power was much stronger and tried to push Catholicism. And they were successful. So, the founder of The Netherlands, William of Orange, had to take action. He contacted the Sultan of the Ottoman Empire, with the thought 'the enemy of my enemy is my friend' and asked for help. The Ottomans were benevolent and gave the Dutch money and weapons to fight the Spanish. The Netherlands won and became an independent state. Thus, with the help of Muslims.

So, there is Islam DNA at the core of the foundation of the country. And every year, and they still do so, people celebrate the defeat of the Spanish.

The celebration is called 'Leidens ontzet', which means something like 'the liberation of Leiden', a big City in the Netherlands. And when they do, they wear little crescent moons on their clothes and they sing, just like the Dutch did over 400 years ago: 'I'd rather be Turkish than Papish', which if we translate to modern day English means: 'I'd rather be a Muslim than a Catholic'.

Conversation with my grandfather

"In the last conversation I had with my grandfather, before he died, we talked about religion, about life, death and beauty. He always told me that knowledge is beauty because he believed it showed a little bit of the Ultimate reality.

"I asked him what he thought about beauty and life in relation to God and religion, and he said to me:

'When I look at it from a religious point of view, especially now in these last days, it's very clear that beauty is to live like you see God, and if you cannot do that, try to live as if God sees you. That's beauty to me.' Then he fell asleep and I went home. I never talked to him again.

"A few months later, I read a hadith of Bukhari where the Prophet (PBUH), said that *ihsan* is to worship God as though you see Him, and if you cannot see Him, then indeed He sees you.

"When I read that for the first time, I was so moved and felt so blessed, that the last words my Christian grandfather spoke to me, were almost the same as this hadith of our Prophet Muhammad (PBUH).

"I thank Allah for that, for the fact that I'm a Muslim now."

3

'My conversion at 16 has caused both excitement and bewilderment'

Ayana Jihye Moon – South Korean celebrity

Twenty-seven-year-old Ayana is today a famous Muslim figure in South-East Asia, with 3.6 million followers on Instagram. She came to know about Islam when she was just eight years old, during the Iraq war. The TV screen filled with images from Iraq, of a people she wasn't familiar with, wearing weird clothes. She searched 'Iraq' on the Internet and that would mark the beginning of a journey that saw her embrace Islam at the age of 16.

ON A beautiful day in 2003, when Ayana Jihye Moon was just eight years old, she was watching TV at her home on the outskirts of Seoul. A news program was suddenly interrupted for a terrible announcement: THE UNITED STATES HAS INVADED IRAQ! America's global war on terror was rolling on. The TV screen soon filled with images from Iraq, of a people she wasn't familiar with, wearing weird clothes, with the backdrop of stunning sceneries from a distant land she hadn't heard about.

Who are these people? What language do they speak? Why do they dress like this?

The images created an inquisitiveness she couldn't resist, prompting her to search 'Iraq' on the Internet for the first time in her life. She understood that Iraqis followed a religion called Islam. Until then, the image of Islam in her mind was of a foreign creed that put all women in veils, but her logical mind couldn't think of 'all' Muslims as terrorists as many people said, an accusation she found preposterous and she wanted to find out about the religion herself.

That would mark the beginning of a journey that finally saw her embrace Islam at the age of 16.

Sixteen?

At a tender age of 16, can a person grapple with the deep philosophical questions of life and draw conclusive, satisfactory answers?

Ayana admits the age of her conversion has been a matter of both excitement and bewilderment. "My journey started when I was in elementary school and I converted when I was in high school. Whenever I tell people that I converted when I was 16 years old, they are so surprised that I'm embarrassed. What do you think a 16-year-old should be like?" she beams.

Ayana doesn't even consider herself as special for probing deep into religion as a kid. "Not all kids only enjoy cartoons. Of course, I also watched cartoons, but as I have said before, I had a presidential candidate who I supported at the age of about eight, the same age when I just knew Islam through the Iraq war. There are many children who are interested in stock markets and talk about the economy. I don't think that I was special or smart."

Despite her assertions, it's indeed her age that makes her story unique, sparking curiosity in older minds as to what thoughts traversed through the mind of a young girl that would lead to her embarking on a life-changing decision that other grown-ups would baulk at.

South Korean decapitated in Iraq

The Iraq war would continue to dominate the headlines in South Korea for some time, partly due to a dangerous twist it took. A few months after the US invasion, the South Korean government, as an ally of America, passed a bill to deploy some of its Armed Forces for medical and construction support in Iraq. Soon, the US government requested a dispatch of more troops under the guise of rebuilding an Iraq completely ruined by war. Unfortunately, an employee of a South Korean company under contract to the US military in Iraq, Kim Seon-il, was abducted and decapitated by an insurgent group called Jama'at al-Tawhid wal-Jihad. A video of Kim, blindfolded and kneeling, screaming and pleading for the Korean government to withdraw their troops, went viral on media outlets all over the world. From 9/11 to Kim's execution, a chain of events created a lasting, negative image of Islam among South Koreans – that all Muslims are ruthless terrorists.

Nonetheless, this didn't stop Ayana from learning more about Islam. At first, exotic images of camels and men in flowing thobes walking through the desert were stuck in her eight-year-old mind.

She discovered that Iraqis are a deeply religious people. She wasn't aware of the concept of religion, as her parents are atheists, but still she wanted to understand how a religion could control so many people's lives and have an impact on all aspects of a society. "I discovered Islam not as a religion but as a culture. I watched all relevant news reports and documentaries available in Korean. My mother used to take me to a bookstore once a week to buy me a book; I picked books about Islamic culture. When I was 10, I saved money to buy a book written by Lee Hee-soo, South Korea's famous Islam scholar," says Ayana.

Her growing interest in the religion and the knowledge she gleaned from various sources gave her a fair picture of Islamic culture, which she expanded by reading the Quran and visiting a mosque in Seoul. Still, she had no intention to convert since it was difficult for her to believe in someone who cannot be seen or touched. Islam as a religion came to her afterwards.

"Looking back, I was a frog in a well in terms of my religious belief. I didn't understand the weight of my choice and what I would go through as a Muslim. I was just happy and excited to share the moment with my close Muslimah friends and felt grateful that they accompanied me on the day of *shahada* ceremony," she reminisces.

Social media star

Twenty-seven-year-old Ayana Jihye Moon is today a famous Muslim figure in South-East Asia, with 3.6 million followers on Instagram, 651k followers on YouTube and a total of more than 17 million views, with her fan base coming mainly from Indonesia, Malaysia, and South Korea.

Many know her as a Muslim model and influencer, but she prefers to define herself as a college student at a renowned university in Malaysia, majoring in political science and diplomacy. She looks very polite and gentle, someone who would never raise her voice, but as she talks, she emerges as a powerful and resolute woman with copious amounts of energy, a flaming gaze and vigour.

Born in 1995 as the eldest daughter of a middle-class Korean family of four, living on the outskirts of Seoul, her paternal grandmother named her as Jihye, not a unique Korean female name. Even though she was the only daughter born in a patriarchal family, her grandmother didn't bother to give her a special name whereas all her male cousins got atypical and unusual names. Ayana cites that as the reason why she chose her Islamic name as 'Ayana' since she wanted to be special, not common. She didn't know the meaning of Ayana when she chose it, and later learned it means smile, beauty, and intelligence – all the good meanings she wanted.

As a little girl, she was curious about foreign affairs and politics partly due to her father who was a businessman. Vivid stories from her father, who travelled all around the world, continuously stimulated her imagination, creating an eagerness to discover new countries and cultures. Under the studious guidance from her parents, she was keen to read books and newspapers and watch documentaries while her friends were more into Disney films and cartoons.

As a secondary schooler, Ayana dreamt of becoming a professor or a diplomat with expertise in the Middle Eastern region and therefore actively participated in Islam-related activities. At the age of 17, she went to the Korea-Middle East Cooperation Forum and had a glimpse of the opportunities that lay ahead. She was warmly and eagerly welcomed at the forum, being one of the youngest participants, and they were even curious as to why she was there, she reminisces.

After saying that she's a Muslim, all questions stopped, as if her status as a Muslim was superior to everything else, though she admits, despite her conversion, she didn't know much about the religion and Islamic countries compared to the experts who were there.

Ayana adds: "Thanks to my identity as a Muslim, I could have a seat right next to the people with power such as ministers and professors. As an ambitious young woman, I found out that my religion could also help in my career."

She admits that her first intention on Islam was impure; however, even back then, she was quite determined to continue her life with her new religion because it was a choice she had made, and it wasn't an easy choice in a society like South Korea, where being Muslim meant wading through a hostile territory.

The road to Islam

Now comes the most crucial question everyone would like to throw at her: What attracted her to Islam?

But here, like many things about Ayana, the answer isn't linear. Her road to Islam didn't pass through a rigorous, intellectual study of its theological tenets, nor was it the result of a meticulous study of the Quran or the life of Prophet Muhammad, (PBUH), but more rooted in emotional experiences in which she felt a personal connection with God.

"To be honest, I am quite surprised to know that lots of people think fiercely about the oneness of God even before converting. I hope you don't misunderstand what I mean, maybe the reason why I think like this is because it's a cultural difference or maybe it's because I converted to Islam from an atheistic background.

"This is my question and the point of view about the religion. Why do we have a religion? Why do we worship God, pray, and strive to live God's will every day? I think its essential purpose, and the reason of all those activities, is for myself and ourselves.

"There are social barriers against Islam and Muslims in Korea. And this acts as a big practical obstacle for many people to study and accept Islam. In this society, when choosing a religion, how I am accepted as a person who has a religion is more important than telling right or wrong about monotheism, the scriptures, and the prophets."

Ayana was deeply influenced by Korean Muslim sisters whose life and conduct as Muslims showed her the way forward. She met them at a mosque in Seoul which she frequented for a year, during weekends.

"I was attracted by Korean Muslim sisters who I could meet whenever I visited the Masjid in Seoul every weekend. Their warmth and the way they behaved externally, internally, and intellectually was enough to make me think that even Koreans, as Muslims, might well be able to integrate into the Korean society. "I didn't know much about the religion, the Quran and the stories of the Prophets well. However, the people who tried to follow the way of Islam in a right way inspired me," she says. "Now, I am learning at an Islamic University and even make time to learn his [the Prophet's] biography. However, I think that the ultimate goal of adopting a religion is to learn to love people, to direct myself on the right path for my own happiness and inner strength. And, I just found it accidentally in Islam and I can say that it was the plan of God."

Ayana says that since she had been learning about Islam through books and the Internet, she wanted to communicate with the real Muslims in real life. "I just asked about their daily life. What I was worried about the most was if I accepted Islam, I would be excluded from Korean society. I wanted to simulate from their experiences what my life would be like if I were to convert. I didn't ask their conversion stories as I knew that I was not a person who is easily inspired by someone's decision or life story except when it comes to academic, business and political achievements. And, I visited the masjid every weekend for a year." She took the *shahadah* at Seoul Central Masjid. "For your information, there is only one masjid in Seoul," she states. Muslim sisters became her witnesses and it was guided by the Korean Imam of the masjid. "I didn't have any surreal feeling, but I could feel I was doing something big for my whole life that I decided by myself, without anyone's compulsion, and thought it would change my life 180 degrees and it did. And from the moment I converted, I thought of living more intentionally as a Muslim.

Intention is the most important in Islam."

For her, it has been a journey of personal discovery. "If you've never been madly intense or desperate for something, you won't be able to empathise with why God must exist. I live so hard and good as a human being, and having no one to guarantee or reward me for this is like telling someone like me not to live hard. And when you get to a position where you can't get advice from anyone, only the Absolute gives you the power to move on. The more I experience and achieve, the deeper and more mature my faith is."

For Ayana, experiences are crucial in the advancement of faith. "People on social media platforms like YouTube say they've had a lot of faith right after conversion. We only can realise God's wisdom and the greatness of His plan when we experience difficulties, joys, rewards for effort, feelings of loss, etc."

How did her parents react? "I didn't share with them as I didn't think they needed to know it. But, of course, they were shocked when I decided to leave Korea to study Islam deeply. I think they reacted just like what you imagine."

Foray into modelling and initial struggle

Her extraordinary experience at the Korea-Middle East Cooperation

Forum (KMECF) instilled in her a desire to pursue a career associated with Islam. After a thorough search, she found out that no Korean university offered a course she was looking for. After discussions with several professors and experts, she decided to study in Malaysia. This caused serious tension between Ayana and her parents, who stopped all financial support. But she was resolute and didn't change her mind. She worked 24/7 to save money for her tuition, working in hotels and coffee shops, and doing odd jobs that could supplement her income. Meanwhile, she used every spare minute she had to study English and Arabic. One and a half years of hard work and determination later, she got a scholarship from a university and flew to Malaysia with her hopes and dreams, where another rude shock awaited her. The scholarship covered only the tuition fee and she didn't expect that she would have to buy water, pillow cover, towel, tooth brush, etc with her own savings. Soon, she ran out of money and lived at a friend's house without rent for a year. She started modeling, being in need of a well-paid job with less investment of time, as she had to focus on her studies. However, navigating work and study proved strenuous, taking a heavy toll on her. A feeling of deep disappointment began to set in at achieving nothing after endless efforts. At this stage, Ayana continues, she was on the verge of abandoning everything and thought of returning to South Korea. Some friends she got to know through modeling asked her to visit Indonesia before her return to Korea; she didn't realise at the time that this would be the second turning point in her life.

In Indonesia, she got a request from a local TV network to make an appearance on a show. She didn't expect anything, but the show proved to be an instant hit all over the country! Her friends in Malaysia started to call and message to congratulate her; and she quickly made up her mind to stay in Indonesia for a while to make a while to make use of some unexpected opportunities. She was hesitant at first, as she was taught by her parents that success can only be achieved by attaining an exalted position such as that of a politician, professor, and journalist. Being a model or a celebrity was never an option for her.

Nevertheless, she decided to chart her own course, and learn from her experiences. She wanted to become an influential individual. By leveraging her value and the fame she had achieved through modeling and as a social network influencer, she could be a brand herself, she thought.

Yet, Ayana says, her goal is deeply connected to politics and studies. "I've met so many big Korean figures who used to be in politics. Even these intelligent people couldn't accomplish what they wanted through politics. How could I, with confidence, say that I could do better than them? What I've learned is that if I'm a professor and an influencer, more people would listen to me. That means that I could make real differences in the world. That's amazing!" explained Ayana.

Later, deepening her relationship with Indonesia, she wrote an inspirational book called *Ayana, Journey To Islam*, which was published by an Indonesian publishing house, which explained her journey to Islam.

Challenges of being a Muslim in South Korea

Moon remembers quite vividly the day she converted. "People expect that, once you convert, you'll receive a message from God or feel completely different, as if you are born again. But for me, it was a down-to-earth experience. I became an independent individual by choosing a religion which would take a good part of my life. It was my choice, no one interfered or meddled. I felt a whole new kind of responsibility."

But something else was in store. She didn't know at the time that her life as a Muslimah in South Korea, where Muslims are a minority, would be this complicated.

Traditionally, Koreans were, for many decades, Buddhists. In 1392, a newly established Chosun Dynasty adopted Confucianism as the ruling principle of the country, but today the peninsula is rather atheistic. According to a poll conducted by Gallup Korea, only 40 per cent of the population have religion as of 2021, in the order of Protestantism, Buddhism and Catholicism. Islam is not even listed on the chart. Moon's family, too, were atheists.

There are many rules to follow for Muslims: pray five times a day, do not eat pork, a strict dress code and so on. But it's hard to find mosques in South Korea, pork is the most consumed meat, dress code is getting less strict, even in the office, and furthermore, South Korea is very homogeneous. It is slowly changing, though the idea of a single race nation is still widespread among its people. Under these circumstances, following religious practices seemed almost impossible in South Korea as people are not accustomed to this behaviour.

In this context, it's not surprising that her friends and family didn't fully support her conversion. Most of them couldn't comprehend her intentions. "It's easier to convince someone who already has religion to convert to Islam as he or she knows already the concept of religion and its practices. But South Korea is homogeneous and relatively closed to diversity. I can understand why it is still difficult for South Koreans to accept us, whereas I could live as a Muslimah in Malaysia where the majority of the population is Muslim. In South Korea, I am made aware of my religion every minute and it becomes an obstacle to my everyday life," adds Ayana.

However, the Muslim community and population are growing in South Korea. But, for Ayana, a growing number doesn't mean all conversion are genuine. "Yes, according to many reports, it seems like we're getting bigger. But when you look at this phenomenon, some convert to open a Halal business or to get a scholarship. If you live exactly like a non-Muslim, what's the point?" she asks.

Still, Ayana doesn't complain about the bitter and traumatic experiences in her own country. Before conversion, thanks to her parents who are wealthy, this top-tier Korean girl never experienced poverty or difficulties, and never had been discriminated against. She was living in a bubble, in her safe zone. But her religion put her in a situation that opened her eyes to what others are going through, much worse than herself. She'd always been part of a majority in all aspects, and suddenly became part of an extreme minority. She is indeed grateful to God, as she now can truly understand other people's tears and suffering. Thus, she never regretted her conversion, she asserts.

Hijab

One day, returning home from the mosque in Seoul, waiting to cross the road, she felt a gaze from two Korean males and overheard them making a rude, risqué comment about what Muslim women wore under their burqa. She brought up this story when she met an imam at the masjid in Seoul. She considered his answer conventional. Regardless of what other people say, he said, "you must keep wearing hijab and following religious rules as written in Quran." Her next question was if he was going to act up "when I'm verbally or physically attacked because I followed the Quran?" And that was the end of the discussion. "I am in a country where very few Muslims live. But is hijab a shield? If someone shoots at me, does it bounce back bullets?" she asks. But, barring the humour, it's a sharp comment on the reality of living as a Muslimah, she says.

There are some situations when Ayana cannot or does not wear the hijab, and she says she is doing her best as intention is the most important. If she knows what it's like to wear a hijab as a woman, she can give better advice to fellow Muslimah, especially the young who will certainly ask the same question as she did.

She also talks about the divisions within the Muslim community. People think there is only one Islam, but there is not. As words can be translated and interpreted in different ways, they bring diversity and confusion and even division in the Islamic world. That's the reason why each Islamic country has a different religious identity.

"A country and a culture can have different identities, but all Muslims must know that we could commit errors as we are imperfect beings. What God says is simple. Violence is bad, judging something by its cover is bad, and hatred is bad. If we follow His words, everything is crystal clear," Ayana states.

Ayana's formula to settle all problems is also found in Islam, which are dignity and nobility. These two are important elements based in all Islamic institutions. For instance, in capitalism, an individual can do whatever is necessary to make profit, and the means you choose to earn money can be justified by your profit. However, Islamic finance strictly bans exploitation of others for one's profit. "It says that you must be ethical; if you have more than others, help the one who has less than you, and do not brag about what you have. What we can learn from this is that God asks us to think about what is right, and to take care of each other, and be humble."

She adds: "I'm not making this up, it's all written in Quran. If we genuinely understand His words, there is no problem that can't be solved."

Professor Lee Hee-soo

There is one person who helped her immensely in her journey - Professor

Lee Hee-soo. "He is the best Islamic expert working in Korea. When the practical difficulties of living as a Muslim in a non-Muslim country and the conscience as a Muslim inevitably collide, I am distressed, and I turn to him. In our society, wearing a hijab is not allowed for social and economic activities, but in Islam, women must wear a hijab.

"No matter how devout a Muslim I am, I struggled a lot when the good deeds I did as a Muslim were downplayed by not doing things [such as wearing hijab] I could never have done in our society.

"In fact, these things are matters between me and God, so I do the best I can and hope for His mercy for the rest, but sometimes I felt it was unfair that only women had to worry about things like hijabs. When I was troubled with all these religious but practical problems, Professor Lee's lectures and efforts to get rid of such social prejudices became a comfort to me," she says.

From zero to hero and energy from religion

God always works in mysterious ways, avers Ayana. "Most Muslims react almost identically when they hear my story. How could a South Korean girl from an atheist family accept Islam? Well, I, too, ask this question," she notes.

And she has found the answers. She says this can be explained by *hidayah* (Allah's guidance). There have been a few moments Ayana felt God's guidance. She was unable to read His intention when she went through crises; however, after each incident, she found something that helped her understand why it happened or came across someone through whom she could find God's hidden message.

When she settled in Malaysia, she had hard times making ends meet. Things were going so badly she felt she was losing her faith. However, the moment she decided to give up her life in Malaysia, she found a second chance in Indonesia, in an inexplicable way, as if God wanted her to send a message that it's not yet time to give up, and to continue her journey.

A couple of years before the Covid-19 outbreak, when she was in Indonesia, the same doubts passed her mind – this time she was safe and secure financially, and she made an announcement: now she was ready to go back to college in Malaysia. Throughout her life, Ayana found God's message at the right time.

It's through crises and difficulties that her faith has been moulded and strengthened.

"If I hadn't gone through difficult times, I don't think that I could be this mature spiritually. The last semester was challenging, as I had to manage both my work and my university life. I was having a hard time due to panic attacks, but I managed all quite well. Often, we delude ourselves into thinking that we did our best, but I think only a few can proudly say that they did. What I learned from God is that there's no shortcut. If I really do my best to pursue a Muslim life and my career, I will receive God's guidance."

A huge difference she experienced in her life after her conversion is that she stays optimistic for her future. She believes that the Absolute would be there for her if she fulfills her duty.

Don't judge others

Ayana says her spiritual journey isn't flawless; she undergoes trials and errors. Born with a very analytic and logical mind, she's always been seeking clear answers, even when it comes to religion. Now she understands that religion is not to be judged right or wrong but is something that you humbly accept. It took much longer to get to this truth knowing that nothing was natural to her as she is not from a Muslim country. Her plan is simple: meet more Muslims, listen to them and study everything related to Islam.

By doing so, she could establish the principles and definition of Islam.

Ayana also considers religion as a subjective matter. In Islam, what matters the most is your *niyyat* (intention). There's only one God and God reveals the holy words – the Quran – through his messenger Muhammad, (PBUH). No one is perfect except God, so if you have a kind intention to follow the essence of His words, you are a good Muslim. That's why she tries not to judge other Muslims by their appearance.

"We must admit that, in modern days, it is hard to live like a book. If you keep God's words in mind and have an intention to practice what He said, you're ok, though you must show it by action. Only God can judge your faith and no one else. I think this is an ideal relationship between God and myself," she says.

Recently, she learned that intelligence is the most highly praised feature of human beings by Allah. "I was comforted," said Ayana, "It means that I, who chose to be a Muslim by using my intelligence, am getting closer to the divine will. I was stunned when I understood His profound message. I feel like I've made a big step in my spiritual journey."

Intention and purpose are her chosen life principles that she learned through her spiritual journey. They are the driving forces that enable Ayana to move forward and make changes for herself and for others. She wants to be someone dignified in front of God and herself as she made an inviolable promise as a Muslimah. She says that her religious journey is still ongoing. Wondering what God planned for her future, she could not wait to find out her next *hidayah*.

Ayana admits she is an ambitious woman. She is based in Malaysia and Indonesia, and she actively participates in politics. She says she has become close to many famous Korean political figures and their fruitful exchanges are expected to see results soon.

Sometimes she has compromised on her religious practices, but she always makes an effort to keep her religious identity when she presents herself in front of them.

"In South Korea, my desire to be an ambitious career woman and my faith are constantly at war. I don't want to lose any. If I give up my career, I will hate myself for failing my religion, and vice versa too."

The question of why she converted at such a young age would vanish if one were to listen to her for a few minutes. Despite her humble claims that she is an ordinary woman, what emerges is a powerful personality, an extraordinary woman of great erudition, integrity, moral courage and spiritual strength that far surpasses her age, who has been moulded in the burning crucible of life through intense experiences.

And, she chooses to answer the question of if her conversion happened too early:

"I think it's neither too early nor too late. Because God's timing is always perfect," she concludes.

4

'I've been Mutah since birth. My parents named me 'the one who is obeyed"

Mutah 'Napoleon' Beale – American former rapper

Mutah Beale's path to truth, marred by a tragic childhood and then glistened by international stardom, was a journey of soul searching and healing his emotional scars. Despite feelings of despair and turning to drugs and alcohol for consolation, a constant in his story was his resolute faith in God.

"ELIEVE IT or not, the first time I ever stepped foot in a mosque," said one Mutah Beale, "I went armed with a loaded gun." Aged 24, he also arrived with an entourage of 20.

"I was paranoid!" he exclaimed. "My whole life up until that point was filled with prejudice against Muslims. So, I took my gun with me – I wasn't gonna take no chances [sic]."

Nonetheless, Mutah would eventually find himself swayed to stand side by side in prayer with the very people he had disdained since childhood. "When I went down into *sujūd*, I spoke to God – I told Him I was tired and needed inner peace. I also asked Him to guide me."

Mutah's path to Islam is a gripping tale of childhood tragedy, international superstardom and eventual overcoming of his demons. After being knighted as 'Napoleon' by 90s rap star Tupac Shakur, Mutah emerged as a lyrical force during hip hop's golden age.

Lines laced with lewdness, expletives and anger, however, were all too common within Napoleon's body of work. For instance, he once boasted of "getting [his] pleasure out of sinnin'" in one of his rhymes alongside the late Tupac.

Amid the excesses of the fast lane, gilded with money and fame, in the dark recesses of Mutah's young mind was a soul in pain. Having lost his parents and religion, he was left yearning for belonging. Mutah thus became embroiled in living the life of a thug – seeking solace in drugs and alcohol to bury his innermost woes. "Truly, I was drowning in depression. I was unhappy and always intoxicated. There wasn't a day I left my house with a sober mind or without a loaded gun," he recollected.

Despite feeling hopeless and seeking guidance in all the wrong places, a continual thread in Mutah's story was his unwavering faith in God's existence. "After my parents' passing, I was raised by my Christian grandmother who was very spiritual. I struggled with many concepts of Christianity, but my grandmother would always say, 'anything that happens is from God', and this was easy for me to understand." He continued: "She instilled in me that no matter what you go through in life, you should always turn to Him. So, I've always had that sensibility in me."

This resolute belief in God, coupled with a pursuit for guidance led the way to Mutah's eventual reversion to his Islamic roots.

Brutal beginnings

"Both my parents were actually converts to Islam," Mutah explained. "I think my father was the first in our family to become Muslim." Mutah's father, Lorenzo, was African American and his mother, Elisha, a Puerto Rican Cuban Latina. Both were captivated by the rhetoric of the Nation of Islam's (NOI) new religious movement, which called for Black nationalism and an independent separatist state for African Americans. Although the NOI was led by Elijah Muhammad from 1934 until his death in 1975, it was a fiery Malcolm X who rose to become the group's articulate spokesperson and representative.

In one of his final addresses after having denounced the NOI, Malcolm prayed for his people to "grow intellectually so that [they] can understand the problems of the world and where [they] fit into in that world picture," – a message that spoke volumes to Mutah's mother and father. "My parents were avid followers of Malcolm X. When Malcolm left the NOI, they followed suit and accepted mainstream Islam, too."

After becoming Muslims, Mutah's parents adopted the names Salek and Aquilah. "Many assume I changed my name after becoming Muslim. In truth, I've been Mutah since birth. My parents named me 'the one who is obeyed'," he revealed.

Tragically, aged just 27 and 22 years old, Mutah's parents' lives were cut short.

On March 21st, 1981, under the headline '3 Slain in Jersey Apartment', the *New York Times* recounted the "execution style killing" of Salek and his wife, Aquilah,[1]. A violent scene that unfolded before the eyes of their infant son Mutah and his two brothers Mooney and Mill. John Clark, the then Deputy Police Chief, surmised the crime was likely committed by someone they knew[2].

In 1996, this tragic tale would later be retold by a 19 year old Mutah through his lyrics on Tupac's 'Tradin' War Stories' track. Rapping as Napoleon, he told the listener of his grapple with flashbacks from that fateful day that rendered him "holdin' in anger because [his] parents missin'." He also remarked in his rhymes that the sight of blood being spilt never fazed him, for it was a visual he was far too familiar with.

After the poignant demise of his parents, Mutah and his two brothers were raised by their grandmother in a Christian household.

"One of my earliest memories of living with Grandma was her having my brothers and I kneel on the floor, fold our hands and say a prayer. I remember this very vividly – it was my first experience with Christian practice." Thereafter, weekly attendance at Church on Sunday became part of Mutah's routine.

His family, like many other African Americans, were attendees of the Baptist denominational church – known for its charismatic overtones. "We've all seen the videos of the church preacher conducting healing sessions. They'd tap the heads of the congregation who would then become visibly ecstatic from supposedly catching the Holy Ghost. This was the

---

1   The New York Times, 1981. 3 Slain in Jersey Apartment. [online] p.19. Available at: <https://www.nytimes.com/1981/03/22/nyregion/3-slain-in-jersey-apartment. html>.

2   Ibid.

environment I grew up in – but it never worked on me, though. Every time the preacher would tap my head, it would have no effect on me." Mutah found himself baffled at the sight of others around him falling over, going into convulsions or speaking in tongues at the touch of the preacher.

He further discussed the Islamophobic sentiments that were collateral damage of his upbringing. "Our grandmother told us it was Muslims who murdered our parents. So, in ignorance, I grew with a strong hatred towards them and their religion." This animosity towards Islam yet persisted despite the presence of some Muslim friends and family he grew up alongside.

"After my parents accepted Islam, my auntie and uncles converted, too. But I would say they were culturally Muslim more than anything," he said, lamenting over the limited extent of Islamic instruction he and his brothers received, which solely revolved around abstinence from eating pork. Mutah thus turned to the Bible for spiritual direction.

"But then," he began, "reading the Bible presented me with yet another dilemma. I remember I could never find any verse or chapter that said Jesus is God and therefore should be worshipped." Mutah's faith was now critically at odds. His infant self would constantly seek answers from his grandmother as to why he was being told to pray to Jesus when the Bible called for adherents to worship none but God instead. "I could never get a direct answer from her," he said. These compiling doubts were further exacerbated by one ill-fated Sunday visit to church.

"On this particular day, the preacher wanted to do a reading on my brothers, cousins and me [sic]. We were all lined up at the church altar, and one by one, the preacher tapped our heads and foretold our futures." Mutah vividly remembered the preacher gleefully announcing to the congregation that his brother would someday grow to be a famed football player.

Whereas for his cousin, his was a destiny of becoming a successful lawyer.

"I was the last one he came to," said Mutah. "He tapped my forehead and in front of everyone said that I was the devil. 'This one is the devil, and we need to get the devil out of him!' is exactly what he said." Before Mutah knew it, he was engulfed by a flock of preachers – some armed with holy water, others with the Good Book, in a desperate bid to expel the evil spirit from within him. "I had water thrown in my face, scripture read over me and, at this point, multiple hands on my head. And I said to myself, 'how can a 13-year-old kid be the devil incarnate?'" From that day onwards, he no longer felt a sense of belonging within the four walls of the church.

A blasé Mutah soon ceased church attendance and leaned towards agnosticism after becoming irreligious. "When I was a Christian," he said, gesturing in inverted commas, "I never one day prayed to Jesus – when I prayed, I always would pray directly to God. Now fast forward to when I stopped going to church – truly, at that time I had no religion. Still, my faith in God never left me – I always had belief in Him."

After rejecting the Christianity initially instilled in him by his grandmother, New Jersey's gangland terrain would form the locus of Mutah's moral compass. "I turned to the streets at a young age. I started hanging with the wrong crowd and was introduced to drugs and alcohol. This is what filled the void of my need for guidance and community."

Chancellor Ave.

Despite being outcast as a persona non grata by his onetime church leader, Mutah spoke of foreseeing his eventual walking away from the church. "I was already struggling with the spiritual substance of Christianity. So, I still would have left eventually – there just was nothing for me to believe.

That incident was just a push for me to go."

The absence of a church community, however, yielded a vacuum in Mutah's existence. "I got caught up with hanging on the streets. Believe it or not, I was rubbing shoulders with drug dealers and murderers." Within the depths of Irvington, New Jersey's underworld, Mutah, his brothers and cousins became local leaders. "From my house, we would walk to a street called Chancellor Avenue – this was where everybody would meet up."

Chancellor Avenue would become a place frequently revisited in Mutah's rhymes once he became a rapper. In the third verse of 'Still I Rise', for example, he details Chancellor Avenue as being "where many turn to the street. Thugs snatchin' bags, preoccupied with makin' cash."

As Mutah grew older, his grandmother's control over him waned apace. "I was at Chancellor Avenue every day and became a wild and crazy teenager. This actually isn't so uncommon among America's inner city youth. Yet, I never lost hope and I believe that's one of the reasons I made it out of the hood. I used to say to myself, 'someday, I'm going to leave this place'." Ultimately, Mutah's lyrical and emceeing abilities proved to be his ticket out of Irvington's concrete jungle.

Thinking back to his days as a youngster at his grandmother's, Mutah remembered his eldest cousin, Sharif, as the one who opened his eyes to the world of rap music. "Sharif had a tape cassette and would play some raps just before we would go to sleep and I would mentally study the wordplay."

As rap began to evolve from its infancy, the likes of Slick Rick and Nas would form the soundtrack of Mutah's youth. "East Coast rap of that time just did *something* to me as I listened carefully to the lyrics. Eventually, I got myself a notebook and couldn't stop writing!"

By the late 1980s, before touching the microphone on the world stage, Mutah was Irvington's very own 'Lil' Mu'. "I became the neighborhood rap star; people would always see me with my notebook of rhymes," he reminisced. "As soon as I'd come home from school, whatever I saw that day, I would make a rhyme out of it. This quickly became my hobby."

The sights and sounds his pen spoke of also depicted the harsh reality of life out on the streets. "The first song I ever wrote was called 'Money and Murder'. A friend of mine helped me write it. The hook was like, 'all this money got me feeling like a star, but murder got me feeling like my death ain't far'. I was just 13 years old when I wrote this.

"This was why I eventually gravitated to the West Coast rap scene. West Coast artists at the time came from the gang environment, so their lyrics were talking about murder and shooting. This was also my reality," he said, motioning at his field of vision to stress all that his eyes had seen.

Dizzying highs of fame

The year was 1995 and Dr Dre's 'California Love' was the anthem blaring through the soundwaves in America and beyond. The track coincided with Tupac Shakur's release from prison, and an exonerated Tupac was to be heard celebrating his freedom. Upon taking centre stage and "serenading the streets of L.A", Tupac told listeners of his being "out on bail, fresh outta jail, [and] California dreamin'."

At this time, Tupac was a newly signed artist to the infamous Death Row Records label and would eventually release the final studio album during his lifetime – 'All Eyez on Me'. Tracks such as 'Thug Passion', 'Run Tha Streetz', 'When We Ride', amongst others, would feature Mutah rapping under his Napoleon alias as part of Tupac's 'Outlawz' crew. Mutah recalled hearing himself on the radio alongside Tupca for the first time –"I couldn't believe it was me!" he exclaimed.

"The thing that has stuck with me and what I appreciate most from that time was the family we built together." Mutah detailed how he and his fellow Outlawz were either related to Tupac or inducted by someone else who was. "There were no outsiders – we really were a solid family unit. We broke bread and would always travel together. Although we sold 60 million record copies worldwide, I wouldn't say this was the highlight of my former career. The highlight was those days spent together as a family."

Yet, Mutah recalled losing himself in the whirlwinds of fame and success. "Looking back, I can't say I felt fulfilled internally. The music industry changed me a lot – I drifted away from being the innocent kid I once was growing up and I became a different person."

Mutah further hinted at being unable to escape the label his younger self was given from what would be his final visit to Sunday church service. "It got to a point where, when I used to write my lyrics, I would want the person listening to my music to think it was written by the devil himself; that's just how far gone I was."

A restless Napoleon can be heard pleading "somebody please say a prayer for me" on Tupac's posthumous 'Still I Rise' album. He further continued to narrate his battle with "seein' demons [and] wak[ing] up screamin'".

Despite his melancholy, Mutah yet had no intent on exploring his Islamic roots for respite from his innermost tumult. "Remember, I still had something against Muslims; they were the ones who killed my parents – I wanted nothing to do with them or their religion."

His enigmatic unrest was exasperated on 13th September, 1996 – the day Tupac Shakur passed away. "Things just became worse,"

Mutah recollected. "On the inside, I was in agony and began to conspire to be the evilest person on earth as a coping mechanism."

He took comfort, however, in the tranquillity he would eventually come to find after having embraced Islam. "Sometimes, I sit back and think about the life I once lived when I was lost, and I thank Allah for guiding me."

A chance encounter

In the years that followed Tupac's ill-fated passing, Mutah went on to feature on two Outlawz albums alongside his comrades – namely 'Ride wit Us or Collide wit Us' and 'Novakane'. 'Novakane's' 'Rize' single went on to be featured on the 2001 soundtrack for Antoine Fuqua's crime-thriller 'Training Day'.

However, 'Novakane' was to be the last musical collaboration of Mutah alongside the Outlawz as he began to lay out the blueprint for his solo career and debut album. "My solo career was short lived – after I became Muslim, the rapper lifestyle just wasn't compatible with the person I was aspiring to become."

Prior, however, Mutah was busy in the studio – despite his work ethic being overshadowed by a never-ending intoxicated stupor. "I was always drinking, so my judgement was clouded and my behaviour was reckless."

One particular studio session especially stands out in Mutah's subconscious. "A fight broke out between my little younger brother and me [sic]. In fact, he had to go to the hospital that day to get stitches because I had beaten him so badly. I just lost it; I was breaking bottles and no one could tell me 'okay, stop!' I was on the rampage."

However, one Mikal Kamil, a record producer, just so happened to be in the vicinity amid volcano Mutah's eruption. "He was a stranger to the studio!" Mutah exclaimed. "Yet he was the only one who was able to break up the fight." He further recounted Mikal's respectful demeanour towards him during their first time meeting one another. "He was soft spoken, but firm. He said to me 'why are you acting this way?' and then asked me my name." It was the latter question that began Mikal's feat to reform the then outlawed Mutah.

"I told him my name was Mutah and he asked me if I was Muslim. I told him my parents were. From there, we exchanged numbers. And because of how he was able to calm me down and dealt with me compassionately, I felt as though I had to repay him somehow. Even in my days of *jahiliyyah*[3], I still had some manners," Mutah chuckled.

However, Mikal wanted little in return – only that Mutah accompany him on a visit to the local mosque. "I accepted his invitation thinking I would go with him just that one time and get him out of my life – by then we would have been even." *Au contraire.*

Upon Mikal's request, Mutah found himself in a South Central Los Angeles mosque – but he was not unaccompanied. Mutah arrived with 20 of his "homeboys" and a loaded gun. "I didn't know what to expect! Plus, I already had a heightened sense of caution from growing up believing my parents' death was at the hands of Muslims." It soon became apparent, however, that his being armed to the teeth was unnecessary. "In the mosque, I saw something I had never seen before."

Historically, Christian houses of worship have been marked by racial segregation in America. Many point to this being a remnant symptom of the nation's history with slavery. In a 2001 journal, Robert K. Vischer cited

---

3   *Jahiliyyah* comes from the Arabic root word *'jahl'*, which means to lack knowledge or be ignorant.

   Jahiliyyah as a concept in Islam refers to the time afore the advent of Islam. As a noun when applied to a person, it can be used in reference to their days before embracing Islam.

Martin Luther King Jr's observation of Sunday morning church hours being "the most segregated hour of the week[4]". Robert further highlighted how little this trend has changed, with 69% of American churches being almost exclusively frequented by White Christians, while 18% are mostly Black[5].

"Growing up in my neighbourhood – and not just my neighbourhood, but America in general – church was, and still is, divided by race," said Mutah. "I walked into the mosque and I saw Black Americans, White Americans, migrants from Africa, Asia and the Arab world all calling each other brothers! I never once saw that in a church." Much to his incredulity, Mutah thought the display of unity he saw that day was all for show. Seeing Muslims from far and wide standing shoulder to shoulder for prayer did, however, spark a curiosity within him and he found himself standing in prayer alongside them.

"Mikal said it was time to pray and that I should join." Mutah went on to explain that this trip to the mosque was at a time when his body and soul were tired. "But I just didn't know any way out – so, although I drank daily, I knew I didn't want to carry on living life like that."

Mutah followed the motions of *salah*[6] he saw – first being stood upright, then bowing and falling prostrate to the floor. "I put my head to the ground and I said, 'God, please guide me to a way of life that will bring me happiness, change and inner peace.' That was the prayer I made that day."

After prayers had concluded, Mutah was gifted an English translation of the Holy Quran and Islamic literature by his new friend Mikal. "I drove

4   Vischer, Robert K. (2001). "Racial Segregation in American Churches and Its Impli- cations for

School Vouchers". Florida Law Review. Vol. 53: p204.

5   Ibid.

6   Five times daily, Muslims are obliged to pray at prescribed times during the day, depending on the movement of the sun. In Islamic theology, *salah* is understood to increase a believer's God consciousness.

home that day and immediately read the Book. From the jump, as a rap artist, I knew that these words could never have been inspired by man. The stories in the Quran – although some were also told to me by my grandmother – the way Islam explained it, I just knew it had to be from my Creator." When asked for a verse in the Quran that spoke to him early on, Mutah recalled two verses in particular. "One of the *ayat*[7] that hit me is when Allah says *Did He not find you orphaned, then sheltered you? And did He not find you misguided, then guided you?*[8] It really stood out because I was an orphan who was misguided. Even though those verses were revealed to our Prophet Muhammad (PBUH), it still touches me every time I read it – even to this day."

He thus concluded that if the Quran came from a Higher Being, His religion must be without fault while His adherents are flawed. "Take the story of Wahshi ibn Harb killing the uncle of our Prophet during the Battle of Uhud. Yet, after ibn Harb came to accept Islam later, the Prophet didn't shun him despite being hurt by his actions. So, even if it were Muslims who killed my parents, that doesn't reflect Islam. Islam is perfect, Muslims are not."

Mutah would later phone Mikal to tell him the news that he wanted to become a Muslim.

One more chance at life

"It was on a Friday. I took my *shahada*[9] before Friday prayers," said Mutah. He, in the presence of Mikal, his younger brother, older cousin Sharif, friends such as Doc Bull, as well as a congregation of Friday prayer goers

---

7   Arabic for verse in the Holy Quran.

8   Quran 93:6-7

9   Profession of faith is one of the five pillars of Islam. It is incumbent upon Muslims to believe that there
     is none worthy of worship, save Almighty God, and that Muham- mad (PBUH) is His final
     messenger. For converts to Islam, declaration of this faith in the presence of witnesses is initial step
     taken to becoming Muslim.

and declared his faith in One God and Muhammad (PBUH) as His messenger. "In the immediate moment after having accepted Islam, I just felt different. I felt as though Allah had given me another chance at life."

Mutah further remembered being engulfed by hugs from well-wishers. "Afterwards, everyone came up to give me a hug. This gave me an instant sense of a new belonging. Even though I had a family in my life, I now felt part of something much greater; a real brotherhood and family that showed me love not for any reason other than me following the same religion and believing in the same God that they do. It was just an amazing feeling."

Brotherhood would become a frequent focal point for Mutah in his personal growth as a Muslim. For instance, three months after taking his *shahada*, he would travel to the Kingdom of Saudi Arabia to perform the Hajj pilgrimage. Laughing, Mutah remembered being asked by a *Los Angeles Times* reporter as to why he would travel to the Middle East region in the midst of the then burgeoning global war on terror. "I told the reporter 'I survived wars in my hood'." It also amused him when his friends told him CNN carried the story of his pilgrimage with the headline 'Gangster Rapper Napoleon is Headed to Hajj'.

Reflecting on his two weeks spent in Saudi Arabia in 2002, Mutah recalled being "cut off from the outside world" and being embraced in brotherhood by Muslims from across continents. "I remember being grabbed by the hand by fellow pilgrims to join them to eat. '*Taffaddal*'[10] they would say to me. I would sit and break bread with people I had never met before – this was a brotherhood I never knew existed." Later, upon coming back to America, Mutah was determined to overhaul his old ways – a task that, at times, proved uneasy.

Despite not being brought up to pray five times daily, Mutah described *salah*

---

10   *Taffaddal* in certain contexts can be used as an expression to invite someone to do something in the Arabic language.

as "the natural thing to do", but simultaneously remembered his initial resistance thereto. "'Are you crazy?' was probably what I said to Mikal when we first talked about *salah*. I also remember telling him 'no one stops five times out of their day to pray'. At the time, it just didn't make sense to me.

"But Mikal sat me down and said, 'Look, Allah gave us 24 hours in a day. Maybe a prayer will take five or ten minutes at most. So, out of those 24 hours, Allah is asking for just 50 minutes — and it's not even back-to-back; it's spread throughout the day. You cannot give Allah that time?' And then it clicked." He further explained: "Keeping up with the five daily prayers brings about a tranquility inside that I haven't been able to get elsewhere before."

While in respect of one's hope, Mutah ascribed prayer as being imperative. "With prayer comes forgiveness. Even the one who deviates 1,000 times can still hope to be forgiven just as much if he prays."

As a then-new Muslim, he also felt it was paramount to clean up his vernacular. "One thing I forced myself to, by Allah's permission, was to stop cussing. I was a rapper that, if a person listened to my raps, every other word was a cuss word. But the more I learned about Islam, I learned that every word that comes out of my mouth is recorded by the angels. I now had to be mindful of what I was saying."

Therefore, when approached by the late Johnny J to do a solo album, Mutah took it upon himself to compose lyrics free from derogatory language and expletives. This took shape in the songs he wrote for his 'Have Mercy' album that Johnny produced. "This was the best music I ever made," said Mutah.

However, his initial endeavour to create a bridge between music and his then-newly found Islamic faith left him conflicted. "I avidly studied the Hadith and found clear guidance advising against music. From there I wanted nothing more to do with the music industry."

Notwithstanding, he feared having to be put in an environment that could potentially lead him astray. "What really frightened me was having to perform and promote my album in nightclubs. As a former performer, I know the majority of people that go to shows are either high or drunk before they get to the club – that's just the culture. A culture I wanted to distance myself from." Mutah, who was unable to break his contractual agreement with Johnny, thus sought forbearance in *salah*.

"Every day I was praying for a way to get out of my contract with J." Then one day he received an unexpected call from his lawyer. "My lawyer phoned to say he got a letter waiving my contract. Not only that, but he said J didn't want a penny back from me. This was my internal battle at the time, but Allah made it easy for me."

Since then, Mutah has channeled his writing skills to spread positivity through spoken word. "I believe if a person wants to put out a positive message, lyrically, the safest bet would be to stick with poetry. We have guidance on poetry in the Hadith – the companions of the Prophet and the Prophet himself were poets." In his 'My Life' spoken word poem, Mutah chronicled his journey of coming a long way from his younger days of "bright lights, to gun play and fist fights" in the enclaves of Irvington, to becoming a devout Muslim – abandoning the lavish lifestyle he once relished. "Before becoming Muslim, I had houses, cars, jewelry; the trappings of this worldly life that people assume would bring about peace and happiness. However, my true
happiness didn't come until I accepted Islam."

Meandering through his memory's museum, Mutah is not a man of regrets. "People reach out to me all the time through social media. Since becoming Muslim, I often get asked whether I would   make any chance to live my life again." He concluded, however, that "everything is written[11]. I never sit back and say, 'I wish I would have done this or that differently' – perhaps, had things panned out otherwise, I may have never been guided to Islam. And even if I was, I might not have accepted it." Instead, despite all obstacles along the metaphorical road through his nostalgically remembered past, Mutah maintains the utmost humility and gratitude. "I'm thankful for everything that has happened in my life. These experiences are ultimately what led me to accept Islam. And for that, all praise and thanks are due to Allah, the Most High."

---

11 *Qadar*, or Divine foreordainment, is the Islamic concept of God having predecreed all that is to happen in the universe according to His infinite wisdom.

5

'I can see why Muslims believe in what they believe, merely based on the sonorous nature of Quranic recitation'

Jennifer Grout– American
singer

While becoming immersed in the classical Arabic and North African music genres as an undergraduate student, a friend's suggestion to listen to Quranic recitation took Jennifer Grout's passion for Arabic singing to new heights – landing her a finalist spot on MBC's Arabs Got Talent show. This was also the beginning of what she described as her 'never ending road' to Islam.

HE first few times Jennifer Grout listened to the Quran being recited, she did so inactively, and yet, even as a non-Muslim, she felt an arrow of faith physically penetrate her psyche.

"It was sheer magic," she said as she remembered jotting down some notes one day, being exhilarated by what would prove to be a revolutionary auditory experience for her.

"Remember, this would have been at a time where I wouldn't have known what the words of the Quran meant!" she exclaimed. "And yet, I came to an understanding of why Muslims are so resolute in their faith just from hearing the Quran being recited. It instantly became self-evident to me," she added.

Since then, as a singer with a magical and mesmerising voice, Jennifer's own sonorous recitations of the Quran have captivated millions. Equally fascinating is her spiritual journey that has transformed her, instilling in her life a new-found peace, purpose and meaning that she missed for so long. Said journey has also incited intense curiosity among millions of her fans to discover the specifics of a journey that she undertook against heavy odds.

In the past decade, the Boston born native has risen to fame with her unique ability to capture the emotions of classic Arabic and Amazigh Tashelhit music. She took the Arab world by storm in 2013 when she made it to the finals of Arabs Got Talent (AGT), an Arab television talent show broadcast by MBC 1 to television sets of all around the world. Jennifer astonished spectators with her ability to sing classical Arabic music - despite not speaking Arabic fluently at the time. As such, she was dubbed the 'surprising new face in Arab music[1]' by *The New York Times* as she rose to become a household name in the Arab world.

---

1   Crouse, L., 2013. Surprising New Face in Arabic Music. The New York Times, [online] Available at: <https://www.nytimes.com/2013/12/04/arts/ music/jennifer-grout-sings-umm-kulthum-hits-on-arabs-got-talent.html>

From stubbornness to surrender

It was while in Morocco that Jennifer made the conscious decision to renounce her former agnostic atheism and embrace Islam. "In the immediate week prior to converting, I remember feeling really bad. If I had to put it in words, I would say it felt as though I physically had knots in my stomach," she explained, recounting a tension of inner tumult that she just could not place. "When I finished university, I visited Morocco for the first time. It was there that the fight in me to resist religion ceased. I felt an unexplainable pull towards faith." She went on to describe becoming rid of her former stubbornness and her heart being open to the possibility of belief in God.

"I found myself in deep thought one day. I was sat on a couch, just staring at the walls, motionless – but inside, my mind was at war. There and then, I told my brain 'I'm going to choose to believe, and I now believe in God!'" She further described this as being a very physical experience.

"Instantly, a warmth overcame me when I made that choice," she remembered. "Not just that, but the knots I was carrying – it felt as though a hand physically reached into my stomach and untied them. So truly, crossing over to the 'other side' was the only relief I could have gotten from my innermost grapples with faith at the time."

She continued: "I initially couldn't explain where those knots had come from, but they immediately went away as soon as I took that literal leap of faith." In her estimation, had she not done so, she still would have remained in a state of unexplainable inner tumult to this day.

Despite this relief, Jennifer also spoke of feelings of fear and uncertainty in venturing into the unknown. "It's like taking a jump in a body of water – you're stood on the other side, and you do not know how deep it is."

She continued: "All it takes is that jump of bravery, and you soon see that everything is okay. You're safe. "So," narrated Jennifer, "my taking *shahada* wasn't done in the presence of others. It was, instead, a *shahada* of the heart." She continued: "When I chose to become a believer, it was specifically belief in Islam that I had in mind." This thought process coincided with hers being a mind that "is just constantly going and going and going and imagining the infinite possibilities of this world." Thus, while the emotional and physical components of her conversion story played an integral role, intellectual cognition was just as important.

"Our actions are shaped by our intellect," she argued. "The state of one's soul will depend on that which was created by our minds. So, in my heart, when I made the conscious decision to believe, I knew that from that moment onwards, I was now a Muslim."

Jennifer further detailed how this winding course enabled her to do something she had not been able to do before – surrender and be humble. "This is really a tale of contrasts; within a matter of moments, I went from being stubborn, uncertain and having questions I just couldn't find answers to. Then, in a split second, I found myself in a different state. I let go of my stubbornness, and with *imaan* (faith) came the ability to surrender and be humble." For her, the latter two constitute core components of the Islamic faith.

"We truly have a lot less control than we think," she explained. "Nothing in this life is guaranteed. When I became Muslim, I surrendered the idea and illusion of control that I thought I had." Despite abruptly choosing to adopt Islam as her religion, Jennifer expressed not being fazed with thoughts second guessing her decision. "I like to look at the bigger picture, rather than the minute details of faith. I sit and ponder over God's creation – His mountains, Earth, His design – this is what keeps me certain in my conviction."

Latent religious belief

Jennifer is the daughter of a pianist mother and violinist father. "But, I was always drawn to singing as it's a more intuitive form of expression. The piano and violin? Those were my parents' identities. Even from a young age, we want to feel like we have own thing!" she continued. As such, music and song prominently played in the backdrop of her younger years.

"Growing up, my idols were comprised of mostly pop and R&B stars like Britney Spears, Christina Aguilera and Aaliyah. And even before that, I began studying classical and operatic singing from a very young age." Yet, a young Jennifer still found herself being pulled to Arabic music.

It was her discovery of Arabic music that proved pivotal to her discovery of the Quran, and subsequently Islam. Conversation then turned to her hearing Algerian singer Cheb Khaled's '*Alech Taadi*' for the first time.

She first heard Arabic music when she watched Luc Besson's 'The Fifth Element'. She was only seven at the time, so, while she cannot remember her exact feelings, she does remember being drawn to Khaled's voice as his song played during the taxi chase scene.

"The vocal melismas that he does," she continued, "and his unique style of singing just struck me. But it wasn't until I started university that I actually began exploring the world of Arabic music in depth."

Regarding the religious landscape of her childhood home, Jennifer spoke of being Baptised as a Christian since she was the daughter of parents who had close ties to the church – "But those ties were social more than anything," she said. "My parents and grandparents have a longstanding parents and grandparents have a longstanding history with our hometown's local church," she explained. "But, we would only ever go to Church on special occasions, such as Easter Sunday." She went on to detail how despite taking an active role in the church chorus during occasional church visits as a youngster, the extent of her religiosity was "vague."

"At the time, I don't really think I knew deep down what being Christian or Catholic even meant. So, I wasn't connected to a religious identity at the time. I almost never read the Bible, but I do remember praying to God directly, though I didn't have a specific idea of what or who God was. I also had a deep-seated need for some type of guidance in my life." She continued: "This is natural – it's an innate force in our *fitrah*."

While religious instruction may not have featured in her upbringing, Jennifer conversely cited music as being a constant. "From a young age, music was a space for me to let out any hard feelings that had been brewing inside of me or any other difficulties; it always came back to music," – including her journey to Islam.

She remembered being unsure about her religious identity as a youngster, since religion was restricted to infrequent visits to church. "In truth, had someone asked me, 'what religion do you follow?' when I was a kid, I wouldn't have known what to tell them. I probably wouldn't have had an answer for them at all," she surmised.

Looking back on this void of religious identity as a child, Jennifer hinted at a sense of feeling insufficiently guided. So, where did her younger self turn to during times of difficulty? She laughed, as she remembered being, "blessed; given that hardship and difficulty weren't a feature in my life growing up. I wouldn't say life really *threw* anything at me, until after I became Muslim!" While there may have been no major instances of tragedy as a youngster Jennifer yest lamented having no recourse to religious counsel when faced with life's minor challenges. "You know, emotional struggles are something we all go through – even something as simple as experiencing bullying at school. Sometimes, I do look back and I wish I had been a believer back then. It would have made it so much easier for me to get through those times."

On the other hand, she did fondly remember the wealth of diversity afforded to her by growing up in Cambridge, Massachusetts. "It truly was a luxury to grow up in such an environment," she explained. "Our society was very open and tolerant to people of all cultures and religions, so I made good friends with the Muslims that I went to school with." She further detailed how her early exposure to Muslims and Islam inhibited her from developing any prejudices thereto.

"I would always know when Ramadan was as a kid because my Muslim friends would say they couldn't eat or drink until after school. Admittedly, I did find that odd, but I never looked upon their religious practice negatively – it was just something different.

"We truly remember the little things," she continued with a smile. "I remember being at the birthday party of one of my Egyptian friends. An image that especially springs to mind from that memory is of a woman taking a nap with a hijab on. Again, at the time, I found it odd, but these moments made Islam familiar to me. Muslims and Islam were part of the fabric of my society – Muslims were my friends and neighbours; I never made a negative association with Muslim cultures and the religion itself." Therefore, she found herself immune to the media framing and rhetoric that emerged concerning Muslims amid the Global War on Terror era.

"I was about ten or 11 when 9/11 happened. In my young mind, it was impossible to make a connection between the Twin Towers attack and Islam as a whole. How I registered it was that bad people flew some planes into two buildings – that's all I remember! This, I would say, was all because of being exposed to seeing Muslims and their religion being lived from a young age."

Primordial steps to becoming a Muslim

When asked about her secondary school days, Jennifer gleefully remembered having a teacher and a fellow classmate who hailed from Morocco. On one particular school day, she stumbled upon the two jamming to Moroccan music. She was unsure about the sound she was hearing, but it captivated her and made her stop in her tracks. "That is just another moment that particularly sticks out to me – it proves that even without being fully conscious of it, I was really, really drawn to this genre!"

After finishing secondary school, she went on to pursue a Bachelor's degree in Classical Singing from Montreal's McGill University. "It was at university that I became more immersed in both classical Arabic music as well as North African genres," explained Jennifer. She further detailed how this would later help her break into the Arabic music scene.

"Art is all about communicating," she said. "And I took it upon myself to become a part of the Arab communities in Montreal. If you're not in a context where you're able to communicate with people through your art, then you probably won't get very far."

Despite affiliating herself with a predominantly Muslim crowd, Jennifer recollected adopting a somewhat atheistic outlook on life. "Well," she explained, "I wasn't completely sold on atheism. But I just couldn't identify with religion at the time." She further spoke of a metaphorical mental wall she would put up which served as a barrier between her being receptive to religion of any sort. "I had reached a stage where I couldn't understand religion or the concept of God.

Yet, I was still very fascinated by our universe. This created a stubbornness within me – I was stuck in a search for answers and explanations about how our world works." Still, when given advice of a religious nature to her uncertainties, she would yet disregard such suggestions.

"When you're not a believer, your brain will actively find any reason to not believe. That's why trying to talk logic, most times, is not going to work – there's always a way to counter that logic."

Jennifer actively sought ways to "outsmart" those who would try to tell her about Islam. "Notwithstanding," she continued, "however well intended my friends at the time were, the *da'wah* I had been given honestly wasn't very good." She surmised that while she understood their zealousness, surface level debates are not always sufficient, especially for philosophical and logically inclined minds.

"*Da'wah* shouldn't just start and end with talking – it's far deeper than that!" she exclaimed. "And, for someone like me," she continued, "who is very philosophical and once was on the agnostic/atheist borderline, Islam and its proofs need to be seen and lived, not just spoken and debated about."

After a series of debates with the Muslims of Montreal, Jennifer was to find tangible proof of the veracity of Islam from an unlikely source. "As I became familiar with Arabic music outside of the lecture hall setting, I wanted to learn more about it on a theoretical level and started exploring the genre more and more alongside my university studies." She then soon discovered her need to reconfigure her ears to become adjusted to the *maqāmāt*[2] of classical Arabic music.

---

2   This is the system of heptatonic tone rows of differing pitches, patterns, and development
     unique to Arabic music.

"I became interested in *tarab*[3] singing and wanted to nail the modulations that the genre is known for. What's interesting," continued Jennifer, "almost all notable *tarab* singers who emanated from the Golden Age in Egypt had a background in Quranic recitation." As such, Jennifer was advised to listen to the Quranic recitations of Egypt's Muhammad Siddiq Al-Minshawi (1920 – 1969).

Jennifer chuckled as she remembered, "The person who told me to listen to Al-Minshawi's recitation actually wasn't Muslim." She continued: "Perhaps because of this, I felt free to listen to it and interpret it as I wanted to and wasn't resistant to his advice. He didn't come with an approach of trying push anything upon me, as I had experienced with other Muslims during debates about religion."

Jennifer found herself listening to Al-Minshawi's recitation of *Surah Al-Fatihah* to *Al-Nas* frequently during her downtime. "It was sheer magic," she said, recollecting her first times hearing it. "It was an auditory experience like no other," she continued. It was while listening to his recitations that she wrote: 'I can see why Muslims believe in what they believe, merely based on the sonorous nature of Quranic recitation alone.'

Outed

Fast forward to Jennifer's becoming an AGT finalist in 2013. This feat garnered the attention of the Moroccan film industry. "I was approached and reluctantly agreed to do a Moroccan film and sing Tashelhit music," she said. Wary from the outset, Jennifer remembered the experience being overshadowed by an unwanted leaked scene from the film.

"I actually saw this coming," she sighed. "I just had this gut feeling after

---

3   This refers to subculture within Arabic music known for its deeply emotive nature. A notable
     singer of this genre would be Egypt's Oum Kulthum (1898 - 1975).

I shot this scene that it would be shared all over the internet and taken out of context. I even went as far as asking the producer to remove it so I wouldn't be outed." The scene in question showed Jennifer reciting *Surah al-Fatihah* and uttering the Islamic declaration of faith. "Unfortunately, I was pressured to do this," she said.

Her efforts of expanding classical Arabic music to a wider audience by making it to the finals of AGT were now eclipsed. Instead, "overnight, videos titled 'Jennifer publicly converts to Islam' went viral – news spread of my becoming Muslim far and fast, but not on my terms." She further lamented, "I didn't have the chance to explain to my friends and family in my own time – they came to know against my will. The whole world came to know that I was Muslim without my consent. This was a hard time for me." Suddenly, Jennifer was thrust into the public eye, under the scrutiny of the Arab Muslim world, and beyond, as to how she ought to conduct herself as a new convert to Islam.

"It was as though I became an infant once again. The only difference was," she laughed, "instead of having just two parents telling me what to do, I now had millions of people telling me, 'do this', 'don't do that', 'you have to do this', 'you can't do this anymore!' What a lot of people don't understand is that this puts the convert under immense strain. This constant social pressure only yields ephemeral results – at best!" The very same pressure that Jennifer came under would eventually became evident to her parents.

"After being outed, I was able to sit down with Mom and Dad and they gradually saw me ease into my Islamic faith. Then, abruptly, I entered an overzealous phase, donned the niqab and began bombarding them about Islam." Looking back, Jennifer attributed this to her subconsciously mimicking her own unpleasant experiences at the hands of overeager Muslims.

"Before I became Muslim, and even after, I disliked being given *da'wah* that came across as forceful and imposing. Yet, I found myself doing the very same thing to others." She went on to regret going against the grain of the mantra she held dear once she accepted Islam.

"I try to always go back to that initial space of surrender and humility, but instead, during this phase, I had deluded myself into thinking I was on the right path because I was following all of the 'rules' – fasting, giving *zakaat*[4] and 'dressing the part'." Jennifer regretted having lost that essence of being humble in one's self, towards others and speaking about Islam from an arrogant standpoint.

"For some, their view is such that in Islam, our deeds are purely transactional. I can understand this linear way of thinking, but I also see it as a dangerous and narrow school of thought. This rigidity can be especially difficult for Muslim converts. As best as one can, one should try to take things slowly. The expectation shouldn't have to be that a newly converted Muslim woman begins covering head to toe in an instant – this is something I wish I would have known back then."

'Allah created us the way we are'

After converting to Islam, Jennifer took a hiatus from the music industry for three years. "This was something hard for Mom and Dad to see," she admitted. "They were the ones who initially taught me about music – it has been a part of my life from the very beginning."

When asked what prompted the abandonment of her passion for music,

---

4   *Zakaat* translates as almsgiving and constitutes one of the five pillars of Islam. Muslims who
     have the *nisaab* level (approximately 88g worth of gold, or its equivalent in money) of
     excess wealth by the end of the Islamic calendar are prescribed to donate 2.5% of said wealth
     in alms.

Jennifer remembered having become convinced that music was forbidden, and thus, should she walk away from it, despite it being something she loves, she would be rewarded immensely. "I was told that I was destined for Hell if I didn't give up music – this was the narrative that forced my hand."

Initially, Jennifer was able to live a life sans music: "But truly I was suffering," she revealed. "My life without music took a toll on me, not only in terms of my livelihood, but mentally and emotionally, I was unhappy and became a shell of myself.

"In my desperate attempt to walk away from music," she continued, "and live up to the pedestalised image that had been imposed upon me as an American convert to Islam, I was living a life where I wasn't happy." This pedestalised image was further intensified as she became renowned for her beautiful recitations of the Quran that she would upload on social media.

"Eventually, after posting videos of myself reciting the Quran, I one day got a message on Instagram asking if I taught Quran recitation classes. This is something I have enjoyed doing ever since!" For Jennifer, not only do her classes enable both born- Muslims and converts to learn how to read and recite the Quran, but: "The classes also are a teaching tool for me, too! Before I have my sessions, I first need to prepare in advance how to pronounce certain letters as well as the motioning and positioning involved. Aside from these mental gymnastics, I too am pushed to be more disciplined in respect to my connection with the Quran." However, Jennifer further recollected not always having a solid link to the holy book.

"After converting, I loved listening to the Quran being recited – much like how I did during my days at university. While I was fascinated by the auditory experience, I didn't have a connection to the depths of the Quran's message. I didn't know the meaning of what was being recited, nor did I make much effort to better my understanding – initially." Jennifer would eventually find herself sat in attendance for the lectures of those she referred to as '*shoyoukh al YouTube*[5]' who offered their exegesis.

"One story that I especially remember as being impactful upon me early on," she narrated, "would be that of Maryam. I often think of her and how she was in a situation of continuous worship of her Lord. I imagine the state of bliss she must have been in, then suddenly, she finds herself shouldered with the difficult trial of bearing our Prophet Isa, *subhan Allah*[6]! But she overcame this challenge, and that gives me strength." Chapter 54 of the Quran would also come to fascinate a then newly converted Jennifer.

"I remember having a deep conversation one day about the mysteriousness of the moon, and how that mirrors my own femininity. That same night, I got up from my sleep and felt the need to read the Quran. At this point, waking up in the middle of the night for worship hadn't developed into a full-fledged habit, so I cannot explain what woke me up that night." After waking, she performed ablution and reached for her Quran in Arabic, alongside an English translation. "It was a pretty large book!" she laughed. "But when I opened it, it randomly opened to page one of Chapter 54 – *surah Al-Qamar*[7]"

She also remembered another instance where her level of *imaan* had declined, and she was not frequenting the mosque as often as she would have liked. "At this point in my journey, I hadn't gone to the *masjid* in a long time. I decided to go one day. This was at a time I felt as though I had drifted far in terms of my faith, but I forced myself to try to reconnect." Jennifer took it upon herself that day to go early for congregational prayer.

---

5   This translates as the 'sheikhs of YouTube'.

6   This translates as 'Glorified is Allah.' It is often used to express amazement in the Almighty's creation.

7   *Surah Al-Qamar* translates as the Chapter of the Moon.

"I was so early in fact," she said, "when I went, there was no one else there! But in the days prior to going, I was asking Allah to reinvigorate my faith and show me a sign I so desperately needed." With the spare time she had on her hands before congregational prayer had started, Jennifer picked up the Quran to read. "I feel it's also important to mention that this incident happened on a Friday – just before *jummah* prayer[8]," she said. "I had done my two *rakaat* before sitting[9] and went to the shelf to pick up a Quran. I opened it to where the bookmark was – you know, where the person who had it last had been reading. To my amazement, the bookmark in the Quran was placed at *Surah al-Qamar*. In an instant, this brought me back to that special moment from before and revived my faith!"

Later, however, after being thrust into the limelight after converting, Jennifer found herself subjected to a deluge of hate comments amid her return to music and uploading videos of herself reciting the Quran without a veil. When asked how she was eventually able to make music compatible with her Islamic beliefs, she narrated a process of "unbrainwashing", aligning herself with likeminded individuals and schools of thought that matched her lived experience.

"I expanded my horizon and took into account the interpretations from renowned and educated scholars who argue that music is not unequivocally haram." She further recounted a piece of advice given to her that quelled her inner struggle in building a bridge between Islam and her love for music.

---

8 *Salah al jummah,* or Friday prayer, is held weekly in congregation after midday in the place of dhuhr prayer. In Islam, Friday is prescribed as a holy day of rest.

9 According to the Prophetic hadith, Muslims are advised to pray two units of su- pererogatory prayers before sitting in the mosque. See the narrations by al-Bukhari, 1167 and Muslim, 714.

"Something I was recently told is that 'Allah created us the way we are'. He created me like this. Why would He give me a voice that I'm not allowed to use? Why would He bless me with this gift, these skills and then tell me I can't use them?" She went on to say: "This advice was so helpful to me. Truly, I was struggling, but now, I am confident in myself again, and no one can take that away from me."

When asked whether the external noise of social media has proven testing upon her faith, Jennifer ascribed this as all being part of the process. "I would be lying if I said that it was easy, but not only has this experience strengthened my faith, it has also taught me the importance of separating my faith from my identity."

For Jennifer, identity is the sense of self we adopt to exist in the environments we find ourselves in. Our identity is also what enables us to relate and communicate with others. "The time for us to exist just as pure souls hasn't come yet!" she chuckled. "We cannot exist as *just* Muslims and ignore our cultural identities. And I don't see why faith cannot exist alongside our unique identities and personalities. When a person is able to separate identity from faith, the latter always remains with you – no matter what the environment."

She also further spoke of her difficulties in navigating Islam. "Where things start making less sense to me is when focus shifts to the 'rules' of faith. This is where different interpretations, schools of thought, translations and cultural implications come into play." While she recognised Islam's history as paramount to the heritage of the religion and its adherents, she also emphasised the importance of one's own lived experience and cultural context.

"The fact of the matter is that I am an American," she asserted. "So, in many ways, Islamic culture couldn't be any further from what I had grown up with." She further remembered a discussion she had concerning the role of culture in Islam.

"Something else I was once told, and I thought it was really beautiful, was that our culture is like a glass – the context, if you will, and then the *deen* is the water. While water is the substance, it still needs a container. We can't just be Muslim without acknowledging our humanity and cultural identities.

"I think in the beginning why I was so chill about being a new Muslim was that I took my then new-found faith one day at a time – I think this is the best approach!" She continued: "The reality is that many born-Muslims cannot appreciate what Muslim converts are going through, and end up approaching us in a manner that comes across as bossy. Unfortunately, this is why some become disillusioned and leave Islam altogether.

"I cannot deny that matters of being steadfast in one's prayer, fasting, paying *zakaat* and other outward acts of obedience are important. However, what I think is really important to stress here is that in the immediate moments after a person embraces Islam, the embellishment and detail that can always be worked out later on. What's key is assimilating the new convert to an Islamic community and understanding that they won't have Islam all figured out once they've taken their *shahada*."

She further surmised: "Islam is a journey for every one of us – converts and born Muslims alike. So, we should all learn to be more gentle with one another".

Jennifer's never-ending road

Jennifer also discussed deeply about Islam being negatively stereotyped by the mainstream media, especially regarding its treatment of women. She was quick to highlight that this discussion is two-sided. "No one community holds a monopoly over misogyny," she explained. "Historically, you will find instances of oppression against women in all ages and no culture is immune from this."

She was also candid about her attitude to certain voices within Muslim communities who subscribe to a stringent rhetoric of the standing of women within society. "I cannot entirely blame those who do argue that Islam is a religion that oppresses women," she said. "There are personalities who have risen to internet infamy shouting at the top of their lungs that, 'a good Muslim woman exists only to please her husband and remain in her home; never to be seen in public, nor show her face and beauty. And, if she does everything her husband tells her to, she will be with Allah'." She went on, "This rhetoric *is* present among Muslims, and you will find people using scripture as evidence of Islam supporting such a stance. As a community, we really cannot just disregard this."

In circling back to her journey to Islam, she described it as a never-ending road. "Concerning the steps leading to me becoming Muslim, it's difficult to clearly pinpoint and explain. The way I see it, I'm *still* in those steps!" She continued: "So, when I ask of Allah, I ask him to let me die in a high state of *imaan*. Like most, my *imaan* is in a constant state of flux. That's why when I supplicate, I ask Him to take me while in a state of firm faith."

Finally, Jennifer offered her take on the affinity of the musician's ear to Quranic recitation and the call to prayer "Music and sounds are vibrations that are moving, despite us being unable to see it." She further spoke of how this phenomenon is akin to the Islamic realm of *al ghaib*. "These vibrations that are going into our body and affecting our psychology, our cells and everything inside of us. And so, a lot of the time, I feel like the auditory experience is a proof in itself because of the way that it restructures one's mind – at least that's what I felt."

She concluded that hearing the Quran and call to prayer are experiences unmatched. "Even without necessarily understanding it, just the phonetics of the language alone – it has a gripping beauty that stands without the need for a translation."

Lastly, she remarked "the Quran speaks to one's soul directly – so our souls feel the enormity of its message instantly. The journey then begins with the pursuit of understanding the message, with the help of a translation, on a human level."

6

From captive to convert: Journey of a feisty war correspondent

Dr Yvonne Ridley – Award-winning British journalist and author

Dr Yvonne found the contents of the Quran liberating, as a blueprint for women's rights and empowerment and a message of equality for all
- including our enemies. She then began to read about the Prophet Muhammad, peace be upon him, and soon realised that he, too, had been demonised beyond recognition by enemies of Islam.

IT IS A mid-morning in the north-west highlands of Scotland in June 2022 and a group of 20 walkers, who had travelled from Edinburgh, Liverpool, Leicester and beyond, prepare for a 10km walk up the hill to the grave of Lady Evelyn Cobbold, thought to be the first British-born Muslim woman to make the Hajj pilgrimage to Mecca. Born in Edinburgh in the late 1800s, Lady Evelyn, a Victorian aristocrat, performed Hajj aged 65.

It was an exhausting walk battered by cold wind and intermittent rains, but spiritually energising. At the tombstone of Lady Evelyn, they paid respects and prayed in a moving moment and a few members of the group, who were Muslim converts, were brought to tears.

One of the members of the group was Dr Yvonne Ridley, a renowned British journalist, herself a convert. Yvonne's own conversion and the circumstances preceding it had made global headlines in 2003.

"I was exhausted by the walk, but the prayers by the grave [of Lady Evelyn] were spiritually moving. There was a stag which appeared on the hill above her graveside which was quite symbolic and moving," Dr Yvonne said.

But the trek was symbolic of Dr Yvonne's own journey to truth 20 years ago – a journey which has all the compelling ingredients of a thriller, but what makes it even more exciting is that, two decades on, she is more firmly rooted in her new faith than when she started. Reminiscing those heady days, Dr Yvonne's face glows with the warmth of faith. "Islam introduced a calmness and routine into my life that I'd not experienced before and I began to enjoy my own company, again something I hadn't really enjoyed in the past. An empty room would prove daunting to me but now I welcome solitude and silence," she says. The words eloquently encapsulate the inner transformation that Islam has brought about in her life.

It all started in 2001 when she was captured by the Taliban in Afghanistan.

At that time, she was known as a feisty war correspondent who worked for British newspapers. She reported on death and destruction from conflict zones at huge risk to her life, while proclaiming to the world the reckless futility of wars.

This is her own hair-raising description of her journalistic adventures:

"I've been caught in the crossfire between government forces in Sri Lanka and the Tamil Tigers, arrested by Libyan fighters after the fall of Muammar Gaddafi, threatened by Israeli gunfire and lost part of my hearing when ISIS lobbed a mortar bomb near a school in Syria I was visiting. Later, I was diagnosed with post-traumatic stress disorder (PTSD) after my work with Syrian female prisoners and Myanmar war crime victims in the Rohingya community."

To top it all, in 2008, she joined international activists on board the first boat to break the 40-year ocean siege of Gaza despite the threatening presence of Israeli gunboats.

9/11 and foray into Afghanistan

The horrific World Trade Center attacks had shaken the world. In the following shock-filled days, the drums for war were beating loudly from Washington and London in the direction of Afghanistan where the ruling Taliban were in control.

As chief reporter of *The Sunday Express* newspaper, a young Yvonne was sent to Pakistan where she was one of 3,000 journalists who had assembled from all over the world expecting a war to begin in neighbouring Afghanistan while the US was demanding the Taliban hand over Saudi-born Osama Bin Laden, the leader of Al Qaida and the man accused of being the mastermind behind 9/11. Being a competitive individual, Yvonne wanted to get an exclusive story ahead of her fellow journalists and so decided to sneak into Afghanistan wearing the all-enveloping blue chador or burqa. All Western journalists had been expelled from the country and, on the very day she entered, the Taliban's spiritual leader Mullah Omar had issued an edict saying anyone helping a Westerner would be executed.

But her curiosity and nerve couldn't be tempered with threats. "Despite the threats, I wanted to get inside the country to find out what life was really like for ordinary Afghan people and for the next two days I was able to discover and bust a few myths. Girls' schools, for instance, were in operation and so were further education colleges where women had been training to become doctors. I planned to write a feature for my newspaper which would not have relied on the narrative that the Taliban was the most brutal evil regime."

But her adventure turned into a fiasco. On 28th September 2001, she was arrested by the Taliban and treated as a Western spy. It was a terrifying experience and she genuinely thought she wouldn't survive. For the next 11 days, she was held and interrogated first in Jalalabad and then in Kabul. At one point, she was invited to embrace Islam by a religious cleric but she bluntly told him she couldn't make such a life-changing decision while she was in prison. "However, I did promise to study Islam and read the Holy Quran if they released me. Against all the odds, while they held on to other Westerners, they freed me on humanitarian grounds the day after the war had started. To everyone's surprise - and in the West, their dismay - I said I had been treated with courtesy and respect by my captors. No one wanted to hear this in London but it was the truth."

From Sunday School to Sunday School teacher

Looking back, religion didn't play much of a role in Yvonne's life as a child, but Northern Ireland politics was a cause of stress and division. The generation of her parents focused more on the bigotry and animosity at play between Catholics and Protestants; Catholic schoolchildren went to the Roman Catholic schools and their Protestant counterparts went elsewhere. There was nothing as exotic as Muslims, Hindus or Sikhs, and all she could remember was one boy at school who was Jewish. Everyone else was Christian. It was a very white community.

Her own family wasn't particularly religious but identified as Protestant and became very anti-Catholic whenever the politics of Northern Ireland arose.

"I found this bigotry and sectarianism very puzzling as I had friends in the nearby Catholic School of St Joseph's in Stanley Front Street and we never argued over religion," she reminisces.

Yvonne always had a core belief in God and went to church for years. She became a Sunday School teacher and was also part of the church choir at St Paul's in West Pelton village near Stanley, County Durham. It was from that church that she went through a confirmation ceremony at 14 which meant she could partake in bread and wine of the Holy Communion on Sundays as symbolism for the body and the blood of Jesus Christ.

"I 'd known very little about Islam although I knew that a prophet's name was invoked by a bunch of book-burning religious men in Bradford after the publication of a book by Salman Rushdie called *The Satanic Verses* in 1988.

"That Prophet was Muhammad, peace be upon him, and I never really knew about him until I reverted to Islam. Now I would stand up till my last breath to defend his name and whenever I get into a tight corner, the first thing I ask myself is: What would Muhammad do?"

However, this transformation would come several years later. Her interest in matters of faith then extended mainly to St James' Church in Piccadilly which she attended maybe twice a month on Sundays and, 'let's face it', she admits, in secular England that's bordering on religious fanaticism!

Journalism as a passion

Journalism was more than a passion, and a dream, though as a student, her careers master discouraged her, giving the impression that university was not for the likes of working class kids like her. But she pursued her dream with tenacity and wrote to every single newspaper group in Britain.

In 1980, at 22, she married her childhood sweetheart who she had met at school, and started her career at *The Stanley News*, a tiny weekly newspaper with a circulation of 8,000. But, by the end of 12 months, the marriage was falling apart and they split; she then moved to *The Northern Echo* from *The Stanley News*, immersing herself in work.

By the time she moved from *The Northern Echo* to a regional Sunday newspaper in Newcastle, she was on to her second marriage to a divorced detective, but all she had done was jump from the frying pan to the fire and found herself back in the divorce courts ten years later.

"I became quite the party girl, playing hard and working hard, and my faith began to take a backseat. I moved to my own flat in Newcastle overlooking St James' Park, home of Newcastle United which, as any football follower will tell you, is like the region's second religion," she says.

The first Muslim she met was a Geordie (someone born in Newcastle) called Brian Hewitt, who was the nephew of her editor Jim Buglass at the *Sunday Sun*. He had changed his name to Ibrahim and was a close friend of another convert called Yusuf Islam who was better known to millions of adoring fans as the musician Cat Stevens.

"I was totally in awe when I met the pair of them and was slightly upset when 'Cat' refused to shake my hand on religious grounds. I would meet him again some years later at a huge Islamic event in London and when we looked at each other we burst out laughing as I said: 'I promise I won't try to shake your hand again'."

Her career was in the ascendancy and she went on to break several glass ceilings, finally entering the prestigious Fleet Street in 1996. After a few false starts, which included a stint at *The Sunday Times* as an investigative reporter, she settled at *The Sunday Express* where she was a royal correspondent. She had already worked on a few royal stories at the height of the Princess Diana scandals and wrote the front page story for *The Sunday Times* on the night she died in the car crash in Paris.

On a side note, Yvonne was captivated by Diana's story. "Just for the record, I don't believe she was murdered, but I do believe she would have ended up marrying a Muslim. I remember discovering a few days after her death that she had asked the famous heart surgeon Dr Christian Barnard if he would give Dr Hasnat Khan a role at his hospital in South Africa.

"I don't know how true that is, but I know she was a manipulator, certainly with the media, and believed she was using Dodi Fayed to make Khan jealous in a last ditch effort to persuade him to marry her. I guess we'll never know her true intentions. Either way, had she survived the mother of the future king of England would have married a Muslim and that would've shaken the Establishment to the core."

She also spoke of an irrational fear that gripped her during those days that robbed her of much-needed sleep. "I existed on around three hours sleep a day because as a teen I had read somewhere around 60 percent of people die in their sleep and since we spend one-third of our lives asleep it came as no surprise then a lot of people die in bed. I developed an aversion

aversion to going to bed and so became well known for partying and working round the clock."

Fulfilling a promise and equality of women

After release from her 11-day captivity by the Taliban, she set out to fulfill the promise she had given to the Taliban cleric to read the Quran, and began reading an English translation of the holy book by A Yusuf Ali. Having observed the Taliban up close for nearly two weeks, she had realised that Islam was more a way of life than a religion practised once a week on Fridays, and was also encouraged by the fact that she could not report accurately on the Muslim world if she knew little or nothing about Islam.

"So, I made full use of the index [of A Yusuf Ali's translation] to try and find out why this religion oppressed women and promoted violence," she recalls with a smile, then little realising that what started as a promise and a professional interest would soon metamorphose into a life-transforming spiritual journey.

As she progressed through the pages of the holy book, she felt a refreshing sense of awe and respect as her preconceived notions began to be demolished. "I understood the language of the Quran very well drawing on my years as a Sunday School teacher. I was amazed that most of the characters in the Bible were also mentioned in the Quran."

The treatment of women, or discrimination, has been a favourite whip for critics to lash Islam with, but what Yvonne discovered beggared belief, and would later turn out to be one of the most significant ideological factors that led her to this faith.

"Far from finding any oppressive passages, it became crystal clear in the pages of the Quran that women were equal to men in spirituality, education and worth," she asserts.

However, what really bowled her over were the messages of justice, peace and equality that ran through virtually all of the pages of the Quran. "As a Christian we were regularly told to show love and kindness and be good to people and, while it is a good message, it is the easiest thing in the world to go about your business being kind to others. What the Quran was telling me was that justice must be delivered to our enemies as well as our family and friends in equal measure; in other words, justice is for everyone and everyone should be treated equally."

She says a lot of this has been drawn up in the United Nations' Declaration of Human Rights, but it could all have been based on the contents of the Quran. "I was blown away by its contents. Chapters on women's oppression, forced marriages, female genital mutilation and other tyrannies blamed on Islam simply did not exist other than in the minds of the ignorant or those who tried to push a distorted message about Islam."

She cites a verse that really stood out for proof of equality between men and women:

*But those who do good—whether male or female—and have
faith will enter Paradise and will never be wronged even as much as the speck
on a date-stone. (*Quran 4:124)

As a feminist, Yvonne took particular interest in what she read and then began reading additional literature about the origins of Islam and great women in the history of the religion. She knew in Islam's formative years, it is doubtful if much could have been achieved without the calming influence of The Prophet (PBUH) and the amazing people who surrounded him and gave their unstinting support when it was most needed.

"But none of this could have been achieved first without the terrific financial boost given unconditionally by one woman. Her name was Khadija bint Khuwaylid and before she met the blessed founder of Islam, she was a successful businesswoman, an international trader who had to be tough to succeed in a ruthless world where women were treated more like commodities than human beings.

"She knew the value of honesty and when she employed Muhammad, peace be upon him, she was so impressed with his transparency, integrity and business dealings that she proposed marriage to him even though he was 15 years younger."

Their marriage lasted nearly a quarter of a century and, although she died before Aisha became Prophet's wife, he never forgot and never stopped loving the woman who supported him throughout the turbulent early years promoting a new faith in a lawless region. She died aged 65 in Ramadan during the year 10 after the Prophethood.

"I read that Aisha, overcome by jealousy of the memory of Khadija asked why the Prophet (peace and blessings be upon him) missed her when he was blessed with a better, younger wife by Allah. He responded: 'I have not yet found a better wife than her. She had faith in me when everyone, even members of my own family and tribe did not believe me, and accepted that I was truly a Prophet and a Messenger of Allah. She converted to Islam, spent all her wealth and worldly goods to help me spread this faith, and this too at a time when the entire world seemed to have turned against me and persecuted me. And it is through her that Allah blessed me with children'. "By the time Khadija died, her entire wealth had already been spent to promote Islam; she left not a single gold dinar nor a silver dirham – but what an investment she made and it is one which keeps giving today around the world. Each and every Muslim who has passed through this life is a living testament to the fruits of that investment."

Yvonne also discovered that the Quran provided women with explicit rights to inheritance, to property, the obligation to testify in a court of law, and the right to divorce - rights which could not even be imagined in most other parts of the world for centuries to come.

"I was surprised to discover Islam made explicit prohibitions on the use of violence against female children and women as well as on duress in marriage and community affairs. Muslim women were equally responsible for ensuring that all religious duties of the individual and the community were fulfilled, in terms of punishment for social, criminal and moral crimes.

As equals, women were also offered equal opportunities to attain the ultimate prize: a place in Paradise and proximity to God – not for their beauty, wealth or power but based purely on piety and closeness to Allah."

Such equality was not available to women anywhere else in the world. And these great women weren't hidden away; they were very active and influential within the fledgling Ummah. While it is well documented that the first martyr to Islam was a woman, the first convert was a woman and when the Holy Quran was finally compiled in to a book it was entrusted into the hands of a woman; and it is perhaps less well known that women took active roles in conflicts on the battlefields back in those early days.

Yet today many Western armies are still agonising over whether or not to put women soldiers in the front lines and in the infantry. In addition, most Muslims know a quarter of the hadith are down to one woman, Aisha, but she was not alone in being a great female scholar – Fatima was also up there as a great teacher who men and women would go to, to seek knowledge.

Women administrators in Medina & Makkah

Yvonne says other incredible female pioneers included Al- Shifa bint Abdullah, an amazing woman who was one of the few of her generation during the pre-Islamic era who could read and write. Regarded as one of the first female teachers of Islam, she taught Hafsa, one of the Prophet's wives, how to read and write. She was also skilled in medical practices, particularly in the practice of *ruqyah* or spiritual healing. Al-Shifa bint Abdullah was appointed as a public administrator in charge of the Medina market. Her position was similar to the combined position of an administrator and accountant. "Now I want you to consider the importance of this – a woman was put in charge of the economy. She was chosen because she was considered to be a scholarly and intelligent woman, and the second Caliph [Umar], a brilliant man in his own right, would regularly consider her opinions and consult her for advice.

"Imagine that. Under Umar, the caliphate expanded at a staggering rate which saw him rule over territory encompassing today's Iran, Iraq, the Arabian peninsula and what became known as the GCC countries, the Caucasus [Armenia, Georgia, Azerbaijan, Dagestan, South Ossetia, Abkhazia], Egypt, large parts of Turkey, much of Central Asia [Afghanistan, Turkmenistan, Uzbekistan, Tajikistan], Yemen and Pakistan and more than two thirds of the Byzantine Empire."

Her appointment was highly successful and so Umar appointed another woman to run the economy in the markets in Makkah - Samra' bint Nuhayk. "It suggests that in those early Islamic societies, there were women shoppers and women shopkeepers. Had the market place been largely a man's domain, a woman would find it exceedingly difficult to discharge her duties as controller, yet neither Al-Shifa nor Samra' encountered such difficulties."

Yvonne contrasts this with the achievement of women in modern history. It wasn't until 1958 that the first female bank manager - Hilda Harding – was appointed at the Barclays Hanover Street branch in London. It was said that the appearance of women in banks was the biggest banking revolution of the 20th century in the UK yet when Islam was introduced in the 7th century, women were running the economies in Makkah and Medina.

"I have given lectures to lots of young Muslim women and told them about these incredible pioneers and urge them to learn more about Islam so they can challenge the misogynists in our societies. I've also spoken of their examples to Muslim men who have tried to sideline women in their communities. Knowledge is power and there isn't a man foolish enough to challenge the word of God or what is written in the Quran."

In short, Yvonne found the contents of the Quran liberating, as a blueprint for women's rights and empowerment and a message of equality for all - including our enemies. "I then began to read about the Prophet Muhammad, peace be upon him, and soon realised that he too had been demonised beyond recognition by enemies of Islam.

"I was so impressed by the purity and goodness of him that some years later I would write a book on his life with the subtitle: *Don't Shoot The Messenger*. I was incensed at the way his memory was being trashed and insulted by outsiders when, in fact, he was probably the most perfect human being ever to have walked the earth.

"So, if anyone asks me who are the big Islamic influences in my life, I can easily say our beloved Prophet Muhammad, his wife Khadija and the late Sheikh al-Qaradawi."

Yvonne admits the oneness of God was initially a bit of a struggle for her because as a Christian, she was told to believe in the Holy Trinity, the concept of God the father, God the son, and God the holy ghost. "It was repeated so often to us. I mentioned this to several scholars and theologians of both faiths but it was an ordinary brother who convinced me with a simple statement. "He said: 'If John the Baptist was a cousin of Jesus why, when he prayed he did not pray to his uncle God? I laughed at the silliness of the question and then he said: 'The fact you laugh says it all. Even you know there is a God and there is a human being and neither can be mixed as one'."

The simplicity of his case was convincing.

"I've since spoken to some other Christian theologians who are also uneasy about the Holy Trinity and fear it was something invented by Rome as it doesn't appear to have been practiced or mentioned by the early Christians."

Conversion and hijab

If it takes extraordinary tenacity and determination to brave bullets and report from conflict zones, the same qualities underpin Yvonne's character, too. Once she got over the obstacle of the Holy Trinity, she didn't baulk at taking the plunge and took the *shahadah* at the end of June 2003, without fuss. "Various groups wanted me to declare my *shahadah* at Trafalgar Square, but I did it in the privacy of my home in Soho, London, with a group of four brothers who had helped me in my spiritual development with advice and reading material."

The conversion wasn't difficult. She had 'practised' being a Muslim by living a more moderate, quiet lifestyle for nearly a year after a lifetime of partying, clubbing, alcohol, cigarettes and working unsocial hours.

"The very first time I prayed was with some sisters who worked for a *dawah* group called Discover Islam in Bahrain. I was on my spiritual journey but was nowhere near ready to make that step when they invited me into their mosque. I asked if they minded if I prayed next to them and I followed their actions. It felt right." The first Friday prayers she attended was as a Muslim in Qatar and the mosque she went to provided an English translation for the *khutbah* (Friday sermon) which was really helpful.

The congregation was diverse and reflected most of the nationalities of immigrant workers in Qatar.

But it was the donning of hijab that brought her the scorching realisation of what it means to be a Muslim.

She didn't wear hijab when she first embraced Islam, but after a year started experimenting with it. She loved the starched, colourful, sculpted designs worn by African women, Black sisters with attitude, but when she tried the style, she looked as though she'd 'piled last week's laundry' on her head.

"The Chechen widow-look appeared to freak out London's black cab taxi drivers so I soon ditched that and I couldn't really get a handle on the headscarf without it slip-sliding away.

"My brutally frank friend, who also happens to be Jewish, roared with laughter at my first attempt to go public with a hijab. The style I opted for was a headscarf which tied at the back of my neck leaving my throat uncovered. 'You look like a Jewish settler or someone who is undergoing chemotherapy,' she said." That look was soon ditched.

"One day I remember being told by an office worker that it was far too hot to wear a hijab, to which I retorted: It's a lot hotter in Hell! I hadn't meant to be that judgmental of her but by the afternoon when I returned to the office where she worked, I noticed she had put on a hijab.

"I laughed about it at the time but today I take no pleasure. I've seen the hijab become such a dominant issue in discussions between Muslims and non-Muslims that I think we've lost focus of what Islam is really about."

Yvonne is angry that wearing the hijab in Europe or America today, for instance, where Islamophobia is reaching alarming levels, is like propelling a woman in to the front lines, short sword fighting in defence of Islam. "We may as well wear a flashing light on our heads which sort of defeats one of the objects of wearing an hijab which is to blend in modestly with everyone else.

"I now live in the Scottish Borders and Muslims are about as rare there as hens' teeth. So, if I wear a scarf that looks as though I've just come down from the Hindu Kush then I will attract the attention of everyone I encounter."

There were a few excruciating experiences. In December 2004, Yvonne wrote an article in *The Guardian* about her hijab experience headlined, *It's only a piece of cloth,* where she asked: Can a woman in a hijab still get a taxi?

"The reaction from some people was unbelievable. I knew I would become a target for abuse from the odd Islamophobic folk, but I didn't expect so much open hostility from complete strangers," she wrote.

Qaradawi's influence

Yvonne says converts to Islam face different challenges to those born into the faith and so need extra support and advice from the scholars. One who stood head and shoulders above all others for her was the late Sheikh Dr Yusuf Al-Qaradawi.

He was a pioneer of what some viewed as a new jurisprudence called *fiqh al-aqalliyyat* - the Jurisprudence of Minorities - covering the growing Muslim communities living outside Arab and Muslim countries. "I remember someone sending me a copy of an al-Qaradawi fatwa permitting a European woman to remain married to her non-Muslim husband after she converted to Islam because of their otherwise harmonious union. This was ground- breaking stuff for converts who face all sorts of challenges while trying to embrace a new faith and lifestyle.

"He also permitted European Muslims to take mortgages on houses and small businesses in order to function and work while living in the West. Both of these practices are normally strictly forbidden for Muslims, but he also recognised the impracticality of forcing traditional interpretation of Islamic law on those of us living in the West.

"He truly was one of the greatest of contemporary Islamic scholars whose life and work had a huge impact on us all in both the 20th and 21st centuries.

"He understood the unique challenges which confront the ethnically diverse Muslims emerging in the West. With wisdom and knowledge, he gave us newbies the courage to stand up to our critics and defend Islam, as well as the understanding to balance our religious commitments and hectic lifestyles, and thus avoid falling into extremist traps.

"As someone who could engage so easily with whoever was at his table, he used Islam to discuss everything from religion to politics, Western democracy and climate change, as well as the challenges facing the Muslim world, including Palestine."

Pork sausage incident

Reactions to her conversion from friends and family were along expected lines, though that didn't make some of her experiences less hurtful. "I've certainly lost a lot of work colleagues and friends who saw my conversion as a betrayal of white culture and British lifestyles and values. However, those friends who've remained with me say I'm still the same but without the cigarettes and alcohol, which is no bad thing. The embracing of Islam split my immediate family and now one of my two sisters does not speak to me and it also caused tensions with my late father."

One particular experience remains etched in her mind, what is still referred to in her family as 'the pork sausage incident'. "I remember bringing some halal chicken to cook at my parents' and my father used the same pan he'd already used for pork sausages. When I mildly protested, a huge row erupted in which all the prejudices and bigotry my parents held towards Islam came tumbling out. I'd really no idea they felt so aggrieved about my reversion to Islam. In their eyes I had become a traitor to 'my people'!", Yvonne remembers with a tinge of heartache.

"Over the years, they saw how content and happy I was as a Muslim and gradually began to accept my change of faith. When my father died, I was asked to give the eulogy at his funeral at the local church, which I did. I think it was a first at St Margaret's Church in Tanfield, Stanley, to have a hijab in the pulpit!

"There have been times when I've faced challenges purely because of my faith but despite the hardships, tests and challenges, I've never once regretted joining what I consider to be the biggest and the best family in the world.

"The immense pleasure I feel praying in a full mosque on Fridays is unparalleled whether I'm in the UK or visiting one of the mosques in Qatar, Egypt, Turkey or elsewhere. The rustling of starched abayas, and the rhythmic motion of fellow Muslims praying side by side is joyous."

And she is still bombarded with that tense question – 'Why did you do this?'. But she says she actually welcomes the question so that she can explain rather than having to deal with a quiet, moody silence from someone who doesn't understand why she did what she did.

Prayers in a helicopter

Yvonne felt blessed to perform Hajj twice and there were two highlights for her. One was what she calls her Malcolm X moment when she was running late for prayers and made an ungainly dash for the mosque from the hotel. As she ran around a corner for the final sprint, she was confronted with tens of thousands of other Hajis, all late for their prayers.

"We were pushing, shoving and shouting. Many languages filled the air. There was a very tall African man next to me shouting over to someone else while a woman was raising her voice in Urdu. Suddenly the first prayer began and, within ten seconds, out of this turmoil there came a unity and discipline that would have made any regimental sergeant major proud.

"We had all snapped into straight lines. Those of us with prayers mats put them down on the street outside the grand mosque in Makkah and we began praying, in the same direction, in the same language, and in one voice to Allah."

The second vivid memory was courtesy of the Saudi military when she was taken up in a helicopter to film above Makkah on Arafat Day. "I remember seeing this huge white mountain, but when we got closer it was moving. The movement came from all the Hajis wearing their *Ihram* (white cloth).

"The pilot then swung back towards Makkah and we performed Tawaf, or the ritual of circumambulating the Kaaba seven times as part of the Hajj, from the helicopter. It's an amusing story and always creates lots of discussions between friends over the validity of my prayers performed mid-air," she says with a smile.

A fulfilling life

Looking back, it has been an emotionally fulfilling and spiritually uplifting life.

"I have always embraced life full-on and becoming a Muslim has not stopped that. In fact, I've achieved far more since I became a Muslim than I had as a Christian. I've become an author, filmmaker and scriptwriter, won awards, was nominated for a Nobel Peace Prize in 2019, and have launched my own companies and charity. Far from slowing down for a quieter life I have achieved and done things I could never have imagined."

In 2011, she swapped her Soho lifestyle for a farm in the remote Scottish Borders. She says moving from the heart of London brought her closer to God and every day she encounters His miracles either through flora, wildlife or her domestic animals.

"Far from craving the company of others I find I'm more drawn now to spirituality, contemplation and wondering at the whole majesty of the world around us. I wasn't a particularly bad person before I converted to Islam but today I'm much more disciplined in my daily routine thanks to prayers."

When asked if she is still haunted by that fear which kept her awake most of the night, she has this to say: "I sleep well these days despite the irrational fears I used to hold about dying in my sleep.

"Islam has taught me not to worry or dwell on things out of our control. When I die it will be God's will and so I will continue to put my trust in Him and I know I have nothing to fear ... although I'd prefer not to be fast asleep when Azrael (the angel of Death) arrives!"

7

From MTV to Makkah:
A journey that filled a
deep void

———•••◆•••———

Kristiane Backer – Former MTV Europe
presenter-turned art dealer
———•••◆•••———

It was in the late 1980s and 90s, and Kristiane seemed to have it all - fame, a celebrity lifestyle which took her all over the world, mixing and partying with the rich and famous, and being adored by millions of fans. Paradoxically, it was at the height of her career that she felt the most lonely and the most empty, and then she discovered Islam.

I FEEL *so ill – much worse than I've felt in a long time. Sick, dizzy, weak, no energy or drive, irritable and jaded. When is this low going to come to an end? It's work, work, work and then I'm alone again* - Kristiane Backer wrote in her diary.

It was in the late 1980s and 90s, and Kristiane seemed to have it all - fame, a celebrity lifestyle which took her all over the world, mixing and partying with the rich and famous, and being adored by millions of fans. But, paradoxically, it was at the height of her career that she felt the most lonely and the most empty, and yearned for something deeper and more meaningful.

She speaks of falling into a black hole of depression, a running out of energy. "I was constantly stressed and didn't know why I was doing what I was doing. I was at the peak of my career and yet I felt like a hamster in a wheel. The only thing that seemed to matter was the next show. As a presenter, for all the glamour and fame, I was under huge psychological pressure, having constantly to improvise in front of thousands or hundreds of thousands when things went wrong, which they did all the time," she says.

A relentless quest to fill that void led her to Islam. She is probably one of the most high-profile people to have converted to Islam in the last 30 years.

Kristiane's story is a stunning example of how success, especially success with fame that millions yearn and tirelessly toil for, can still leave a deep void that can't be filled with worldly components. Or, how a resplendent career with its package of pleasures and gleaming incentives can't guarantee happiness.

Kristiane Backer is internationally famous as a former MTV Europe presenter and is currently an art dealer in London.

Meeting with Imran Khan

While she was at the height of her fame at MTV, Kristiane met the then-Pakistani cricket captain Imran Khan who would become a central figure in her subsequent conversion to Islam. "God knows what He is doing and works in mysterious ways.

If Allah at that time had sent me a long-bearded mullah, I probably wouldn't have taken to the faith in the same way as I did when I met Imran – he was very passionate and idealistic and explained Islam from a conceptual, philosophical point of view. I had always been idealistic myself and went into journalism initially because I wanted to search for the truth, highlight scandals and do something to better the world. I ended up on MTV which wasn't quite my plan but it put me on the map internationally. My introduction to Islam was one of a kind and am very grateful for that," she says.

"When we met, Imran had just won the World Cup for Pakistan in 1992 but he used to say it wasn't 'me' or 'us' who won the World Cup, it was because of God."

At the time, Imran Khan was fundraising for a cancer hospital in Lahore in memory of his recently deceased mother who he had to watch die over a period of time when she was in a considerable amount of pain. Winning the World Cup had increased donations for sure and Kristiane and other friends accompanied Imran Khan on trips around Pakistan where she witnessed poor people, especially, give him money for the hospital.

"With the Muslims I met, I noticed their whole life was infused by Islamic teachings. Allah was at the core of most Muslims' being. I had never experienced God taking centre stage in people's lives to such a degree. When things would go wrong, for example, like planes being delayed or cancelled, Imran would just say 'alhamdulillah', resigning to destiny as God's will, which astonished me because I was more accustomed to seeing people getting angry when such things happened in the West. Imran would say: 'Maybe the plane would have crashed'; this was a good lesson in a dignified acceptance of God's will.

"I was learning about God being the centre of life, the Creator of life, our reference point, our anchor and destiny. I was discovering the reality of the next life and how our actions in this life affect our position in the hereafter. Understanding these concepts and many more became life-changing."

Travelling and interacting with people in Muslim nations gave a beautiful insight into a living Islam and the Muslim way of life for Kristiane. Pakistan, in particular, left a profound mark on her – the people, the nature, the music, the architecture and the philosophy. The hospitality she experienced in Pakistan and in other Muslim nations eclipsed that in the West. People might have had far less money but they were rich in faith and very giving. Kristiane speaks of a detailed conversation she had with Imran about the void in her life and Imran's pithy replies. She writes in her book *From MTV to Mecca* (published in 2012):

"During a rare quiet moment over lunch at a French restaurant near his flat, I explained to Imran that I'd had practically no contact with Islam in my life and had never really given it much thought. I assumed that Muslim women had no freedoms and were oppressed by a patriarchal system and I imagined the Quran to be a strict, antiquated book of rules. But I was happy to be enlightened. 'The Quran is actually not written by man, but is the word of God,' Imran explained. 'Belief in God is the basis of Islam,' he said. Okay, so far so good, and I did believe in God. 'But how can the Quran be God's word?' I asked him. 'The Quran was revealed over a period of time by the archangel Gabriel to Prophet Muhammad (PBUH) who is the last Prophet,' he explained. I didn't really understand, and I thought he believed in Allah and not in God. 'The Arabic word for God is Allah,' Imran retorted. 'Allah is the same God that all people believe in. Islam actually means "surrender to the will of God". And it has a second meaning that is "peace". In other words, those who submit to God and place their trust in God will find inner peace.'

What exactly did it mean to submit to God, I wondered. All I knew was that in my world, there was neither God nor peace. I had no connection with religion as such, and God meant little more to me than distant childhood memories. My parents had just got divorced, and I felt as though I was emerging from some kind of existential crisis. If I was honest with myself, I couldn't remember the last time I'd felt inner peace, even though I had all the success a young person could have wished for. Deep down I felt empty and a bit lonely, and I thought that what I needed was a partner. But the truth was that no human being could have filled my inner void."

Books that changed her life

Imran gave her books to read on Islam that would challenge her value system – such as Ali Shariati's *Man and Islam*, Gai Eaton's *Islam and the Destiny of Man*, and *Road to Mecca* by Muhammad Assad. Kristiane would later get to know the late Eaton well and he would be a wonderful teacher and friend and a major influence on her spiritual life.

Kristiane quotes words from Iranian sociologist Shariati's book which instantly resonated with her, which shone a new light into her search for meaning. "Man can free himself from the prison of nature and history with the aid of science. He can free himself from his social order with the aid of sociology. But in order to free himself from the prison of his self … he needs religion and love," wrote Shariati. He believed that love could help us transcend our ego and find true freedom. This love, he believed, came from God and was for God.

Eaton's book, too, opened a new world of knowledge to her. "I was flying to L.A. to go to the MTV awards with *Islam and the Destiny of Man* in my luggage. In my spare time, instead of partying, I was reading my Islamic books – it was a stimulating and exciting awakening process for me."

Kristiane also read English scholar Martin Lings' *Muhammad: His Life Based on the Earliest Sources*, which brought her to the realisation that what she knew about Prophet Muhammad (PBUH) was just hearsay. She liked this incident in particular: Every day, when the Prophet set off to the Ka'ba, a Jewish neighbour would throw litter in his way to show her disrespect for him. One day, he was surprised to find no litter scattered on the path, and concerned for her well-being, the Prophet paid her a visit. The woman was afraid to see the Prophet. She wasn't ill, but just hadn't managed to sweep up her own litter in time to throw it outside. The Prophet said he had come because he was worried about her as he hadn't seen any litter on the path. Muhammad's words melted the woman's heart and she embraced Islam.

She also discovered that the Quran contained all kinds of scientific facts that were not known at the time of revelation and were discovered by scientists only centuries later. For example, the Quran states that the planets moved in elliptical orbits around the sun. Imran later said German scientist Johannes Kepler only discovered in the seventeenth century that planets move around the sun in ellipses. The Quran also described how mountains had roots as deep as the mountains themselves and that none of these facts mentioned in the Quran have so far been disputed by scientists.

Kristiane said she learned "so much that was beneficial for my daily life: The idea that we are not in control of our lives but Allah is. This is why we should always try our best to achieve whatever we are aiming for and leave the results to Allah. We will receive reward for the efforts we make and accepting God's will. God judges our actions by our intentions."

"Or the fact that we are born pure, not as original sinners and that we are not responsible for anyone else's mistakes but our own. (A particular poignant lesson being German.)

"When feeling overwhelmed it is reassuring to know from the Quran that 'God does not burden a soul more than with what it can bear'.

"I was also very pleased to see a lot of commonalities between Islam, Christianity and Judaism, discovering that all biblical figures such as Abraham, Moses, Mary and Jesus were featuring in Islam as well and were revered as Prophets. It made sense to learn that God always spoke the same message to people, just through different messengers."

But Kristiane still struggled with some issues when it came to Islam, and especially those relating to the rights of women such as the inheritance laws, polygamy and the hijab. She would debate these regularly with Imran Khan. A particular sticking point was the verse in Surah Al Nisa where Allah says: "As to those women on whose part ye fear disloyalty and ill-conduct, admonish them (first), (next), refuse to share their beds, (and last) beat them (lightly); but if they return to obedience, seek not against them means (of annoyance): For Allah is Most High, Great (above you all)."

Imran invited the former rock star musician and famous Muslim convert Cat Stevens (Yusuf Islam) once to meet Kristiane and share some of his conversion experiences. He brought an Islamic scholar along and Kristiane asked her questions about this particular verse. The scholar said that only in extreme circumstances were men allowed "to beat women lightly, for example with a tooth brush or a newspaper." This did not sit well with Kristiane.

She could not believe that Allah would sanction the beating of women, however lightly, in his sacred book, knowing also that Prophet Muhammad (PBUH), who she read so much about, never beat a woman himself.

Imran Khan told her if something did not make sense, not to get entangled in a particular point, of the religion and nit- pick or search for holes, but rather to look at the overall spirit of the religion. She could always come back to the details later, he said. This was great advice, Kristiane said and she is glad that she followed it. It took her another 19 years to resolve the issue when the Canadian shariah scholar Yasser Auda pointed her to a book on marital discord written by Abu Sulayman who explains the Quran through the Quran and says that the Arabic word *"dharaba"* should be interpreted to mean "separation" rather than beating.

Fascinated by the unseen

Kristiane Backer was born in Hamburg, Germany, in 1965, to a nominally Christian but not very religious family. Despite this, she was confirmed as a Protestant, although religion didn't play a major role in her home life. Nevertheless, Kristiane always believed in God as a child and would pray to Him in her simple way.

She had a comfortable, even pampered, upbringing in a middle-class home with her parents and younger sister. Her father was hardworking and catered for their financial needs while her mother devoted her whole life to her children, ferrying the two sisters here, there and everywhere to make sure they fully participated in extra-curricular activities. Kristiane grew up to be a confident, active girl who did well academically and had an inherent sense of optimism and adventure.

It was this sense of adventure that led her, at the age of 16, to spend a year in the United States with two host families where she learned to speak English fluently. She spent the year making lots of friends and travelling around the country – two things that she would continue to do throughout her life.

Upon her return to Germany and straight after secondary school Kristiane trained as a journalist at a radio station and it was here that her dormant spirituality saw its first expression. She became fascinated by the unseen world and did reports on witchcraft and the Ouija board, which is used to summon dead spirits at a seance, for Radio Hamburg. She often talked to the Institute of Paranormal Studies to verify the facts and was fascinated.

"I had this interest," she says. "Some kind of religiosity was clearly in my DNA – my grandmother and her sister were very religious and went for 50 years to a Pentecost Christian church, but it had jumped a generation as my father was not interested – so it was very vague and unguided. As for Islam, growing up I had no inkling about it, other than the basic ABCs and that it was a strict religion."

At the age of 24, Kristiane got her big break – she landed a job at the American cable (and satellite) channel MTV which was launching in Europe and needed video jockeys to present their music videos. MTV became hugely popular and revolutionised the music industry, television and youth culture across Europe, becoming a household name, and was referenced countless times in popular culture by musicians, TV channels, and shows, films and books. The job offer presented Kristiane with the opportunity to move to London, which delighted her tremendously, and the city has been her home ever since.

"I've always loved London because it's truly international, it's so diverse, you can find anything that you're interested in here at a very high level – the studies, for example, that London offered me I could never have done quite like this in Germany. I took a lot of different classes, most recently in interior design. Previously I studied natural medicine and after four years of part time studies, I qualified as a   Homeopath. I also started to learn Arabic although I still need to take a lot more [lessons].

"In Germany and the rest of Europe it is very different. All over Europe, there is a lot more Islamophobia, those societies comprise of monocultures, whereas the UK is much more diverse, even historically, hence it becomes more difficult to be a Muslim in Europe, to be natural, content and accepted."

Kristiane stayed at MTV for over seven years – which was a long time as the channel usually changed its on-screen presenters frequently. During that period, she had the red carpet treatment wherever she went with her camera team. Her programme, The Coca Cola Report, took her around the world. She interviewed and met stars such as Mick Jagger, David Bowie, George Michael, Annie Lennox, Sinead O' Connor and Prince. She would party with celebrities in nightclubs and mountains of fan mail would pile up in her office. Moreover, some of the stars she met at MTV in the 90s remain her friends to this day.

Parallel to her work on MTV, Kristiane was asked by a German production company to create a Youth Music show for Germany, which she did. This became very popular and she hosted huge music events alongside her weekly show on Bravo TV.

While her MTV years were a non-stop adrenaline rush, she was happy to leave by the time it came to an end. She had presented almost every show on the channel and there was nowhere else to go really. Aged 30, she had outgrown this youth channel. And the MTV lifestyle – which was fuelled by alcohol, parties and drugs – was increasingly at odds with her burgeoning interest in Islam. After seven years at MTV the company decided not to extend Kristiane's contract, although they did keep her on in a freelance capacity for some time. The end coincided with heavy media speculation about her impending conversion to Islam. When she was asked by a German journalist at the 10th anniversary celebration of Bravo TV, whether she had converted (she hadn't at the time), she replied that she was "a Muslim at heart." This was enough to lead to hysterical media headlines which didn't go unnoticed at MTV and at her German youth show for which she won several TV awards.

"The German media was very hostile about my faith," she says. "When it emerged before my conversion that I had met Imran Khan and developed an interest in Islam, headlines in the German press asked: 'Is our MTV girl going to be First Lady of Pakistan and leave it all behind to go behind the burqa?' This led to some very controversial articles and chat shows and I was basically finished - I lost my entire entertainment career."

She once appeared on a chat show where every stereotype about Islam was thrown in her face by a presenter determined to play on Islamophobic stereotypes. She had the intention of using her appearance as an opportunity to explain Islam to an audience in Germany (where she was still best known), but soon realised that the dice were loaded against her so she limited her appearances in German media from that point onwards.

"Yet no regrets. It was meant to be. Later on, I found it much more satisfying going on stage and talking about my journey to Allah and making a contribution to building a bridge between the West and Islam. I became a well-known convert and it gave me much more satisfaction to do something meaningful rather than just introducing music bands on TV or on stage."

Her family wasn't amused either because all they knew about Islam was stereotypes from the media. They actually thought it was a phase that she would grow out of, but as the years passed by, they eventually realised it was permanent and even came to appreciate the fact that it had made her a more considerate family member. Kristiane says her family are accepting of her Islam now.

As for her friends, some of them found her journey inspirational and were impressed that she could be so passionate about her new- found value system; others didn't care or simply exited her life.

Conversion at the age of 30

Kristiane formally converted to Islam in April 1995 at the age of 30. She did this in a mosque in North London, the UK headquarters of the prominent late Sufi Sheikh Nazim Al Haqqani – a Turkish Cypriot Muslim scholar and one of the most influential guides of the Naqshbandi Order of Sunni Islam. Although it had taken Kristiane a few years to formalise her Islam, she says she was basically a Muslim at heart for some time prior to her conversion. As a Christian she found Islam to be a very inclusive religion as it didn't deny Jesus, Moses, Noah, Adam and Eve.

"I knew now that Islam was the path I wanted to follow. All I had to do was place my trust in God. He would always be there, and I was accountable to Him and Him alone. The message of *tawhid*, the absolute oneness and sovereignty of God, was clear and ultimately irresistible to me. I knew I was ready, from the bottom of my heart. The sense of independence and security this realisation brought me was an extraordinary source of strength to me, and one I couldn't wait to tap into. There in my room in Cornwall, I stood and prayed to Allah for the first time.

"Most people convert for intellectual reasons because they see the logic - Islam is more logical than Christianity. The concept of *tawhid*, the oneness of God, is very powerful. In Christianity you have this whole confusion about the Trinity. Who do you pray to, God or Jesus? Islam actually emphasises the feeling I had when I was a child and I prayed to God - There is an innate monotheism in a child.

"I also found the fact that we are not responsible for our parents' sins. I didn't believe Jesus took all our sins away so that we could do whatever we wanted. It is more logical to have self- responsibility and atone for our mistakes and not be burdened with them forever. We can repent and God will forgive us if we are sincere and give up our sins."

Kristiane was also attracted by the fact that Islam was a way of life which constantly reminded one of God. Everything was an act of worship – even marvelling over the beautiful geometric patterns and arabesques in the art and architecture of Islam, which are designed to symbolise aspects of Allah. This was especially evident during the month of Ramadan. She contrasts this to the Christian festival of Christmas which has become a consumerist frenzy after doing nothing to earn it.

It's clear that Kristiane's relationship with Imran Khan was a serious one and they wanted to get married as soon as the cancer hospital was opened. But, with the endless delays, marriage didn't happen. Then, in March, Khan confided to her that his spiritual advisor had told him the relationship would not work out and shortly after it was all over. Khan then married the heiress Jemima Goldsmith in May of the same year. The couple divorced again nine years later in 2004. Over the next 22 years Khan would slowly build a political career before becoming Prime Minister of Pakistan in 2018.

Although the split hurt her, and it was clearly Khan's decision, Kristiane learned to accept it as Allah's destiny and found it in her heart to not only forgive Imran but to become friends again when he got in touch years later. Her faith certainly inspired her to become better rather than bitter. Her increasing devotion to Allah was not dependent on her relationship with the Pakistani cricketer and was to outlive it. He was the catalyst, chosen by Allah to call her to Islam, and when that role was fulfilled, there was no more need for him in her life.

Kristiane admits that she was far from the perfect Muslim after she convered and it took her a while to completely give up certain bad habits. Abandoning alcohol was one such struggle as it was an intrinsic part of Western culture and work in the entertainment industry. Fasting during Ramadan was also initially difficult.

"Becoming a Muslim is a process. It does not happen overnight. My first Ramadan was dismal. I had gone out clubbing the night before and the next morning I lay in bed with a pounding headache. In the afternoon I gave up, Ramadan was not for me. But eventually I realised that on the path to holiness I could not continue drinking alcohol, so I gave it up and by the grace of God have been flying through every Ramadan since.

"With this experience I discovered an important secret of Islam as Prophet Muhammad (PBUH) said: If you walk one step towards God, He comes ten steps towards you. The secret is, you have to sincerely take the first step and then God makes things easy for you."

Kristiane said she that felt Islam helps to foster a closer connection to God as it is a way of life and not just something done once a week. With the five daily prayers, *dhikr* - remembrance of God - the fasting for four weeks in Ramadan coupled with evening prayers, charity and the pilgrimage, but also Islamic art, music and literature as well as exercises to purify one's heart- and all aspects of one's life. It is not just an academic exercise – when sincerely practicing, Islam has a transformative effect on one's whole being," she says.

In January 2006, Kristiane made the Hajj pilgrimage which is incumbent on a Muslim who can afford it (and is physically capable) once in their lifetimes. She deliberately chose a basic Hajj package because she realised that this was not a holiday but rather an arduous spiritual experience. She says among the lessons she learned was to be mindful and patient, to keep an inner connection with God at all times, and that self-improvement is a never-ending struggle.

She speaks of her surreal experience during Hajj in her book: "I placed both my hands on the Ka'ba, and prayed with all my might for my family, my friends and myself, for relief of suffering and peace in the world. It was a deep conversation with God. Eventually, having said everything I could think of in that moment, I took my hands off the stone wall again, and the flow of pilgrims carried me forward. I felt happy and alert, concentrating on my prayers. Walking around the Ka'ba, I realised that God truly was the centre of the universe."

Reinventing career

And, as the saying goes, one door closes but another one opens, and after leaving MTV, Kristiane hosted a new daily TV show on NBC Europe and, as a well-known Muslim convert, she was offered many public speaking opportunities. She also did journalistic work and fronted campaigns for Islam. In 2009, the Exploring Islam Foundation invited her to be a global ambassador and to be one of the faces of their "Inspired by Muhammad" campaign. This focussed on disseminating the teachings of the Prophet (PBUH) to dispel misconceptions about Islam. Her face was plastered on posters and billboards across London with slogans such as "I believe in women's rights, so did Muhammad" and "I believe in protecting the environment, so did Muhammad."

It was in 2012 that Kristiane published her book *From MTV to Mecca: How Islam Inspired My Life* in which she shared her highs and lows as she adopted Islam; from the difficulties of finding love, to discovering and embracing Islamic practices in day-to-day life, to dealing with prejudices, misconceptions and professional struggles. The book goes into detail about her success and failures and her travels around the world which will be of great interest to a Muslim or non-Muslim reader.

After the TV years and publishing her book, she reinvented her career and moved into Fine Art. "I studied all different aspects of the art business as well as art history at Christie's and Sotheby's and at University of Westminster. London offers so much to everyone. And I feel very comfortable living here as a Muslim. There are so many interesting events, there is an intellectual scene, Islamic art and culture, finance, etc. and it's relatively easy to find halal food and a mosque not too far away."

Charitable activities and speaking engagements also keep Kristiane busy these days. She volunteers at a soup kitchen in London every Friday, distributing food to the needy.

She also focusses on helping converts. During lockdown she created a weekly Zoom Forum for New Muslims from around the world, in partnership with Al Manaar Mosque in West London. She invites the speakers and sometimes organises events where those who are in the UK can meet in person. There is also a thriving WhatsApp group where participants share inspirational messages. There are around 650 converts from the UK, Europe and beyond and anyone is welcome. "The idea is to support each other in our journey to Allah," she says.

"Being a convert can be a very isolating and lonely experience if you're not married and in a family context. Interestingly, there are a lot more female converts than male ones and most of them convert for conviction rather than convenience. In other words, they don't convert because of marriage; they convert because they really believe Islam has something to offer them that they don't find anywhere else. They like the values which are more akin to Victorian values. It's very good for a woman basically, not to be just used and abused and get thrown away but to be treated well in the marriage context as a wife. Islam, contrary to popular belief, has a lot to offer, especially to women.

"But, as a convert, you are a minority within a minority and it can be hard to fit in with very set born Muslim communities. As a convert, do you go to an Urdu speaking mosque? Or a Moroccan, predominantly Arabic speaking, one? Or a Turkish mosque? It's very hard for us to find the right fit. *Khutbas* and sermons in the English language should be mandatory in all mosques, so as not to alienate the natives, or the youth who may not understand those languages so well anymore. Some converts get ostracised, they lose families, even parents who don't agree with them being Muslims. Or some of them marry a Muslim who turns out to be a misogynist suppressor of women."

And, if the truth be told, Kristiane has also struggled at times to fit in with other Muslims. Her second marriage to an Arab man was a case in point where West seemed to clash with East. Her then husband, according to Kristiane, insisted on banning every, even platonic, contact with all men, including her elderly religious advisors, such as Gai Eaton. Eventually that marriage broke down and cultural differences seem to have played a part. This was particularly difficult for Kristiane because she was keen to prove that East and West could live harmoniously together, something she still believes in. But in her case, this was not to be. She is now happily married to an Englishman.

As a Western woman, she admits, she would probably struggle to adapt to some of the more conservative societies she has visited in the Muslim world where women are not seen or heard. But that is cultural and not Islamic and as a convert one learns early on to try and differentiate between culture and religion. "I signed up to the religion but not to every culture of Islam. If someone tells me I must do this or that I could find it stifling and might feel claustrophobic. In my case I submitted voluntarily because I realised the guidance comes from up above. There is no coercion in religion.

"The inner transformational effect of Islam is what I love - the poetry, the art, the literature, just to have the sacred dimension in one's life is such a blessing and it's the best thing."

She adds: "The white converts usually get invited everywhere but it's like we are a trophy on a mantelpiece that should not be touched. Born Muslims generally still prefer to stay and marry among their own communities and for white Muslims it's still quite hard to get married, but the people who really experience racism are the African converts and this kind of racism amongst Muslims has to stop as Prophet Muhammad (PBUH) taught us the contrary through the examples of his own life."

And how comfortable is Kristiane in her Islamic skin today?

"Today I'm comfortable and happy as a Muslim, alhamdulillah. I've found lots of friends who are Muslims, we have *iftars* together and meet and support each other. I enjoy when at a dinner to step out and pray together with whoever prays. We also meet up to go to talks, classical Islamic concerts or art exhibitions. It took a while to build this network but I have many friends now and a lot of them are Pakistanis because I have a huge Pakistani connection still."

Twenty-seven years after her conversion, Kristiane remains as committed to Islam as ever, as committed to dispelling stereotypes about Islam as ever, and as committed to proving that a Western woman can be as comfortable a Muslim as anyone else.

8

She fled the cult of the self for the love of a desert Prophet

**Lauren Booth – British writer
and actor**

An activist and writer, Lauren's nearness to political events has long challenged mainstream narratives on Islam and Muslims. Her road to enlightenment combines spiritual wonder with historical observation.

IN A refugee camp home, all but empty of belongings, an impoverished mother busily laid out *iftar* for her honoured guests. The nightly meal taken by Muslims during the holy month of Ramadan can be an exciting display of a host's cooking skills and her love for her family. In the poverty of the camp, the paper plates on the floor held just three simple ingredients: Hummus, bread, salad leaves.

Instead of feeding her children and herself first, after a hot, day without food and water, Um Mohammed, laid the humble spread before the journalist and her camera man, visiting to deliver charity meat.

'Don't eat the food Lauren', the cameraman whispered 'It will come out of the children's mouths - we can eat later at my home, God willing.' Half a dozen, small heads peeped around the only other door in the dwelling, drawn by the exciting smell of the take away meat - a rare treat indeed.

Their mother, pointed the visitors to the floor, around a plastic tablecloth. She then piled most of the food onto plates for them. Leaving little more than a couple of mouthfuls each, for herself and her children.

Lauren felt a wave of rage engulfing her, forcing her to her feet. She had been besieged in Gaza for almost a month, having arrived on the siege-breaking mission 'Free Gaza' sea mission. She was, she says, 'frustrated by the patience, the infuriating goodness of the people' living beneath bombs and watchtowers. Facing the perplexed mother, she was almost shouting:

'You say your God loves you, but He makes you hungry for 30 days. After that you are still poor and hungry. So what's the point? You say your God loves you but He makes you thirsty for 30 days, and after that you don't have one day of clean water to drink. So what's the point? Just give me ONE good reason that you fast in Ramadan, just ONE!'

The Gazan mother's response would act as a signpost; towards a path which would change the course of her life, two years later.

Fourteen years on, Lauren now lives in a religious district of Turkey's capital, Istanbul. She and her husband are both journalists and both converts to Islam. She dedicates her time to using multiple platforms to share stories and perceptions from the Muslim understanding of life, to the western world she came from. She creates short films on Ottoman history, writes scripts and articles and hosts meetings for women in her local and online Muslim community.

She can, 'hardly believe the transformation in my life and my habits' which have taken place over the past decade. These days she doesn't smoke or drink. She controls her tongue 'to the best of my ability.' The life she lives is one that is a far cry from the one which appeared to be laid out before her, in the bourgeois hippy enclave of North London, where she grew up in the 1970s.

British way of life

Lauren's birth name is Sarah-Jane. She was born in 1967, to a fashion model, Pamela Riley (better known as Susan) and the handsome, infamous 'Till Death Us Do Part' TV actor, Tony Booth. Her father had other daughters, the eldest of whom were back in his hometown of Liverpool. The eldest, Cherie would become a brilliant barrister attaining the title Queen's Counsel. In 1997, she would also enter Number 10 Downing Street, on the arm of her husband, Prime Minister, Tony Blair - an event that would eventually bring Lauren into direct opposition to her brother-in-law's political alliances and chart her course as a writer and human rights activist.

Hampstead Garden Suburb is a charming area of greenery on the northern reaches of London. Here, Lauren's parents lived a life best described as fashionably, 'down-at-heel.' Beautiful people in the midst of an artistic scene, externally glamorous, they were both, alcoholics. Not that this was a problem in that era. An entire 'scene' had been created to enable adult heavy drinking and drug taking and label it an aspirational 'happening'.

As a child she spent an equal amount of time in the home of her maternal grandparents, in Wembley, North West London. The traditional 'Queen and Country' values espoused by Sid and Frances Riley, were fast falling out of style.

The British way of life underwent a social revolution from 1964 to 1974. One that upended society so radically and so quickly, that a generation of spiritual refugees floundered in its wake, says Lauren. The 'you do you' mantra of today, has its roots in the people of Britain and America who stopped going to church, believing in a fixed family structure or a social moral contract, back then.

This 'transcendental' parenting was uncomfortable for the children living through it. Her home life combined a 'seen not heard' Victorian ideal, imposed on her and her sister - with a 'let it all hang out' zero expectation standard, upon the adults around them.

"A family day out was a trip to the Hare and Hounds, the Bull and Bush or the Coach and Horses. My sister and I would be sat in a smoke-filled corner of the pub while my father held court and my mother was admired by old drunks. We were told to 'shush' or we would be kicked out by the landlord. These trips lasted up to 4 hours. Still, on warmer days we were sat on the step outside with a cola and a packet of crisps where we could watch people walk by. That was a real treat!'

The British code of conduct had once been attached to Christian values. One man for one woman, for life, in marriage. Hard work and 'fair play old chap!' The 1970s, however, was YOLO on acid. It left many western children to raise themselves as parents went out to work, then enjoyed the new socially acceptable 'freedoms' - parties, pubs, marital affairs and marijuana, remembers Lauren.

Despite the tone of those times, Lauren's mother described her as 'a weird kid who always prayed.' In the midst of the adult turmoil around her, she took hope in a certainty that, as messy as daily life was, God was in control of all things and everything would be okay. This led her to a positive outlook, even in the bleakest of times. And things got very bleak for the family, including a drunken fire accident in which her father was almost burnt to death.

"I was taught the Lord's Prayer by my grandmother. I loved the potent message: God is in Heaven, He runs everything. Obey Him and He will provide everything you need. I read the Bible at break times at secondary school – yes I was bullied - how did you guess?' She laughs.

Elsewhere, God was out of fashion, replaced by a fascination for mantras, meditation and mind reading. On evenings when there wasn't enough loose change for the pub, Tony Booth would sit his daughter down to do experiments in mind reading using a pack of cards. They would sit, cross-legged together, on the ash- stained living room rug and communicate without words.

Holding a card to his chest, her father would say: "Using your mind's eye, concentrate on what I am 'sending over to you. It's a picture, see it and then say the FIRST card that comes into your thoughts." Sometimes they would get a run of 10 even 15 cards in a row. Ten years later, this early interest in external realities and powers, led Lauren to play with tarot card reading. Her parents meanwhile, would even experiment with witchcraft to try and get out of debt. Something Lauren links to her father's burns.

This was the age of gurus, chanting and ganja-induced highs. Hinduism was espoused by the Beatles and other pop icons.

Islam though, remained invisible to the non-adherent's eye. Pakistani men, seen working in stores, on buses or as doctors, were simply presumed to be Hindus as well, or to worship some other colourful, foreign deity, perhaps made of stone.

The family went to Church once in her childhood that she remembers. When Lauren was an 11-year member of the Scouting movement, founded by Lord Baden Powell in 1908. "Dedicated to Queen, country and doing good deeds." She was chosen for the prestigious responsibility of presenting the Brownie flag to the altar, at the local church, during Easter Service.

"In my young mind, I felt as though I was not only presenting the flag to church, but to God Himself. My reverence for the occasion overcame me. Instead of placing the flag in the holster, turning round and walking to a seat, I backed up, head bowed, step by step, like the courtiers in black and white films about Henry the Eighth. Everyone was laughing, except Dad, who totally got that I was trying to be respectful."

What stopped her going deeper into the Christian doctrine, was the confusing idea of the Trinity.

"A man had died on the cross for our sins. That made him God, although he had already been a part of God all the time. I just couldn't grasp it. Jesus as a servant of God, taught a crowd how to pray to God. Which is why the Lord's Prayer begins 'Our Father, who art in Heaven'. If Jesus knew himself to 'God', then wouldn't he have told his followers to kneel before him and say: 'I am the Father, who art right now here on earth, hallowed be My name, My Kingdom Come, My will be done?' I ignored the Trinity to keep my faith."

Except that keeping such traditional beliefs became impossible in the face of teenage hormones, atheistic friendships and what she describes as a burgeoning love affair with her own perceived 'brilliance.' In 1989, having completed her Drama Diploma, she embarked on an acting career that would take her on long haul European tours of Austria and France. It was at this time, she changed her name, in order to be accepted by the actors' union, Equity. Her brand name, 'Sarah Booth' was already taken. She so she chose the name 'Lauren.'

On 1 May 1997, her brother-in-law, Tony, was elected as the British Prime Minister.

The next day, Lauren's phone began ringing with invitations to jazzy lunches at Kensington bistros with Fleet Street editors wanting to get to know 'Blair's sister-in-law'.

She describes herself as taking the opportunity to begin a writing career with both hands. At the same time, the attention persuaded her to join a very popular cult. A membership of which she would hold for almost quarter of a century: The Cult of The Self.

"That name change and having a famous relative, led to the creation of an alter ego with few inhibitions. That version of 'Lauren' played the role of minor celebrity, for all it was worth. She also became a 'high functioning' alcoholic, like, at least half of my media colleagues. Celebrities are encouraged to be bingers, then exploited for news stories when they do. Welcome to 1990's Ladette culture."

That era, she feels, spelt the end to any of her early innocence. The child's human nature, the light leading to faith which the Quran calls *Fitrah[1]*, was doused out by celebrity, ego and Jack Daniels.

The cult of the self

The dreamy child she had once been, became a 'spiritually moribund adult. Showing off and flashing witty soundbites on TV, Radio and in print

---

1   Fitrah is understood as an inborn natural predisposition which cannot change, inclined towards
     right action and submission to Allah, the One God. (Quran 30:30)

for large sums of money. Like a million celebrities before and since, the need to be constantly applauded led to flirtations with different types of risk taking behaviour. Today she looks back at the time of premiers and private drinking clubs with a shudder.

'So many of my acquaintances of that time are already dead of overdoses, suicide or heart attacks. What was the point of all that supposed 'fun' - where does it get you?"

Two major life experiences would reawaken in her a yearning to understand the purpose of life and to seek a connection to The Divine.

Near death and new life

"In the year 2000, aged 33, in the space of just 6 months - I almost died in a freak accident and I gave birth for the first time. Both of these events held elements of a supernatural experience." The wedding to her long term boyfriend, was covered by the celebrity magazine 'Hello'. In return for exclusive photos of the big day and the honeymoon, the publication paid for everything, including 10 days on Canouan, an island in the Grenadines. A photo shoot on the third day, would end in a shock.

"My husband and I were asked to pose together in the swimming pool by the photographer from the magazine. He set up large lights next to the crystal blue salt water and we posed in the water.

'Smile!' He shouted, time and again. Then, as he moved to get a different angle, his foot caught in the cable connecting a set of huge lights directly to the mains. Dozens of bulbs and thousands of amps of electricity lurched towards the water. The splash came and I held my breath. Things actually went in slow motion. Death! I remember that I didn't think about my loved ones, or see my life flash before my eyes. There was just one crystal clear thought. "Shouldn't I have done more?' And then, 'Done more what?'

A silence stretched out as no one dared to move. I knew in that moment that 5* holidays and fame were not the meaning of life. I promised myself that, if I lived - I would to find out what was."

Five months later, Lauren gave birth to her first daughter, Alexandra, in the Royal Free Hospital, London. She and her husband had agreed on a drug free birth with as little professional intervention as possible. Again, she felt, in that experience, an existence far greater, more beautiful and complex than the materialistic understanding of reality.

Driving past Hampstead Heath on the way to hospital, she remembers the beauty of the trees and the morning mist impacting her with a sense of absolute wonder until tears fell down her cheeks.

"How had I ignored the magnificence of the oak and elm trees thrusting towards the sky? I began to whisper, 'Thank you. Thank you. Thank you."

Who was she thanking?

"The One who made everything. When we really look at nature, stare in wonder at it, we know it is created by God alone, without partners or comparison," she says.

A year later, in 2001, events of September 11, sparked a series of wars. Set in motion by the US President George W Bush, they were fully backed by her brother in law, then British PM, Tony Blair. Lauren remembers watching the Twin Towers collapse on the BBC News. Being aware of geopolitics through her work with news outlets, she recalls asking her husband:

"Which poor Muslim country do you think will be made to pay for this?"

She was determined to do something more useful with her public voice at this time and began to write and to give speeches for the campaign to hold the UK government accountable for its activities in Afghanistan. She rallied against the 'war-mongering' arguments made by politicians, for invading Iraq. A vocal supporter of the Stop The War Coalition, Lauren began to attend fund raisers for refugees and orphans of war. For the first time in her life, she began to spend time in the company of Muslims.

At first, she wasn't impressed.

"There was no alcohol. Whenever there was an event with Muslims, I thought 'this will be boring - no booze!' I even smuggled vodka miniatures in my handbag because, I was so used to drinking at events."

After several occasions, the calm of those gatherings, in comparison to the bling-bling, media events she was used to, began to affect her. In diaries from that time, she describes feeling 'like a hardened, sarcastic adult in a playground of lovely, innocent, children.' Another element was new to her. At these events she was mostly a speaker. She was astounded to go onto and leave the stage to silence - rather than applause. She found out that this was because Muslims believe in praising only God and that feeding the human ego through congratulations and applause is considered toxic to spiritual health.

This was something she could completely understand having trained and worked as an actor. At first, she felt irritated when directed by the male hosts to all female tables. Gradually she took time to engage the Muslim women around her and began to recognise an "unexpected" depth and cleverness amongst the women in hijab[2] or even niqab[3]. Her internalised preconceptions were challenged. Far from being 'merely' homemakers,

---

2   Hijab: Arabic: "cover" or "barrier" an obligatory garment expected to be worn by Muslim
      women.

3   Niqab: Face veil which is not an Islamic requirement upon all women but can be a personal
      choice. It was an obligation upon the wives of the Prophet Muhammed pbuh.

these women could be highly accomplished in those fields AND in business, health, academia or politics. Who knew, she wondered that Muslim women who lived their faith could also have the head space, intelligence and social freedom to earn PhDs and run major organisations.

"When it clicked with me that as well as being chefs, attentive wives and school run mums - they could have other accomplishments too, it was actually irritating. I felt kind of shocked, like we western women were actually under-performing in many areas."

February 19 2003, three weeks after the birth of her second daughter Holly, Lauren gathered her newborn and two-year- old Alex, onto the London Underground to join the largest demonstration in English history; against the invasion of Iraq. Breastfeeding one under a heavy coat, with the other on her shoulders, she joined more than one million members of the public, braving freezing conditions to try to prevent the murder of innocent families thousands of miles away in the Arab world. Tears iced her cheeks for the babies of the Muslim parents, about to die "as if their lives were somehow worth less than my own children."

The horror she watched unfold on the TV bulletins, was called 'shock and awe' by the White House. Murdered women and children were labelled 'collateral damage.' This increased her resolve to help bring 'truth,' from the Muslim perspective, into the mainstream news domain.

Perhaps it was inevitable that with this intention, Lauren would become involved in challenging the final colonial project, supported by western governments, Zionism.

On leaving Downing Street in June 2007, Tony Blair was appointed by Russia, the USA, the UN and the EU as their Special Representative in the Middle East. By this time Lauren had already made trips to the West Bank,

Jerusalem, Gaza and Lebanon. Palestine and the Right of Return for refugees as a result of her experiences, became her 'calling and purpose'.

The activities attached to her raison d'être, would take her in a different direction different to the political path on which she at first set out. Bringing her into a realm of believers in One God, who followed a book she had been taught to suspect - The Holy Quran.

During this period, she continued her work and her visits to London for Sky News and the Mail on Sunday. This meant constantly hopping in and out of taxis. The majority of cab drivers she came into contact with came from Afghanistan, Iraq, Sudan or Somalia - Muslim majority nations. These drivers began to give her lessons from the *seerah*[4]. "Whether I wanted them or not" she chuckles.

Somali drivers were especially determined lecturers.

One cabbie introduced her to the Prophet's legendary humility. When great leaders came to the mosque in Medina to meet the now powerful regional leader, they were unable to tell which person was the Prophet of Allah, and which a humble farmer or merchant. So modest was Muhammad, peace be upon him, he sat on the floor (not a throne) whilst wearing the same clothes as those around him.

Being a cat lover, Lauren remembers being especially moved by the true story, in which the Prophet's cat Muezza, was asleep on his cloak when he needed to begin a lecture for his congregation. Multiple narrations report that he cut the hem of his only cloak instead of disturbing the animal's rest.

With tears in her eyes she sat in the back of the taxi thinking "Who does that? Who cares that much for the feelings of a small creature?" Already, at this

---

4   In Islamic sciences 'Seerah' means the study of the life of the Prophet Mu- hammed pbuh.

point, she was feeling a change in herself, for which she wasn't prepared.

"After one taxi lecture on the Prophet, my heart was lurching so hard, I felt like the 'Grinch' - as if I was beginning to feel again after decades of hardness. I was a bit scared to realise, I seemed to be falling in love with a man who had lived in a desert, more than 1400 years ago," she said.

Then she went to the Holy Land, Palestine.

For eight years between 2005 and 2013, Lauren Booth visited different regions of Occupied Palestine on an annual basis, both as a journalist and a siege-breaking activist.

Her first visit was to the West Bank, on commission for the *Mail on Sunday*. She was researching a major magazine feature on the first elections of the Palestinian Authority (PA).

"I went in search of *truth*. The truth about what was really going on in the Middle East. I wanted to find a hard hitting story. Behind that, I wondered if I might find an answer to what I was really seeking. An answer to the question: Why are we here?'

She hitched lifts across the region, made friends with local families, travelled to multiple cities and villages, from Bethlehem to Nablus, Jenin to Nazarath. She reported being met with a great affection, generosity and kindness, one that felt almost like a family's love.

"Every time I went out I was met with the word, 'salam'[5] and this really moved me. The children, mothers and shop keepers would all say, 'Welcome home to your country'. I asked an elderly rug seller about the welcome, and he said: 'Whatever your faith, this is your home. Come in peace, Jewish or Christian believers, and you will find all the Prophets here, and inner peace, *insha' Allah*[6].'"

---

5   Arabic *salām*, meaning literally, peace.
6   Arabic term, literally 'Should Allah (God) want to.'

She found the people in the refugee camps especially generous. At one visit to a family in Jenin, a young boy of around 10, brought her in a homemade, red, shield. On the front was a rough outline of Masjid Al Aqsa[7]. Normally the women would clap and laugh when a gift was given. But this time, says Lauren, there was a shocked hush.

"The item was made by Salim's father who he had never met due to his being held in an Israeli prison since before he was born. When the boy's mother told me it was the only thing he had from his father, I tried to give it back." But the boy refused. Why did he do that?

The response was the pointing of a finger towards a large book. 'Our blessed Quran, our Allah, tells us we should be kind to the traveller and the guest - you are both,' he said. Lauren has the precious item in her home, to this day. It was the fact of meeting people who were 'actively living their faith in the twenty first century' that struck her most. That, and the utter certainty that Allah was taking care of them.

In 2006, in the Old City of Jerusalem, an English translation of the Quran was placed into her hands by a young Palestinian man, as they shopped for souvenirs. It was a chance encounter.

"There is no such thing as chance" Lauren corrects.

"Each meeting in this life, each incident, each test and blessing are meant to be it is the Qadr[8] of Allah, The All Knowing."

The meeting took place after a distressing tour of Gaza. Seeing the hardship of the people under siege, left her emotionally wrung out. Even leaving Gaza had not been easy. Eight hours at the dangerous Eretz Israeli crossing, where her phone had died and she had lost contact with her Jerusalem taxi driver, Jamal.

---

7   Jerusalem mosque that was the first direction of prayer in Islam
8   Qadr, Islamic Arabic term meaning Divine intervention in the affairs of humans, predestination.

Finally, emerging, alone, into a dark, truck park, she feared a night walk through the hills. Or sleeping under the wheels of an empty lorry. Suddenly, a car reversed towards her at speed. Her driver, Jamal threw open the passenger door. Once driving, she asked "Why did you wait 5 hours, not even knowing if I was still coming through?" His answer was typical of the Muslim mindset she was coming to respect.

"I waited" he said "because as a Muslim, I could never leave a woman alone or at risk, no matter how long the wait.' His words made her cry so hard, Jamal threatened to drive her to hospital as she was clearly 'hysterical.' That made her laugh and cry at the same time, she recalls.

The next day was her flight home, from Tel Aviv to Paris. Jamal drove through the hectic streets of East Jerusalem dropping her at the Lions 'Gate entrance to the Old City, promising to meet her in an hour, after her last minute souvenir shopping. In amongst, near-empty Arab market stalls, she pulled out a shopping list. Beneath 'Olive tree cross for mum' and 'toy camels for the girls' an afterthought had been scribbled. 'Quran in English. 'Buying the book, she says was just an act of curiosity - definitely 'not a sign of conversion'. Christianity suited her at the time. It had minimal demands, so much easier than the expectations of the Islam she was witnessing.

"Five prayers a day and helping people out all the time. Are you crazy?" She laughs at the memory of how imposing it seemed. A young man, in his late teens, with a rangy look, offered to assist her in souvenir hunt. Half an hour later, she remembers having 'at least' eight bags of gifts worth quite a lot of money. She had yet to pay a single shekel. She was mentally prepared for some serious bartering.

'How much do I owe you?' She asked the young man.

It was raining. The young man's black curls clung to the collar of his leather jacket. Then he shrugged. The words he would say, were another push in a direction that was starting to feel inevitable.

'You don't owe me anything. Please take these small things to your family with salaam from Al Quds[9]. 'How could she take that amount of goods from poor shopkeepers? The goods were worth at least 100 pounds sterling. She began to argue, but the young stopped her.

"He looked me in the eyes" she recalls, and said: 'Just one thing I ask from you. Don't forget Palestine when you go home. Remember us. Please.'"

That was how a Quran in English came to her. As a gift from a Palestinian youth in the holy city of Jerusalem, asking for his people not to be forgotten.

Back in France, she began to feel the English language Quran, sitting on her home library shelf, was calling her to read it.

"I was wealthy and living a life of ease, when I first picked up the Quran. I didn't 'need' it. It was just, I could no longer resist opening it."

On a Spring afternoon, Lauren washed her hands (remembering the Muslims she had seen do the same) and picked it up. The first page said 'Al-Fatiha', translated into English as 'The Opening'.

"I read page one not having any idea what to expect." She was surprised to find the verses sounded similar to the Lord's Prayer. 'Praise be to God, the Lord of the worlds, the Most Merciful, the Most Compassionate; the Master of the day of Recompense. You alone do we worship and You alone do we turn to for help. Direct us on to the Straight Way, the way of those who You have favoured, who did not incur Your wrath, who are not astray.'

---

9   Al-Quds is the Arabic name for Jerusalem, translated it means the holy one ie holy city.

But was it the same God she had always known, the God of Adam and Jesus? She began to read the second chapter titled Al- Baqarah, 'The Cow.'

'This is the book of God, there is no doubt in it; it is a guidance for the pious, for those who believe in the existence of that which is beyond the reach of perception, who establish prayer and spend out of what We have provided them, who believe in what has been revealed to you and what was revealed before you and have firm faith in the Hereafter. '[10]

This was the moment Lauren says that she *knew* the author of the book was none other than The Creator of all existence. She describes recognising the same commanding voice from some verses of the Bible. The question was asked - had she actually 'established prayer' by going to church every couple of weeks, but sinning in between? What she read next, terrified her.

'There are some who say; "We believe in God and in the Last Day," while in fact they do not believe. They seek to deceive God and those who believe, but they deceive none but themselves, though they are not aware. In their hearts is sickness, and God has increased their sickness. They will have a painful punishment because of their denial.[11] '

She describes feeling the words speak directly to her. As if the author could see every shred of hypocrisy in her weak faith, and was calling it out. It was a warning. One she did not want to hear. But believed in, totally.

That was January 2009. A year after meeting the Gaza mother who had offered her food on a paper plate, in a refugee camp. The mother who had explained her reason for not eating and drinking in daylight hours, for a month out of each year. "I fast to remember the poor" she had said, "…to remember the poor."

---

10   Holy Quran 2: 2-5
11   Holy Quran 2: 8-10

Ten years into her life as a practising Muslim, Lauren Booth recognises that her condition needed to change for the final piece of the puzzle to fall into place. She feels that her wealth and status led her to believe that she "ran the world to some degree. That I was in charge. Everyone listen to me!"

By September 2010, she found herself on her knees, emotionally at breaking point, in a rented flat back in London. Divorcing, bankrupt, the family home in France repossessed. After an agonising 18 months of loss over which she had little to no control. She made her first prayer using the name of God, 'Allah'.

"I was in a complex custody battle for my children. Our life in France was finished. Marriage, gone. And much more besides. I begged Allah with all my heart: 'Just my kids please Allah. I get it now, you alone are in control. Just my kids, please."

Weeks later, having won the court battle, she went to sleep in a mosque during Ramadan and awoke absolutely certain that there could be no God, except Allah and that Prophet Muhammad, was His last and final Messenger.

"Meaning and saying those two phrases changed everything about me. What I liked, what I thought, how I lived. Every day, I cry with the gratitude at being given Islam in my heart and in my family."

What does she miss from her old way of life?

"Nothing. Not even bacon! Islam took only the worst habits from me. It replaced them with Divine love and light. *Alhamdulillah.*" [12]

---

12   Alhamdulillah is an Arabic phrase meaning "praise be to God."

9

The curious Consul whose journey to Islam began abroad

Consul General Seifeldin Usher – British diplomat

Aged just 24, Seifeldin Usher found himself on a diplomatic mission to Sudan – a time he fondly remembered as his 'spiritual reawakening'. There, not only did he witness, but he learned just how much faith can mean to an individual; how it can be a guide and source of support throughout a person's life.

INDIA – a nation comprised of over 1.3 billion inhabitants – is the abode of one of the largest Muslim minority communities in the world. This South Asian republic would also form the locus for one inquisitive diplomat encountering literature, albeit critical, about Islam for the first time.

The year was 1991, and 21-year-old budding diplomat Stephen Usher – whose illustrious career now spans him having toured China, Jordan, and Iraq amongst other places – was posted on assignment to India's first city, New Delhi. It was there that the Consul spoke of becoming immersed in a wealth of cultures, faiths and ideas. A melting pot he described as worlds apart from his English seaside hometown of Morecambe.

"The first time I ever thought about Islam would have been in an Indian bookshop," the Consul began to narrate. Whilst sauntering through the store, one hardback especially caught his eye – Maxime Robinson's *Muḥammad*. "To be honest, I wouldn't recommend it!" he laughed, "his rendition of our Prophet's story is unsympathetic – to say the very least."

Robinson's secular biographical account of the Prophet's life was from the purview of his Communist-Marxist stance, and therefore heavily emphasised the material, rather than religious or spiritual, circumstances surrounding the emergence of Islam. "This would have been the first instance of our Prophet (PBUH) ever coming onto my radar," he confessed – "which just goes to show how ignorant and narrow minded I was before."

When asked about his days of ignorance, words and phrases such as 'blissfully self-absorbed', 'partygoer' and 'avid traveller' instantly sprang to mind – traits which became more pronounced once he left sleepy Morecambe for London, aged just 18. Prior to the move, which laid the foundations of his would-be diplomatic career, the Consul detailed his childhood Catholic upbringing.

"I wouldn't say my household was strict," he said, "but it certainly was very practising." He went on to discuss how, despite an abundance of orthopraxy – such as regularly attending church, Mass, catechism classes and so on – orthodoxy was left wanting in his juvenile cognisance. As such, by the time he became a teenager, his religious practice was more out of 'duty', rather than belief and conviction.

"When I left home at 18, religion wasn't really part of my life anymore. However," he continued, "it was never an issue of whether I believed in God or not – I've always had belief in Him rooted in me. It was more a question of whether what I was taught to practice had any meaning."

He described this gripe stemming from what he referred to as the 'complicated' rites of Catholicism. "Becoming a Catholic is a very long drawn experience, necessitating exams," he said. "It's quite a process." He further touched upon how the structure of Mass, wherein bread is declared sacred as the flesh of Christ, as well as the concept of the Trinity, would have been a struggle to absorb – not just for his teenage self, but many of his peers at the time.

Later, Seifeldin was to discover what he dubbed the "very simple and straightforward" nature of Islamic *ibadah*[1]. "Let's take the physical act of prayer in Islam. Truly, it creates its own sense of wellbeing, even if your head's in completely the wrong place. And, let's face it – sometimes life's like that. Yet, we still pray." He continued: "It doesn't get any simpler than that, does it? Having a simple, daily structure where you're directly praying to God – it just fits together exceptionally well."

Before, however, to drown out his ecclesial doubts, Seifeldin partied hard

------

1   Linguistically, *'ibadah'* is an Arabic word derived from *''abd'* – which means servant of God. 'Ibadah' is thus typically associated with acts of worship done with humility and in servitude.

in his 20s and became a frequent flyer, climbing the ranks of his diplomatic career. A lifestyle devoid of connection to any religious tradition. "It was in India that I first became conscious of Islam, but seeing it as a lived religion in Sudan – that changed everything for me!"

From stagnation to motion in Sudan

Three years later, a 24-year-old Stephen found himself in transit from New Delhi to Khartoum for his latest posting. It was 1994 – a few years after the 1989 Sudanese coup d'état. "Those were tough times for the people of Sudan," he recalled. "It was clear to see that the aftermath of the uprising put many families, and society as a whole, under strain." Yet, he remembered that at the backdrop of Sudan's societal blues existed an evident framework that helped guide them through the tough ordeal: the religion of Islam.

"My time in Sudan served as a major education for me," said the Consul. "In hindsight, I probably wouldn't have realised it at the time, but looking back, the sights and sounds of Islam in Sudan truly were the initial steps as I went down my path to discovering Islam."

In the immediate aftermath of the 1989 coup, the vast majority of the Sudanese populous found themselves struggling to afford the bare necessities and blighted by poverty. Despite the gloom and doom, Seifeldin vividly remembered his time in Sudan being marked by a distinct thread of reassurance among the people that Islam provided a context that meant there was purpose in their struggle.

Seifeldin, who laughed at often finding himself being greeted with the not-so-honorific title of *khawaja*[2] by Sudanese schoolchildren, did stick out like a sore thumb and attracted the attention of locals wanting to tell him

---

2   Within the Sudanese lexicon, *khawaja* means, as aptly put by the Consul, "foreign gentleman".

about their religion. "Before becoming Muslim, no one took it upon themselves to proselytise me. But what has to be understood here is that within the Sudanese milieu, Islam is an integral fabric of everyday life. So, naturally, as I began to forge close friendships, the importance of Islam, both on an individual and societal level, would come up in conversation." It soon became imperative for Seifeldin to rid himself of his ignorance, and he began studying to become Islamically literate.

About his era of self study, he remarked on having always been an avid reader which, aside from his initial curiosity, prompted him to find out more about Islam. "Well, it wasn't so easy in those days – remember, back then there was no internet," he said when asked how he sought to self educate. Thus, Seifeldin buried his head in the work of Western scholarship about Islam – penned by the likes of AJ Arberry, Reynold A. Nicholson and William Montgomery Watt who wrote extensively on Islamic culture and tirelessly translated Arabic and Persian poetry.

Although admitting Western scholarship of the 19th and 20th centuries is fraught with Orientalist biases, for him, such texts spoke from a perspective that he, as an Englishman, would have been familiar with. "Naturally, there would have been a *slant* to their writings, but at the very least, their work did help me a great deal in raising my general knowledge of Islam to a more decent level."

Beyond Orientalist scholasticism, he also remembered being gifted English Islamic literature from his Sudanese friends – namely, an old paperback written by Iranian philosopher, Seyyed Hossein Nasr. For the Consul, Nasr's *Ideals and Realities of Islam*[3], amongst other titles, were 'constructive' in guiding him through his self-education.

---

3   Originally published in 1966.

He was also given a translation of the holy Quran and was quick to remember a passage that instantly struck a chord with him early on.

The Quranic connection

"*Surah al Hadid;* verse 20," he said. In part, it reads:

"*Bear in mind that the present life is just mere amusement; a diversion, an attraction, a cause of boasting among you, of rivalry in wealth and children* (Quran, 57:20)."

"Here, Allah is calling for us all to be mindful of the pleasures of this life – and this resonated with me." For the Consul, this very verse transported him to a time where he was somewhat lost, caught up in a maze he described as being filled with "life's little irrelevancies," but bereft of true significance and meaning. "Reading this verse probably would have been the first time I deeply connected with Quran's words." In contrast, he also spoke of an experience common among many converts – finding a way to navigate Islam's Holy Writ in a way that suits them.

"Reading the Quran cold, especially coming from the Christian tradition, isn't always easy. Within the Bible, we're familiar with a structure of stories being presented as parables – the Quran isn't like that!" For Seifeldin, each individual has to seek out an approach that makes the most sense to them – "whether that be first hearing the beauty of it being recited, and then reading a translation, or for those like me who had to learn Arabic, it could be a case of reading the Arabic text in tandem with a translation." He continued: "Even though a full understanding of the Quran can take a lifetime's work, it is incredibly worth it to do so."

When asked whether he was struck by the parallels between the Quran and the Bible, it made the Consul chuckle to remember a youngster who, although a keen reader, was not so keen on reading his Bible. "As I went on my path to Islam, I never once felt any desire to directly refer back to the Bible – however, I was aware of the overlap, such as the concept of a chain of Messengership, between the two." In many ways, he found this useful in being able to reorient himself in his newly developing Islamic faith.

In a similar vein, he further remembered becoming engrossed in Dr Safi Kaskas' *'The Quran - with References to the Bible: A Contemporary Understanding'*. Dr Kaskas' publication is an analysis of the Quran in light of Biblical references – a project whereby he enlisted the help of Dr David Hungerford, MD, a practising Christian, to see to fruition. In an interview, Dr Kaskas highlighted how germane such a cross sectional study of the two holy books was – especially in America's post-9/11 context. "There are many verses in the Bible that are similar to the Quran," highlighted Dr Kaskas. "[Notwithstanding], I think [America] can prosper with pluralism […] and we all live together, like a salad bowl [sic] - we're all different, but together![4]"

Narrating through his long and winding road to eventual conversion, which took him on an 18 month journey, Seifeldin spoke of difficulty in pinpointing the checkpoints from ignorance to awareness, and then the subsequent genuine reawakening of faith. However, he easily identified a constant throughout – the mere meaning of Islam itself.

'You have reached your destination'

"What was it that convinced me to convert?" he asked. "I think ultimately it was about peace," he concluded. For him, Islam aligned with

---

4   Shadeed, K. and Kaskas, S., 2016. Scholar"s Chair - Interview with Dr Safi Kaskas.

   - YouTube. [online] Youtube.com. Available at: <https://www.youtube.com/watch?v=s2l9P6KP4DU>

his frame of mind and answered the questions latent in his subconscious of why we are here, as well as what the purpose and meaning of life are.

"Looking back, in many ways, it's as if with Islam, I was able to shift onto a different rail track and suddenly, in an instant, things clicked together." Regarding said shift, Seifeldin circled back to his days as a young Catholic lad, who not only become disillusioned with Catholicism, but at one point, resentful towards religion altogether.

"In terms of religious identity, I truly was uncomfortable when I was younger – in the sense that there was always an internal conflict I had with there being intermediaries between God and I. So religious practice made no sense to me," he revealed. "Broadly speaking," he continued, "I think if you're going to practice a religion, then it ought to make sense to you." As such, a younger Seifeldin found himself "switching off" and begrudging those who would talk to him about matters concerning faith.

"Really, the English aren't great at talking about religion," he laughed, "especially teenagers. So, I was aimlessly following in Mum and Dad's footsteps, but I didn't know what the meaning of it all was." This was in stark contrast to what Islam was able to offer him – "an explanation of life that made sense."

"What I was silently rebelling against as a youngster," he continued, "was practicing, and seeing others practice, faith, but not having anything of substance behind those actions – an absence of genuine understanding and belief, if you will."

Finally, in 1995, Seifeldin concluded his direction was set and the final destination was embracing Islam. "I think it was a slowish [sic] process for me, but by the time I met my wife and formally converted, I'd suddenly found myself in a very comfortable position religiously."

When asked about the day he took his *shahada*, the Consul was quick to say that it was a day he remembers very well. A Sudanese friend of his had taken him to a local mosque in Khartoum – "Of which, as you can imagine, there are many," he said, laughing as he chimed in. And it was there that he sat with a *sheikh* and recited the Islamic declaration of faith. Although he admitted that that would generally be considered a defining moment, he did not recall having such feelings at the time.

"I'd like to say the skies opened and the sun's light suddenly shone brightly upon me, but it wasn't like that. I think because the actual act of saying the *shahada* is a very, very quick thing," – especially in contrast to the rites involved in adopting Catholicism. For him, however, although central to embracing Islam, the Consul also spoke of how in his estimation, his faith was not just about uttering the *shahada* – "For me, faith was about the noticeable change in my spiritual bearings, and this was already evident to me from my journey's humble beginnings."

At the culmination of said humble beginnings, the Consul, formerly known as Stephen, became Seifeldin. "I changed my name!" he exclaimed. "Although, I didn't have to. Nor did I choose Seif to make a bold statement or anything of the sort. For me, in terms of setting out the person I was becoming, changing my name was just the logical thing to do."

When pressed further as to the story for him choosing a name as striking as Seifeldin[5], the Consul laughed as he remembered his early days trying to perfect his Arabic proficiency. "Admittedly, I chose it because it meant the initials of my name would stay the same. That, and, back then, my Arabic was terrible! 'Seifeldin' would have been one of the very few names I could properly pronounce – and that's as simple as it gets!"

----

5   Which translates to 'the sword of faith'.

While for Seifeldin, his becoming Muslim was a logical conclusion to a one-and-a-half-year personal voyage of rediscovery, he hinted at his parents surmising otherwise. "'Why couldn't you have found faith in your own faith?' was an especially tough question they had for me," he sighed. "This is a question I really struggled to answer. I didn't want to sound ungrateful to the upbringing that they had given me, nor did I want to push back on their framework of faith," he continued. Despite what he described as an initial shock, he further spoke of what came to be an eventual understanding between him and his family regarding his conversion.

"It is understandable," he said. "Mum and Dad grew up in homogenous 1940s Britain – they would have had zero exposure to Islam. But, with time, they came to understand my decision better and actually concluded they would rather have their son believing in God and practicing faith – even if that faith just so happened to be Islam – rather than having no belief system at all." He further happily remembered an instance of his mother defending Muslims during a heated conversation with her friends. "Mum wasn't even talking about me specifically, but it was touching to hear from her that she took it upon herself to do that. It was quite something."

Fulfilling the fifth pillar of Islam

Incidences such as 2001's 9/11 and 2005's 7/7 attacks, and subsequent media portrayals ever since, have arguably created an unpleasant media landscape goading Muslims to actively counteract how they have been represented on the world's stage. "However, such incidences have never shaken my faith in Islam – not even by an inch," he asserted. "During my time in Sudan, the way I saw Islam being practised – whereby despite being a relaxed society, its people are still very pious, meant that the very idea of intolerance, hate and violence on the grounds of religion would always be a natural anathema to me."

While he did not recall instances of being embroiled in antagonistic discussions with his fellow diplomat colleagues, he did remember them, like many others, trying to make sense of all that had unfolded. "There certainly would have been questions along the lines of 'why do they hate us?' But, I never found myself being told, 'You're Muslim and therefore, you're responsible.'" He continued, however, "Certainly, when people do meet me, they most likely won't immediately guess that I'm a Muslim. But, of course, after they come to know my name – then the game's given away, right?" As such, he explained, not only does this put the convert in the already difficult space of having to defend Islam against stereotypical media framing, but also, "You find yourself in conversations where you're having to give your whole life story and explain yourself. It's not uncommon to hear things like, 'Well, you don't look Muslim'. And I think such discussions pose a unique challenge for converts, versus someone who's born into the faith."

More recently, however, in July 2022, Seifeldin posted on his social media platforms of his first time performing the Hajj pilgrimage. "I was always hoping to perform Hajj while I was posted in Saudi," said the Consul, in reference to his mission in the Gulf Kingdom drawing to a close in August of 2022 – after serving there for four years.

"In my first year working in Saudi," he explained, "on behalf of the UK government's initiative of helping Brits abroad, I would often go visit British pilgrims in *Mina*[6]– that was one of the highlights of my role. I would go around, from tent to tent, talking to them and listening to their expe-

---

6   Also commonly referred to as 'the city of tents,' Mina is situated approximately 8km southeast of Makkah. It is an important stop on a Hajj pilgrim's itinerary to complete the necessary *jamarat* Hajj rite of stoning the devil. Said ritual is in commemoration of Prophet Ibrahim's stoning of three pillars thereat to ward off temptations from the devil. Pilgrims re-enact the pelting to symbolically rebuke becoming strayed.

riences – it was lovely!" He further recounted wanting to have performed Hajj earlier but being unable to do so due to Covid-19 restrictions that saw the quota of pilgrims slashed from upwards of 2.5 million, to around just 1 million. "But *alhamdulilah*," said the Consul, "I'm glad I was finally able to do it."

Regarding his experience there, Seifeldin recalled being asked about it many times prior, and always struggling to give a "great" answer. "Hajj is just such a complex thing," he began. "It's wonderful. It's amazing. It's noisy, it's uncomfortable. It has its moments of frustration. And I think it's supposed to be like that. It's supposed to be something of a trial." He further juxtaposed the trial of the modern day Hajj to that of old.

In the Quran's *surah al Hajj*, it proclaims:

"And call all people to the pilgrimage. They will come to you on foot and on every lean camel from every distant path (Quran, 22:27)."

"Today, no one spends 20 days on a camel from Damascus or longer from countries even further away," he chuckled. "Those aspects are now long gone – we just hop a plane for a few hours and are then transported to a coolly air-conditioned hotel room." As such, the nature of the modern pilgrim's trial has completely changed. For Seifeldin: "I think the great challenge today is digging out the kind of spiritual marrows so that, on a spiritual level, you feel enriched." While he did speak of feeling a sense of achievement as a Muslim for having fulfilled this religious duty, he also said it would necessitate more time to deeply reflect on a personal spiritual level what else he had achieved.

A forgotten past

Towards the end of the conversation, Seifeldin discussed Muhammad Marmaduke Pickthall, Lord Headley and Lady Evelyn Cobbold - figures from Britain's bygone Victorian era who, although important in spreading awareness of Islam in Britain and beyond, have very much become erased from the nation's remembered history.

After Christianity, Islam is Britain's second largest religion. A British Social Attitudes (BSA) survey found the frequency of Islamic identification leap from just 1% in 1983 to 6% in 2019[7]. Islam's prominence in the North Western European island arguably stems from the nation's historical interactions with millions of Muslims during the era of the Empire. Subsequently, Islam proved to garner the attention of Victorian aristocrats who most times, through their travels to Muslim lands under colonial rule, intimately developed an understanding of the religion and later embraced it as a way of life.

As penned by Lady Cobbold, the first Western woman to perform Hajj, the history of Victorians embracing Islam ought not to be regarded as a strange phenomenon – "[especially when] one remembers that Islam is the natural religion that a child left to itself would develop. Indeed, as a Western critic once described it, 'Islam is the religion of common sense[8]'."

For the Consul: "While people like Marmaduke Pickthall may be recognised among British Muslims for spreading Islam to an English-speaking audience, the fact of the matter is, Victorian Muslims are simply from a different era, and I think this conversation can be situated in the wider context of relevance in terms of how people access information and find meaning. Remember," he continued, "in my day, there wouldn't have been YouTube where, with a click of a button, one has access to a deluge of

---

7   Voas, D. and Bruce, S., 2019. Religion: Identity, behaviour and belief over two decades. [ebook] London: The National Centre for Social Research. Available at: <https://www.bsa.natcen.ac.uk/media/39293/1_bsa36_religion.pdf>

8   Cobbold, E., 1934. Pilgrimage To Mecca. 1st ed. London: John Murray.

information." He further continued explaining that, although times may have changed, creating a bridge so that wider society can access and understand Islam is a challenge that yet persists.

"In the Victorian era, people like Pickthall and others were speaking about faith in an era where people intrinsically had faith – it was just a different faith. Now, speaking of faith is, in itself, very challenging – especially in terms of how it resonates to people generally." For instance, the 2019 BSA survey further revealed a sharp rise in the British populous expressing "very low confidence in religious organisations" and becoming "very" or "extremely" irreligious[9].

"Within the British context, I think as we go from generation to generation, overall, understanding of faith is going to become more difficult. This is generally going to be a challenge for Muslims in the West where we are a minority community." He continued: "Given the widespread lack of understanding about Islam, compounded by the overwhelming negative stereotype found in the media, we are going to have to deal with first, getting over the hurdle of not only explaining why our practices are different, but why we even believe in God and practice in the first place!"

He went onto contrast the situation of an irreligious West with the ubiquitous desire to pray and practice in African and Middle Eastern countries – "Not just among Muslims, but Christians and Jews there, too," he said, chiming in. "These are areas where, generally speaking, most people have an understanding of faith, so it's much easier to strike that dialogue to foster communal understanding. While in the West," he concluded, "it isn't so straightforward."

---

9   Voas, D. and Bruce, S., 2019. Religion: Identity, behaviour and belief over two decades. [ebook] London: The National Centre for Social Research. Available at: <https://www.bsa.natcen.ac.uk/media/39293/1_bsa36_religion.pdf>

This backdrop was further intensified by a situation he described as "both great and terrible at the same time". For him, the wealth of information at one's fingertips by virtue of the worldwide web, can, at times, prove to be a double-edged sword. "If a person is lucky, they will stumble upon information grounded in guidance that is helpful to them." Alternatively, however: "There's just as much chance that they stumble upon advice that is terrible or somebody spouting uninformed nonsense."

Despite this set of challenges, for the one who has the drive and desire to find information about Islam, Seifeldin reassured those wanting to know more: "The sources are all there and the information is all there, too. There are ways that you can go forward to find what you need to get to the path that you wish to be on."

Last of all, in returning back to his own personal pursuit for information and subsequent journey to truth, although at times uneasy, Consul Seifeldin expressed thankfulness to Allah for having been guided to a framework of faith that aligns with him in every way. "I've been very fortunate to have entered into a faith that's given me not just a system, but a comfort, and ultimately, a peace that I was once searching for."

10

'All I wanted was an answer to a simple question – *'why are we here?"*

Abdurahman Afia – British Business Consultant and verified TikTok user

As the heir apparent to his family's lucrative textile business, Abdurahman was a boy who had it all. One night out, however, changed everything. A mere question challenged his atheistic outlook and sent him on a two and a half year search for answers. In his tear-jerking story, his journey to self discovery led to strained familial ties and disownment - but an eventual spiritual triumph.

"**T**HERE IS a difference between having fun and being happy," began Abdurahman Afia. "As a youngster, I was known for having fun and partying – that was all I would have cared about all the time."

However, he confessed, his was an upbringing devoid of happiness. "At the end of the night, after coming home from being at a nightclub, when left alone with my thoughts, I remember feeling very sad," he sighed. "There was definitely something missing from my life," he continued. "And as I got older, I started to become more aware of that."

Abdurahman, who took great pride in sharing the same birthplace as Paddington Bear, described himself as once being a 'natural atheist'. Today, however, he uses his TikTok platform – which has garnered an immense following worldwide, to share his journey to Islam, how he celebrates Islamic festivals, such as Eid, with his family, as well as poking fun at those who are fascinated by how he, as White man, is the father of mixed-race children.

However, he explained, "in my household growing up, we never spoke about God. Sure, we would put up a Christmas tree every December, but looking back on this, I find it bizarre – my parents had zero connection to religion – there was absolutely no religion in the house!" As such, Abdurahman detailed how religion grew to be internalised as a matter concerning only lunatics of old.

"Although my parents weren't religious, they did at one point put me into Sunday school." But, as he revealed, his time there was sporadic and very short lived. "Mum and Dad put me into three different Sunday schools – I kept getting kicked out because of misbehaviour and fighting – I thought religion was all nonsense! I simply didn't believe in anything – I rejected religion even from a young age!" He further remembered his disappointment on hearing the news of Yusuf /Cat Stevens embracing Islam.

"I was about 15 years old," he said. "I came back home from school and there he was on TV giving an interview about how he became Muslim." Although ironic now, at the time when he saw Yusuf on screen – clad in a thobe[1], turban and sporting a beard, he thought to himself, "This man clearly took too many drugs back in the day and now his brain has snapped!" He continued: "I really didn't like what I saw, and I don't think the media helped to make Yusuf look good – instead, his story of becoming Muslim was juxtaposed by terror-related incidents committed by Muslims that dominated the airwaves – even back then."

Instead, Abdurahman was preoccupied with what he thought was going to be his definite succession to running the family business. "When my grandad passed away, Dad took over Afia Carpets – the family carpeting and textile business. Dad made the company very successful." Under his father, Afia Carpets grew to achieve the prestigious Royal Warrant as their textiles gained popularity amongst British royals.

"So, you could say I did grow up with a silver spoon in my mouth – money was never an issue and I had no worries in life." He continued: "In my mind, no matter what I did in my life; whether I did well in school or not, I'd be taking over my father's business – I'd not have to want for money or anything – ever!"

In living up to his carefree outlook on life, not only did Abdurahman find himself being expelled from Sunday school, but every other institute he was put into. "I went to 11 schools in total," he said. "I never stayed in a school for more than one year before getting kicked out of it. Eventually, after becoming so angry with my repeated expulsions, Mum and Dad put me in a state school."

---

1   A thobe is a long-sleeved, ankle-length male garment.

It was at this point that Abdurahman found himself having interactions with Muslims for the first time. "I was this posh kid who had gone to boarding school. Now, I found myself having to interact with a demographic of people I had never met before." And he found himself making fun of his Muslim peers – not necessarily because they were Muslims, according to him, but because of the outward displays of religiosity he saw which he so disdained. He further detailed how, although he was having day-to-day interactions with Muslims, paradoxically, Islam as a religion was something he had no knowledge of. "To be honest," he chimed in, "I really wouldn't have known that Islam as a religion existed!"

All this was to change when, aged 16, his one-time conviction in atheism suffered a fatal blow amid a marijuana-hazed conversation. "In many ways, my journey to Islam begins at a party – of all places," he laughed.

Simon says: *Why are we here?*

"I was at a party with my good friend at the time, Simon," said Abdurahman. A party just like any other, or so a young Abdurahman thought, took an unexpected turn when posed with a question that induced a would-be overhaul of his worldly outlook.

"We were sat on a sofa, just chilling out," said Abdurahman. "Then Simon turned to me and said, 'Joel,' – that was my birthname – 'Joel, why are we here?'" Up until that point, said question had never featured in his young mind. "Nor had anyone ever asked me such a question," he said.

"I didn't like the question at all!" he exclaimed. "In fact, I said to Simon, 'I think you've smoked too much – we're *here* because we're at a party!'" Yet Simon persisted and kept asking his friend Joel, 'why are we here?' "He also said to me, 'are we here to be just like our parents – live, make money, die and then that's it!?' Are you sure there's nothing more to life than this?"'"

The more Simon kept prodding, the more annoyed Abdurahman became. "I remember thinking, 'why is he bringing this craziness to me?' – 'I can give you 99 topics that we can talk about,' I said to him, 'and this definitely isn't gonna be on that list – at all!'"

"I'm dead serious!" Simon would retort. "Why are we here? What's our purpose in life? Why are we even alive?" To which a disgruntled Abdurahman replied, "If you carry on like this, you're not gonna be alive for much longer!"

In the days and weeks that followed, Abdurahman recalled Simon's barrage of questions lingering in his mind. "Simon's questions weren't prominent in my thoughts," he explained, "but it would be at the back of my mind – sometimes resurfacing at the most unexpected times. I could be at a restaurant, or even another party and his questions would just hit me - *Why are we here?*' I think this would be the start of my faith in atheism getting knocked."

Abdurahman's silent existential grapple would remain passive for some time, until he found himself (somewhat) preparing for an upcoming exam at St. John's Wood Library. "I would love to say I had tunnel vision for my exam revision," he laughed, "but in reality, I paid no mind to any of the tasks I had at hand." Abdurahman, now 16 and a half years old, found his eyes wandering to the sights of the library and stumbled across the religion and philosophy shelf. "And then instantly," exclaimed Abdurahman, "the questions sprang into my mind again!" Perhaps the answers to Simon's questions lay nestled on the bookshelf.

"'Maybe it's worth having a look,' is what I thought," he said. "I still was an atheist, yet, I got up and had a look through the books."

There, Abdurahman found literature on Christianity, Judaism, Communism, Buddhism, Hinduism. "And just about every other -ism you could think of! But nothing about Islam."

Week in and week out, Abdurahman embarked on a self study in a desperate bid to rid himself of the mental struggle he found himself embroiled in. "But I found nothing," he revealed. "There was nothing that I found that I felt any connection with at all. For instance, I disliked how I found Jewish scripture presenting Jewish people as being superior to others. I may have had a prejudice against religion," he chuckled, "but I hated racism — starting from my early teens, it was just something I couldn't and wouldn't tolerate."

Most of all, Abdurahman could not find the answer to the question he was seeking — *'Why are we here?'*

Two special gifts

A year later, Abdurahman's quest for answers had not yet been completed. "At 17, I became resolute that Simon's questions had no answers, and gave up looking." Until, one day, while on his way to sixth-form college, he was struck by a sight that stopped him in his tracks.

"It was a Friday," he began narrating. "I was on the bus to college and the drive went past Regent's Park Mosque. To be honest, I had gone past the mosque thousands of times prior, but assumed it was a Hindu temple," he confessed. As it was a Friday, a 17-year-old Abdurahman saw Muslims from far and wide, bedecked in traditional gear for congregational *jumuah* prayer.

"I saw people wearing traditional Pakistani clothes, people in very bright African clothes, there were also Arabs wearing Arabic clothes — just a spectrum of different people, different colours, all walking down in the same direction." Abdurahman cut his bus ride short and went to see what all the commotion was about.

"I got off the bus and found myself walking to the mosque – or what I thought was a Hindu temple. But as I got closer and closer, I spotted women in veils and thought, 'This must be where the crazy Arab, religious people congregate'," he chuckled. "So, I ended up not going inside the mosque – but I was curious. I do remember thinking that just maybe, this group of people might have a book that could answer Simon's questions."

To quell his curiosity, Abdurahman sat on a nearby wall outside of the mosque. "At the time, I wouldn't have known what Islam was or who Muslims were, but I did want to know more." So, he remained sat, listening through the entirety of the *jummah khutbah*. "All I could hear was shouting in Arabic from the speakers. I said to myself, 'Yeah that's the crazy people shouting – that's what they do!'" After the prayers, however, Abdurahman was met with the sight of happy Friday prayer goers, greeting and well wishing one another as they left the mosque.

"'I wanna speak to someone – I'd really like to know more', is what I was thinking to myself, but I looked down at my watch and saw I had missed the first two hours of class, so I dashed to the bus stop to see what could be salvaged of the rest of the day." As he retraced his steps, he caught the attention of someone who was making his way out of the mosque.

"A Sudanese man came up to me and asked, 'Can I help you with anything?' I told him 'No – I'm alright.' He then asked if I was Muslim. Again, I told him 'No'." Then Abdurahman was asked whether he could be given a gift. Before he could answer, he was told to wait while the man went to go fetch something special for him.

"Honestly," confessed Abdurahman, "I was ready to flee – I was paranoid, I thought this man, along with anyone religious, was crazy - I didn't know what he was gonna bring me! But then he came back with two books in his hands just for me." The man said to Abdurahman, "Here is a translation of the Quran – our holy Book as Muslims. Please look after it, keep it clean and in a tidy place". The man continued: "I also got you a book about Islam – please take these two books, and if you ever have any questions about our religion, you can come back and ask us." Abdurahman was given a copy of Suzanne Haneef's *'What Everyone Should Know about Islam and Muslims'*, thanked the man and went on his way.

When he got home that day, he perused through his new gifts. "I remember looking at the Quran for the first time - it looked like what a holy book should look like in my mind." Abdurahman opened it up, glanced through the introduction and started reading the opening chapter: *surah al Fatiha.*

"I would love to tell you that, instantly, the words had a profound impact on me, and from there I became Muslim," he said, "but the reality was I couldn't understand a word I was reading. It was a translation in very classical English, and I was someone who hated learning about Shakespeare! So words like 'thou', 'knowest' and 'doth' just put me off." Further, looking in retrospect, Abdurahman described his younger self as "not being ready" to grasp the message of the Quran. "Truly, it would have been too much for me to read and understand." His younger self thus wrapped the Quran in a clean sheet and tucked it away in a high cupboard in his room.

"Interestingly enough," he revealed, "I did find myself going back to the Quran a few times after that initial read – if there were stressful situations, such as an exam coming up that I had done zero studying for, I would pick it up and read again." Each time, however, Abdurahman found himself unable to fully comprehend what the Book was saying to him.

Hesitancy to become a *'full Muslim'*

Fast forward to when Abdurahman's days as a 17-year-old began drawing to a close – he recollected a boy who was partying harder than ever. "This was an era of more partying, more alcohol, more drugs and more craziness," he said. All this, he confessed, was to, in some ways, mask the emptiness that had grown more and more prominent in his life. However, this was all to change over the course of the next six months.

"Hyde Park's Speakers' Corner was a real turning point in my life," Abdurahman narrated. "I heard about Speakers' Corner from two old ladies talking about it during a bus ride," he laughed. "They were saying how crazy and mental it was out there – so, naturally, I made a detour to see if it really lived up to the hype."

One Sunday afternoon, Abdurahman alighted at Hyde Park to take a gander at the sights and hear the sounds of the Sunday soapbox. "I was hit by a wave of noise!" he said. "There, I saw a Christian man, a Hindu, a Jewish man – and so many other people preaching about what they believed." He listened intently to what each person had to say. "But I found myself growing impatient," he confessed. "Remember, I still hadn't found an answer to Simon's question. And that question was simply, 'Why am I here?' It shouldn't be that difficult a question to answer, right?"

After a series of soapbox hopping, Abdurahman found himself at the makeshift rostrum of a Trinidadian Muslim. *"Ma Sha Allah²,"* he said with a smile, "he was dressed so beautifully in his pristinely white thobe and turban – he just looked good!"

"All of us are here for a reason!" Abdurahman recollected the man bellowing to the crowd. "Instantly, he had caught my attention just with

---

2   This is an Arabic expression that translates as "what God has willed has hap- pened". It is commonly used as an expression of awe and amazement.

those few words alone!" he confessed. "He then began explaining – 'In the Quran, it says this, thus and so'. His breakdown was helpful to me since, initially, it was a remote book that made no sense to me." Abdurahman remained listening to the man speaking, until eventually, the clock struck six.

"To be honest, I don't think I would have believed what he was saying initially," he said. "I still had a lot of questions, like how do we know the Quran is *the* book? How can we prove there is a creator? I wanted to know all these things, and I found myself, week after week, going back to hear him speak."

After seven weeks of meandering to Speakers' Corner every Sunday, Abdurahman confessed to being completely rid of his atheistic outlook. "I later came to know that the Trinidadian man's name was Kaja. Listening to him speak week in, week out – it just became obvious to me that there must be a creator. Kaja would pose thought provoking questions, such as, 'How can there be creation without a Creator?' Something so simple but it caught me so off guard – there was no arguing Kaja's logic.

"Kaja also spoke about the many flaws in the Big Bang theory – and it seems so obvious to me now, but I guess when I was younger, I was just regurgitating what I would have learned at school. But then Kaja would ask us, 'How can such order and perfection of Earth, our solar system, the universe, the galaxy, have come from the chaos of a random explosion?'"

Blown away by Kaja's preaching, Abdurahman concluded there must exist a higher power who created us. "I was no longer an atheist," he chimed in. "And yet," he continued, "I still didn't fully understand who God was. Kaja kept on referring to the Creator as Allah, but I still needed more convincing that that was the case."

As the weeks went by, Abdurahman listened as Kaja explained how it would be unjust for the Creator to create His Creation and not send the proper criterion as to how they ought to live their lives in accordance with His will. Kaja further spoke of how this was delivered through a chain of Messengers and Prophets, each fortified with revelation appropriate to their respective times and places – this was in order for creation to know what their purpose in life was.

"I would record his speeches on my Walkman," said Abdurahman, as he described the now bygone portable audio device. "I'd play back his talks and say to myself, 'This makes sense!' And I became convinced in the existence of Allah and that the Quran wasn't a normal book." Abdurahman detailed how easy it became to accept the Quran as a Holy Book, and the veracity of the Prophet that it was sent to.

"I would have only known the basics of the Prophet Muhammad (PBUH) at this point. From listening to Kaja, I knew he was a man born over 1400 years ago – a layman who couldn't read or write. A man whose existence isn't only celebrated in Islam, but also verified by Western historians." He said further, "The miracles mentioned in the Quran, the depth it goes into explaining science – these are all details that no one would have known at the time. I was once someone who believed Prophets and religious scripture were things of fairy tales, but Kaja changed all that within me."

After a six month stint of visiting Speakers' Corner at the end of every week, Abdurahman felt it necessary to speak to Kaja about his remaining burning questions. "I thought Kaja wouldn't have the time of day for someone like me. I was someone who came from a completely different background, I was still partying and drinking – I thought he might shun me, but I knew I had to speak to him." Abdurahman plucked up the courage, staying to the end of one of Kaja's talks, and said to him, "I know you might not have time for someone like me, but I think I'd like to be a Muslim someday-

But I still need more information."

Prior, Abdurahman recounted seeking knowledge about Islam in a more discrete manner. "Before actually speaking to Kaja, I took myself to Edgeware Road thinking I would be able to get some books I could read in my downtime. I went from store to store, asking if there were any books about Islam I could buy. There were plenty of books on Arabic calligraphy, art and history – but nothing about Islam. So, I had no choice but to talk to Kaja!"

"You say you'd like to become a Muslim?" asked Kaja. "Well yes, but not today – today I just want some more information – I've been coming to listen to you speak for months now, and there are some questions I'd like to ask," replied Abdurahman.

A delighted Kaja invited Abdurahman to a nearby bench and there began their exchange. "If the Quran has the last and final message for mankind, what happened to all the messages before?" asked Abdurahman. Kaja explained to him that the Quran has remained unaltered since its being revealed as it was to be a book of all times thereafter. "There was no need for other texts to be preserved," said Abdurahman. "Kaja explained that they were for a fixed time and place – and it made sense to me."

"Do you now believe in Allah? Do you believe that there's none that should be worshipped except Him?" asked Kaja. "'Yeah, man! Of course!' I said to him. In truth, I already started believing in what he was preaching months ago." Kaja continued: "Do you believe in all the Prophets? Moses, Abraham, David, Jesus and Muhammad, may peace and blessings be upon them – do you believe that they were messengers of Allah that they all brought a message?" Abdurahman gladly nodded in agreement.

"If you believe all this in your heart," asked Kaja, "then are you willing to say this with your tongue?" Abdurahman immediately replied 'Yes!'. "This is probably the reason why I have gotten into so much trouble in the past!" he laughed. "I'm someone that, if I think something, I'll say it!" "Would you be willing to say your faith in Arabic?" Kaja asked once more. "Yes!" Abdurahman replied.

Ashadu' an lā 'ilāha 'illa -llāhu, wa-'ashadu 'anna Muḥammadan rasūlu -llāh recited Kaja.

"I said, '*ash* what?'" laughed Abdurahman. "I really couldn't say it properly, but in the end, I got there." Unbeknownst to Abdurahman, fully engrossed in his conversation with Kaja, a large crowd had gathered, watching in anticipation.

"Kaja then told me to say it in English: 'I bear witness that there is no deity but Allah, and I bear witness that Muhammad is the messenger of Allah'." Before he knew it, Abdurahman was engulfed by a roar of celebratory cheers from onlookers and a warm hug from Kaja.

"You're a Muslim now!" Kaja said with glee. "I told Kaja, 'No, no! Not today! I can't be a Muslim today – I'm doing so many bad things; I'm still a drinker, I'm still a smoker!'" He asked, "Can't I just be a mini-Muslim today, bro, then maybe in the future, I'll be a full Muslim?"

"Today, you are a new born," said Kaja with a smile. "Don't worry – take this step by step, day by day. The Muslim is the one who merely believes in their heart that there's none worthy of worship except Allah. And they believe in the Prophets, with the final one being Muhammad (PBUH) – if you believe that, then you're a Muslim!"

Abdurahman recounted passers-by greeting and embracing him as he had newly accepted the Islamic faith. "One person even reached into the pocket where my cigarettes were – he said, 'You won't be needing these anymore!' I told him, 'Actually, I'll definitely be needing those – all this has been a lot for me!'"

"Will you be joining us for *salah*?" Abdurahman was asked, as it had just gone time for prayer. "'Definitely not!' is what I said back —suddenly becoming Muslim was more than enough for one day!" The crowd slowly began to dissipate as the onlookers made their way for *salah*. "They all left the park to go to the mosque, and I just remained sat there by myself." He continued: "This was my six month journey to Islam – or to be more precise, two and a half years, starting from my conversation with Simon. But I remember being sat on the park bench alone after taking my *shahada*, watching the sun go down and thinking, 'Joel man, this is the best thing you've ever done in your life!'"

A hard pill to swallow

"During my six month journey to becoming a Muslim," said Abdurahman, "I started reading the Quran more frequently to try connect with it [sic]." One particular instance sticks out in his memory of the initial barrier between him and the Islamic Holy Writ being broken.

"There was one summer where I worked at Harrods in Knightsbridge," he explained. "I was working at a hair and beauty salon – I decided I wanted to learn to cut hair. As the months went on and I was becoming more engrossed in Islam from listening to Kaja's talks, I started taking the Quran with me to work." He continued: "I would read it during my lunch breaks. This one time – I think this would have been just a week before taking my *shahada*, I was on my break, standing on the roof of Harrods – I had a bird's-eye view of London right before me. I had a cigarette in one hand, and my copy of the Quran in the other. I opened the Book to *surah Al Baqara*". It read: "*Alif, Laam, Meem. This is the Book in which there is no doubt, containing guidance for those who are mindful of God* (Quran 2:1-2)."

"I immediately threw my cigarette to the ground and reread those verses.

It just hit me – this is guidance! Not just for me, but for the whole of mankind! This is the manual on how I was meant to live my life – this is why I'm here! It just struck me so deeply and made me tear up."

In the fortnight that followed his conversion, Abdurahman recollected a brief period of stagnation in his religiosity. "For about two weeks, I really did nothing – I wasn't sure what to do next, to be honest, and I was still taking everything all in." Conscience-stricken, however, Abdurahman felt it necessary to act upon his new-found faith.

"I felt guilty I wasn't doing anything," he confessed. "So, at around *maghrib* (evening prayer) time, I took myself to Regent's Park Mosque to pray." There, he heard an awe-inspiring recitation of the Holy Quran.

"I remember feeling very, very scared!" he revealed. "I just never heard anything like this before in my life. The *tajweed*[3] I heard was similar to that of reciters like Abdul Basit Abd us- Samad[4]. It was absolutely beautiful to my ears!" However, a perplexed Abdurahman ended up sticking out like a sore thumb amid the crowd of congregational prayer goers.

"I was looking around the whole time – it was clear I didn't know what I was doing," he chuckled. Fortunately for him, after prayers had concluded, those next to him took the time to educate him on how to perform the daily *salah*.

"They wrote down the transliteration of *surah al Fatihah* for me, some other short *surahs* and what to say while in *rukū*[5]. In the early days, I would stick those pieces of paper in front of me on my bedroom wall and read along

---

3   Within the discipline of Quranic recitation, *tajweed* refers to the rules governing pronunciation, such that the recitation of the Quran is done similarly to how the Prophet Muhammad (PBUH) would have recited.

4   Abdul Basit (1927 - 1988) was an Egyptian Quranic reciter, famed worldwide for his uniquely melodious recitations.

5   In *salah, rukū* refers to the act of bowing from the waist whilst standing. This is done before falling prostrate onto the ground – an act referred to in Arabic as *sujūd.*

whilst praying."

Initially, Abdurahman tried to keep his conversion a secret from the folks at home. "But Mum could already see the changes in me. She asked me one day if something was wrong – 'Girls aren't calling the house anymore, you've stopped going out to parties – what's going on? Is it drugs?' she asked me." Abdurahman chuckled at the juxtaposition of him no longer abusing drugs and alcohol sparking a cause for concern within his household. "At the time, I didn't tell Mum or Dad, but I had to eventually, right?"

After another six months, Abdurahman finally took the plunge and told his parents of his embracing Islam. "There was no way I could hide it any longer – I began growing a beard and wanted to start wearing a *kufi*[6]. I had to tell them!

After taking a deep breath, Abdurahman broke the news. "Mum, Dad – I've become a Muslim!" His revelation was met by hysterics from his mother, and laughter from his father. "Dad thought it was the funniest thing he had ever heard – and I guess I can't blame him too much; nobody saw this coming." He further explained his mother's tears as the subtle changes she had witnessed in her son dawned upon her. "I said, 'Mum, don't cry. Don't cry – everything's good."

Alas, the household dynamics thereafter turned out not to be good. "When I would pray *Fajr* (morning prayer), and I have no idea how, but somehow Dad would be awake at the same time, too. He'd always walk in on me praying and shout at me – saying I was making too much noise so early in the day. In truth, I wasn't making any noise – I took extra care to be quiet! I even went as far as keeping a bowl of water in my room

---

6   A *kufi* is a close-fitted, brimless, cylindrical hat donned by men from West, North and East Africa, as well as South Asia. The hat has also gained popularity among Black communities in the United States and the African Diaspora.

so I could make *wudhu* (ablution) quietly rather than causing noise by going to the bathroom." Sadly, things took a turn for the worse one fateful night during a family outing. "It was our family tradition to go to La Casalinga – a famous Italian restaurant in London. I thought it was a normal night out – just Mum, Dad, my sister, Jenny, and I – as always." However, his father told him he would no longer be allowed to pray in the house.

"'You have a choice to make tonight, Joel,' my dad said. 'Either, you go back to normal, stop praying and come back home with us tonight, or consider yourself no longer my son.' I honestly thought he was joking," sighed Abdurahman. Although an upsetting experience at the time, in retrospect, he now better understands his parents' apprehension – "They didn't understand the new sense of peace I got after becoming Muslim. And, at the time, we just didn't have the tools to have a calm and collected conversation – it would almost always end up antagonistic and hostile." That night, Abdurahman found himself homeless for not relenting in his faith. "'Dad, I love you,' I said to him. 'Mum, Jenny – I love you all

so much. But I love my Creator even more.'" Abdurahman was met with disownment by his family and left alone.

Rendered homeless with nowhere else to go, he walked the long road in darkness to Regent's Park Mosque for shelter. Although heartbreaking, he was somewhat prepared for this eventuality amid growing hostility towards him in his household. Abdurahman, however, arrived at a mosque whose doors were firmly shut. "I remained sat at the mosque's doorstep for five hours," he explained. "Five hours later, I was able to go inside when it was time to pray. I prayed *Fajr*. It was the mosque that became my place of work, and *very* humble abode, until I was able to get back on my feet."

Every hardship is accompanied by ease

Bitterness between Abdurahman and his parents would prove unable to
settle until the passing of 10 years. "It was very difficult for me," he admitted.
"This was the first time in my life where I had absolutely nothing – all the
privileges I once had were gone in an instant." Despite the sheer strain, he
also recalled being able to practice his religion with ease and actively learn
more about Islam. The Islamic books he once searched far and wide for in
Edgeware Road prior, were now readily available for him to peruse through
– "truly, I learned a lot during this time.

"Not just that," he said chiming in, "It was also at the mosque that I got
introduced to my wife, who is also a convert to Islam. Together, we have
four children."

He further explained, happily: "My wife and I take great pride in that we
have built this new generation of Muslims and our children have a very good
relationship with their grandparents. In fact, all our non-Muslim relatives look
to us as Muslims who are contributing to doing good in the world – they see
good examples in our children, and that's such a blessing."

Regarding how the young man formerly known as Joel became
Abdurahman, he laughed as he remembered initially thinking his name
change would be temporary; "All I needed was a visa to go for Hajj!" he
exclaimed.

After learning about the fifth pillar of Islam, Abdurahman was bent on
making the pilgrimage – but was met by a snag. "This was in 1992," he
began to narrate. "When I showed up at the Saudi embassy in London, they
said since I didn't have a *shahada* certificate, a Muslim or Islamic name –
they couldn't issue me a visa." So, he found a loophole – change of name
via deed poll.

With £5 in hand to pay the fee, he found himself sat in a solicitor's office
to legally change his name. "Okay Joel – what would you like your new na-

me to be?" asked the solicitor. "I honestly have no clue – give me a few minutes, and I'll phone my friend," he replied to her. He excused himself to the telephone and dialled Kaja's number. After hearing his predicament, Kaja said: "You know what Joel? You strike me as an 'Abdurahman' – that will be a fitting name for you."

With his deed poll signed and stamped, he took himself to Her Majesty's Passport Office for an emergency passport. "24 hours later, it was processed – I now had a new name and ID. But most importantly, I could get my Hajj visa."

Upon his return from Makkah, Abdurahman planned to change his name back to Joel – but destiny had other ideas. "Everyone around me started calling me Abdurahman, and it grew on me! It was only supposed to be my ticket to perform Hajj but after a while, I started to love the name." During this time, he also remembered stumbling upon a saying of the Prophet Muhammad in the Hadith:

Call yourselves by the names of the Prophets. And the names dearest to Allah are Abdullah and AbdurRahman.

Upon reading that, his then-new identity as a Muslim had become entrenched.

"There were many challenges along my journey to Islam," said Abdurahman in conclusion. "But, my faith is what has gotten me through. I realise now that life is the greatest test, but my Lord has reassured me, and reassured us all that *'verily, with every hardship comes ease. And again, verily, with every hardship comes ease.'*"

---

7   Here, Abdurahman has quoted from *surah al Sharh* – which can also alternatively be referred to as *surah al Inshirāḥ*. In this 94th chapter of the Quran, verses 5 – 6 assert: *"verily, with every hardship comes ease'. And again, verily, with every hardship comes ease"*.

11

'Some things in this life are indescribable. The same goes for my embracing of Islam'

———•••◆◆◆•••———

Amir 'Loon' Muhadith – American ex-rapper

———•••◆◆◆•••———

As a musician, Amir Muhadith felt accomplished but not spiritually fulfilled. Caught in a whirlwind of fame and success, an emptiness resided deep with- in him. When one has reached the pinnacle of their success, "where do you go from there?" he asks. For- tunately, all this was to change when he 'abruptly' found Islam.

AMIR Junaid Muhadith's first sight of someone prostrate in prayer harks back to a 2006 trip to Senegal. This display of outward religiosity had a profound impact on him and raced his mind back to his days growing up in the streets of New York.

"That's such a vulnerable position to be in", he said pondering over the prostrations of *salah*. "Remember, I was brought up with the street mentality – in that position, anybody can run up and kick you in the head or get you from behind. So, it intrigued me - who would a person do that for?" he reminisced.

A rapper of worldwide fame, Amir, who was known by his 'Loon' pseudonym, was invited to Senegal to perform his smash hits. Curiously, the trip had something else in store for him that would spark the life-changing journey he was to undertake.

That day, far removed from the electric atmosphere of a party earlier, the sight of a man prostrating in prayer gripped Amir's attention. A sight he saw, of all places, at an afterparty in full swing.

"The afterparty went down in a Senegalese model's mansion. She said we shouldn't walk in front of the man since he was praying. That sight alone of seeing a man placing his head on the ground, and then being told he was in prayer – the word 'submission' instantly came to mind. That's honestly what it looked like to me; 'submission'."

His curiosity in Senegal was further piqued when he stumbled upon a book that was foreign to him at the time. "Later that night when I went back to my hotel room, I spotted a copy of the Quran. I wanted to pick it up – just to take a look, but the girl I was with wouldn't let me touch it.[1]" Amir found it peculiar that the same lady he had been clubbing and drinking with a few

---

1   There is a school of thought within Islam that asserts the Quran may only be touched whilst one is in a state of ritual purity. As such, it is argued the Quran may only be touched after having performed *wudhu.*

moments prior suddenly changed her demeanour altogether regarding matters of religion.

"Something just changed in her," recalled Amir. "This memory really sticks out because she wasn't veiling, nor showed any other outward signs of religiosity. Yet, her reverence for the Quran was so strong in her heart, she felt she had to defend it. I was curious about this book I couldn't touch, but didn't act upon this curiosity."

While in Kazakhstan, he was introduced to the diversity found among Muslims. "Before travelling there, it was my understanding that Islam was only the religion of Arabs, South East Asians and West and North Africans. But then," he continued, "I found myself in Central Asia and saw a new demographic of people who were Muslim. That for me became fascinating – to learn that this thing called Islam expanded even more vastly than I had initially thought."

He then reminisced about hearing the call to prayer for the first time in the United Arab Emirates (UAE) – an experience he described as "purity" to his ears. "With the *adhaan*[2], there was no beat at the backdrop, no adlibs or overdubs – none of the things that are used to manufacture hit songs. Just a single cry from one voice, urging that people hasten to worship God upon hearing it. That's something no song can ever achieve."

He experienced a state of conflict when he first came to know what the call to prayer meant – feeling a pull to want to pray, but not knowing how. "I remember being in Dubai and asking the people chaperoning me around town what that sound was that I would hear five times a day. They told me it was the call to prayer. 'Y'all going?' is what I would say to them and most times they would say no."

---

2   The *adhaan* is the Islamic call to prayer made five times daily to announce the tim- ings of the obligatory prayers.

He would usually be given the excuse that prayers can be delayed.

"I remember saying, 'are you kidding me?' I just couldn't believe the excuses I heard!" he exclaimed. "I remember thinking to myself, if I knew what *salah* was, I would drop all that I was doing and go follow that voice to go pray – but I couldn't. I didn't know how to do so. Plus, I was following them; they didn't go to the mosque, so I didn't go either."

For Amir, it was these cumulative experiences abroad that served to educate him on "the beauty, variety and dynamics of Islam." Said discovery overwhelmed him – he now had a new- found expansive understanding of what Islam was and who its followers were. "From there onwards, I knew that the way of life that Muslims were upon was what I wanted to be upon, too. It was everything I perceived to be good in this world. I came to understand that Islam is not restricted to just three or four different ethnicities and that, every day, Muslims are instructed to withdraw from the busyness of their days and worship their Creator."

When asked for the very moment in which his mindset was changed and he knew he wanted to become a Muslim, Amir was quick to interpose – "it really isn't a matter of mindset. More correctly, it's about the *heartset*."

"So, to pinpoint what exactly made me convert, the honest truth is that some things in this life are indescribable. The same goes for my embracing of Islam."

For Amir: "I'm simply only able to detail the events that led to my conversion. But remember, Islam wasn't what I was looking for." He continued, "This change in me came so abruptly and perfectly timed that you can only attribute it to Allah and Allah alone. No one fully understands His wisdom, except Allah Himself." As such: "I didn't need to be sat down and told the stories of the Prophet (PBUH), nor did anyone have to present me with the Quran. Islam in itself just clicked!" **Reminiscing about his former** career as a recording artist, Amir, born Chauncey Lamont Hawkins, highlighted how his creative writing talents got his foot in the door of showbiz. "A lot of people don't know that I was an artist before signing onto Bad Boy," he said. "My career began in ghost-writing for other artists; I initially was avoidant of the limelight."

Although being born and raised with the Methodist flavour of Christianity and attending church six times a week, Amir hinted at his younger self being two minds about self-ascribing as a Christian. "With my Baptist upbringing, I was taught that Jesus was the begotten son of God. With that came a lot of reverence, reliance and seeking refuge in him.

"However," he continued, "with the understanding of *tawheed*[3] that I now have as a Muslim, I see that that excessive devotion to Jesus was in fact undue worship of him. And interestingly enough, even as a youngster, that excessiveness just never sat right with me."

Amir was brought up by his grandparents and learned about Christianity from his devoutly 'prayerful' grandmother. "My mother and father were unfortunately products of the streets of New York and so were unable to take care of me. It was my grandparents, *Allah yarhamhum*[4], that raised me. Later on though, they became Muslims after me."

Despite his uncertainty in the Christian faith instilled in him as a boy, Amir asserts never having doubted God's existence. "Throughout my journey to becoming Muslim, I can honestly say I was always attached to my *fitra*. I always knew God was there with me and never wavered from that

---

3   The concept of *tawhid* enshrines the Islamic doctrine of monotheism – namely, that Almighty God
     is one and there is none that can be likened unto He.

4   This translates as "may Allah have mercy on them." Said phraseology is commonly said after
     mentioning of those deceased.

fact. 'There *has* to be a God', is what I would tell myself, but I just couldn't find the right teachings. The teachings I received as a kid didn't add up to what I felt in my heart was just to God."

He went on to detail how, despite his yearning for answers, Islam was never what he was seeking. Yet, he also described the day he accepted Islam as being such that: "All the pieces to the puzzle I was once looking for were found. It just clicked and I knew being Muslim was what I wanted."

A curious mind

When asked about the role religion played in his upbringing, Amir recollected a boyhood of being fully immersed in the church. "I was at church almost every day of the week. I was in the church choir, I was an usher, I played the piano at church – the list goes on really!" Simultaneously, however, he also described how common is it for African American youth to not necessarily practice their beliefs by virtue of the presence of those devout within the family.

He explained: "In our community, it's very common to hear statements like, 'I have a prayerful grandmother', or 'I have a praying mother'. So, many of us grow up with the mentality that we should rely on our mothers, grandmothers or the older generation to exercise that spiritual relationship, rather than doing so ourselves." Yet, he also detailed having an initial drive to emulate his grandmother's faithful devotion.

"I do remember trying at times to follow in her footsteps," he said. "Both my grandparents were my voices of reason growing up. They taught me how to conduct myself – how to have self-respect and respect for others. But, in terms of matching my grandmother's Christian devotion, I came across too many things that corrupted those efforts. For instance," he went on, "I struggled with the concept of rejoicing."

He recounted his younger days spent frequenting the church being marked by a quintessentially African American Baptist 'celebratory' overture. "Baptists are very celebratory. That's why the choir and church band are so important for rejoicing – this is prayer through music and dance." Unfortunately, however, for his younger self, although gifted musically, his dancing abilities were not so flattering.

"The bulk of church worship was in the form of rejoicing, and I just couldn't chime in – I'm not a dancer!" This fundamental aspect of church worship left him feeling isolated. "I couldn't align myself with rejoicing, so I felt alienated and on the fringe of that practice." Therefore, he instead sought belonging within a space where he thought his inquisitiveness would be nurtured and encouraged.

"I was drawn to Bible study," he said. "I felt it was a place where I could develop an understanding of my religion by studying scripture. However, what made Bible study difficult for me was the underlying rule that asking questions was forbidden. "That bugged me," he continued. "Why, in a studious environment, prohibit questions?" And his main bone of contention that he sought answers for from his Bible teachers surrounded the concept of Jesus in Christianity.

"A question I just couldn't shake was, if Jesus is God, or the son of God, then why does the Bible say that he prays? Who was Jesus praying to?" He went on to say, "I think this question is very common among curious minds; if we agree that he is God, then it wouldn't make sense for him to pray to himself. And in going along with the argument that he's the son of God, my young, curious mind was still confused about why he would need to pray."

This led him to a seemingly never-ending road in search of answers.

"Truly, I was confused and trying to find clarity, but I never got it. I really wanted to know how to pray to God. For instance, the Bible talks about Moses kneeling, and then putting his face down on the ground in prayer. But this wasn't what I was being taught." He further lamented, "All this was so challenging for me to have to grapple with at a young age and it stirred up so much confusion within me." A confusion that was to be amplified within the educational setting.

Hallelujah versus *Alleluia*

Amir described the religious instruction he received while a student at Catholic school as being "worlds apart" from what he was taught within the Baptist church setting. "Although I was born and raised as a Baptist Christian, I was educated in a Catholic school," he said. It was there that during the weekly Mass, Amir took part in Holy Communion. "This only confused me even more. I always found myself asking, 'why are we consuming the flesh and blood of Christ?'"

He did, however, recall hearing a word that gripped him. A word he remembered as one of the few things that stuck with him – even after leaving school. For him, said word marked an important checkpoint in his journey to Islam.

"One thing that has stayed with me, and I find it truly amazing, was how during Mass, *'alleluia, alleluia, alleluia'* would be recited. The first time I attended Mass was in second grade, and I can still clearly hear the chants of *'alleluia, alleluia, alleluia'* in my head to this day." He continued: "While in the Baptist setting, the same word would be chanted but, with a totally different twang altogether. Rather than *'alleluia'*, they would say *'hallelujah'*."

Amir went on to describe his younger self experiencing an unplaceable unease towards the recitation of *'hallelujah'* he would hear while at his onetime Baptist church. "Even at a young age, I knew *'alleluia'* and *'halle-*

lujah' were not one and the same and the latter never drew my attention the same way the former did." He continued, "Later on, I came to know that linguistically, '*alleluia*' is similar to *alhamdulilah*."

Reminiscing on this, he concluded: "I believe that Allah was trying to show me something early on – everything else that I was taught at Catholic school really went out the window, the only thing that stuck with me was the word '*alleluia*'."

'Where does one go from here?'

The year 2003 saw Amir release his eponymous debut album, 'Loon', under Puff Daddy's Bad Boy record label. In its first week, his album went on to sell 80,000 copies[5]. A smirking Amir can be seen on the album cover, donning an '*iced out*[6]' chain with a crucifix.

"We're all products of our environment," he said. "Christianity was what I was exposed to as a child, so it's natural that I went ahead and bought a crucifix chain." However, when asked about the religious significance of the jewellery, he revealed: "It was really just there for show.

"Never once did I take my diamond encrusted crucifix and use it in prayer. It was just a status symbol that said, 'I made it!' and, 'hey, look at me – I got money now!'"

Amassing astronomical wealth as a recording artist was what he described as being his goal from the start of his superstar career. "When I was just a budding artist, I wanted to make enough money to take care of my grandmother, everyone else I cared for and those around me who loved me.

---

5   Wiederhorn, J., 2003. Clay Aiken Goes Two For Two, Tops Legends And Loon On Albums Chart. [Blog] MTV, Available at: <https://www.mtv.com/news/2gvjut/ clay-aiken-goes-two-for-two-tops-legends-and-loon-on-albums-chart>.

6   In reference to jewellery, the term 'iced out' refers to ornaments decorated with copi- ous amounts of diamonds.

"I can definitely say I felt accomplished as a rapper, but fulfilment? That's a different story." He continued: "Fulfilment was what I later came to find in the religion of Islam." Yet, as a rapper, his skyrocketing success soon became an internal impediment.

"The emptiness that resided through the course of all that success was tough and almost inexplainable. After achieving what you set out to do, in many ways, you find yourself in a position of loss – where does one go from here?" he asked. "It got to a point where the things I once craved: the fame, money, cars, women, intoxicants – were all at my disposal." However, he explained, after reaching the pinnacle of such success, the lines between being the user of vices and being the thing used soon become blurred.

"After you achieve all of the grandeur and the accolades that come with being successful in the music industry, it's difficult to plan past that." He continued: "After a while, fame then becomes burdensome upon a person and that burden is usually drowned out by their vice of choice. But gradually, over time, the situation becomes such that rather than being the person using the vices, they eventually become used themselves."

He further explained how, "as time passes in that rut, one's health, and to a certain degree, their self-respect deteriorates. The person supplying the vice of choice is just getting rich off you while your health progressively worsens. A person may even come to no longer want to indulge in such vices because of the toll it takes on them. But it becomes so habitual that the cycle is hard to break. That's an artificial existence – that person's no longer living.

"It was bizarre," he continued. "I felt I had made something of myself. My grandma, who more than anybody wanted me to become successful in life, saw my successes, so I felt like I achieved that both for myself and for her." Despite being the man who had everything, he yet felt a void in his life.

"There no longer was a next move. I always found myself asking, 'what do I do next?' Do I just gradually wither away until the next big superstar comes and replaces me? Or, do I increase my consumption of drugs and alcohol to while away time?" To remedy the burgeoning abyss in his day-to-day, he sought refuge in reexploring his Christian heritage.

"I was at a very low point in life, and briefly started reattending church. I got nothing out of it, though. My church experience at that time didn't feel real – people would always stop, mid-session to point and whisper, 'oh look – that's Loon sat over there!'"

When asked what it was he was in search of when he began reattending church, he confessed, "Truly I was lost and looking for a sign from God. I was searching for clarity and how to be a better person." He continued: "And church was the only place I knew to turn to."

He further confided: "People who have been Muslim since birth truly don't know how fortunate they are to have been born upon the truth and have an in-depth understanding of what clear guidance is from the very beginning." He juxtaposed this with the mental misery he experienced amid his then-rap star success. "At the time, I didn't have guidance. So, even though I knew continual substance abuse would be my downfall, I just couldn't find relief from my troubles elsewhere."

A series of fortuitous events

A year after signing onto Puff Daddy's label, Amir left Bad Boy. "I had something to prove," he said. "I wanted to show the world that I can establish the same level of success on my own without Bad Boy; that's what my goal was."

It was this solo venture that ushered in his travels across continents – namely to Senegal, Kazakhstan and the UAE. "I wanted to expand my horizons and no longer be isolated within the four walls of the United States. I wasn't looking for faith, but *alhamdulilah*, through my travels, Allah showed me Islam."

Senegal, Kazakhstan and the UAE all happen to be Muslim majority countries. "However," said Amir chiming in, "I never travelled to those countries to learn about their religion. In fact, most times, I was invited to perform at major parties and festivals that were being hosted there."

He continued, recollecting how that era of globetrotting served to rid him of being entrapped in not knowing his full potential: "This world is so vast and travel truly is the best education. I not only learnt about myself, but how big of a deal the world really is." Further, the sights, sounds, and encounters Amir faced while abroad triggered an intrigue within him that led to his eventual conversion.

However, he recollected his earliest encounter with Muslims and Islam while still on home soil. "My first exposure to any semblance of Islam," he narrated, "was from my boxing trainer and mentor as a kid – Kenny Willis. Kenny," he continued, "was a member of the Nation of Islam (NOI)."

He detailed how the NOI, especially at its inception, was able to hold such sway on the African American community. "What a lot of people outside of America don't understand is that our inclination to anything that resembles us, or gives us a sense of belonging, honour and pride – we gravitate very quickly towards those things." He continued: "When the NOI was founded, it spoke a language that was empowering to Black people and preached aspects of Islam, such as implementing good manners and cleanliness. This uplifted our community and gave rise to figures such as Muhammad Ali."

However, the rendition of Islam presented by Willis and the NOI was also puzzling to a young Amir. "When I first met Kenny, I was already struggling with the concept of anthropomorphism in Christianity, so the NOI's teachings still couldn't give me the answers I was searching for." Despite this, Amir attributed his being under Willis' mentorship as the only reason he had a tolerance for Islam and its adherents. "You know, I looked up to Kenny," he beamed. "Not only that, but growing up, I didn't have a father figure around. That was a struggle for me, but in many ways, Kenny alleviated that struggle."

While overseas, however, his eyes were opened to a belief system that not only reformed his 'Bad Boy' ways, but provided a much-needed end to his search for answers.

When asked why he took the life-changing decision of converting, he humbly replied, "Ultimately, even to this day, I will always have a heightened sense of gratitude as to why Allah chose me – what made *me* a candidate? On the outside, Muslims, and maybe even non-Muslims, want to know why I embraced Islam, when on the other hand, I'm trying to figure out 'why me?'"

He further remembered the day he took his *shahadah* as being 'natural.' "At that point," he explained, "everything just fell into place. The day I accepted Islam was the last day I smoked, drank, fornicated or listened to music. Those things became unnatural to me – I didn't need them anymore."

For him, the *heartset* is at the centre of his journey because his "was a heart that once was corrupted and poisoned. Allah took favour upon me and cleansed it. So, the difficulty doesn't come in adopting a new lifestyle prescribed by Islam – the difficulty comes in the pursuit of trying to protect that newly changed heart."

He went on to liken his scenario to being akin to that of recovery after successful bypass surgery. "The convert becomes protective of this new heart that they have – as though they had heart surgery, and they are now healing from it." He continued: "One naturally becomes cautious – you're not going to let people get too close to your chest when you still have stitches or staples there, right? You're not going to let kids run around too wildly around you because they might accidentally run into you. So, it's like protecting a healing heart – you'll do anything to prevent injury!"

'What's in a name?'

After embracing Islam, the former rap artist adopted the name Amir Junaid Muhadith. "My Muslim name was given to me by a brother named Mujahid – I met him during my Bad Boy days at 'Justin's'; one of Puff's restaurants in New York," he said. "Mujahid used to do Puff's security. He too is a convert to Islam. "Admittedly, during our first encounter, I was a bit of a hot head," he laughed. As per the dress code, Mujahid requested for him to remove his hat while inside Puff Daddy's restaurant. "You know, at the time, I was a young star, I was rich, so I really wasn't interested in entertaining Mujahid's request," chuckled Amir. Yet, he went on to tell how Mujahid maintained the utmost decorum and spoke to him calmly and respectfully.

"He's actually a black belt holder. Between you and I," narrated Amir, "he's a dangerous guy! He could have easily *dealt* with me there and then, but he chose not to. Instead, he reasoned with me, and I appreciated him doing that." After their heart-to-heart, Amir eventually complied and took off his hat. From there, the two developed a mutual respect and became close friends.

Naturally, when Mujahid eventually caught wind of Amir's conversion, the news came much to his delight. "Later on, he told me he had actually been praying for me to become Muslim someday and I'm glad he got to witness his prayer come true."

Not only this, but Mujahid had the honour of gifting Amir his new name.

"'Let me give you your Muslim name!' he said to me after I converted." But Amir had one condition – not to be given a name that included an attribute of Allah. "I didn't feel worthy," he said. "I didn't want to be named as the servant of one of Allah's most beloved attributes and then fall short." The two agreed on this term and Amir was told to wait for a week to be given his new name. Little did he know that the process of him getting his new name would in fact span three weeks.

"I called him up a week later after we had that initial conversation. He told me: 'Your name is Amir.' I said: 'Amir? I like that! What does it mean?' He said: 'It means prince or leader. You always have been a leader; I've never known you to follow anybody. So, your new name is Amir.'

"'Muslims are known for having long names', I told him. 'So, what's the rest of my name?'" Amir was instructed to wait yet another week. "I remember thinking to myself, 'what's up with all this having to wait a week stuff?'" he recollected. "But," he continued, "he already gave me the name Amir, so I couldn't wait to hear what he would think up next. I was ready to tell everyone my new name – 'Yo, I'm now Amir ibn something something, or I'm Amir this and that,' you know? That's what everyone else's Muslim name was like."

After the passing of another week, Amir was informed of what his second name would be, and he was given the name Junaid. Mujahid had told him that Junaid was Arabic for a small warrior, with the heart of an entire army. Looking back on this, Amir admitted Mujahid may have stretched the truth a little bit – "But it sounded nice to my ears and it made me happy. But now that I understand Arabic, I know *jundiyy* is a soldier, and *junaid* is a small soldier.

"Remember, I was given the name Chauncy Lamont Hawkins at birth," said Amir. "So I was expected to be told my last name, too." Much to his dismay, he had to wait for a third week to hear the news.

"My Muslim name took three weeks in total to come to fruition. At the time, I remember thinking 'this is ridiculous!'" he exclaimed, "but in actuality, *sabr*[7] is a fundamental of our religion. I think Mujahid was subtly trying to teach me the beauty of *sabr*."

After the third and final week: "I called him. He said 'Muhadith'." Once again, Amir asked what his new name meant and was told it means, 'interpreter' or 'one who interprets'. "What he didn't mention to me at the time was that it can also mean one who is a scholar of Prophetic hadith." He continued, chuckling as he remembered trying to avoid being given one of Allah's names, only to be named as one who is a scholar of Hadith by Mujahid. "Go figure!"

"Funnily enough," he recollected, "I've had encounters where people have asked me whether I really was a *muhadith* in the scholarly sense. I'd say to them, while I may not be a scholar of Hadith, I am someone who can interpret anything I learn – I have a very photographic memory. If someone teaches me something, I can interpret it for people who may not understand it. So, to have gotten this name, and my other two names from Mujahid, was truly a gift for me."

Triumph twice over

Circling back to his feelings of accomplishment as 'Loon' the rapper, Amir expressed feeling doubly accomplished as a Muslim. "Like I said, as a rapper, I was able to take care of those closest to me financially. Then eventually,

---

7   *Sabr* is Arabic for patience. The virtue of sabr in Islam is an admirable trait of piety that Muslims strive to uphold, both in times of ease and difficulty.

by Allah's permission, after I became Muslim, I was then able to uplift them spiritually." After his embracing of Islam, Amir's wife and the grandparents who raised him soon followed suit.

Despite his grandmother once being a 'prayerful Christian', Amir painted an antithetical picture of his grandfather prior to subsequently becoming Muslim. "My grandfather truly was a renaissance man – he was a war veteran who served as an army engineer and rose to become the first African American Captain. But," he continued, "he didn't adhere to Christianity like my grandmother did when I was growing up. He rolled dice and bet on horses, and, like the rest of us, hid behind my grandmother's Christian zealousness."

After embracing Islam, Amir gifted his grandfather with a book he initially used to better understand his then new-found Islamic faith *'Interpretation of Kitab At-Tauhid* (The destination of the Seeker of Truth)' by Saleh bin Abdul Aziz Aali Shaikh. Amir remembered his astonishment after coming to know his grandfather read the book cover to cover. "I stopped by to visit him one day with a few brothers from the mosque.

In the middle of our get-together, he, unannounced, joins us. He said, 'Who can tell me the first thing that Allah created?' Then he said, 'The pen, and Allah commanded it to write!' and turned around and walked straight back to his room." Amir and his friends were astounded by what they had heard from his then-Christian grandfather. "Although it came as a surprise to me, that moment is a very dear memory of mine. That moment right there showed me he was paying attention to his grandson, and eventually, he came to accept Islam," he recollected. After his grandfather eventually became Muslim, Amir was now tasked with giving him his new name. "'Pops, you're Yahya now!' I said to him. 'Yahya?' What' Yahya mean? he asked me. I told him it's John in Arabic."

Reminiscing about his grandpa Yahya's last days, Amir recounted their final conversations together. "My grandfather died aged 96. When he was dying, with every phone call we would have, I would always say, 'Remember what I told you, pops – if you feel like you're getting close, what is it that you will say?'" Amir delightedly remembered his grandfather uttering '*La illaha illa Allah*' (There is no God but Allah) at the end of every phone call they would have leading up to his passing.

"I never hung up the phone with him unless I knew that he knew what to say whenever he felt he was approaching his time. So, the fact that he accepted Islam and continued to have *kalimat al tawheed*[8] on his tongue, I felt at ease when it came time for him to return to Allah."

He lastly explained how his ultimate goal as a Muslim being is to serve as a caller to those yet to embrace Islam, and a reminder for those who already are Muslim. "This is what I ask of Allah when I pray," he said.

"I want to live up to my name and be a soldier in inviting all to Islam, especially the youth. I believe wholeheartedly in our young people, and should Allah ever favour me again with an abundance of wealth, by His mercy and permission, I would utilize that wealth to establish a complete resurgence of Islam amongst the youth. They are the future of our religion."

---

8   This translates as "the words of tawheed" – that being the testification that there is none worthy of worship, save Allah Almighty.

12

Vivo: Spreading truth and hope in Brazilian favelas

César Kaab Abdul – Brazilian former rapper

One of the founders of current Brazilian hip hop, César's journey to truth is unique and fascinating, a story which is inextricably intertwined with Brazil's own complex social mosaic, of which the fabled favelas are an integral part.

Suddenly, César Kaab Abdul's phone went berserk and wouldn't stop ringing all day. The unanswered calls and messages piled up; suspicion fell on him and acquaintances started to distance themselves from him. But it wouldn't stop at that. Every dawn appeared with new graffiti calling him and his family 'terrorists' or accusing them of being part of the Islamic State. Setting a foot on the street without being subjected to threats, insults and mockery became impossible, César says, his face visibly downcast at the mere thought of those horror-filled days.

The trigger for the tortuous tornado of accusations and insults was an article published in a widely circulated Brazilian magazine called *Veja*, accusing César of links with terrorism on the grounds that a man accused of terrorism had visited a mosque he was associated with.

César is a former rapper and one of the founders of current Brazilian hip hop and a convert to Islam, which made his story sensational enough for *Veja* to celebrate.

The article was followed by another report reiterating the same accusations, on Record TV, one of the most influential television stations in Brazil with links to the Evangelist Church. Shortly afterwards, the security forces in charge of maintaining order during the Rio de Janeiro Olympics in 2016 identified him as a possible threat.

A reputation derived from a lifetime of serving the community and built on integrity, compassion and principles was blown to smithereens.

"In addition to the constant threats I received, there were media outlets that put cameras on helicopters to film me every time I left my house, and they made terrible reports against me," says a saddened César, who needed years to recover from that 'defamation campaign'.

According to César, there were never any formal charges against him, nor evidence to open a judicial investigation. He was arrested on one occasion, during the infamous Brazilian police raids during the Olympic Games but, after a few hours, he was released without charge. "It was always fallacies, they had never had anything on me," says César.

But the reason that instigated the media to launch vitriolic attacks against him was the same as that which gave him the courage and determination to overcome them – his new faith. It required fortitude of enormous proportions to wade through the trauma unleashed by the media trial, but what is equally remarkable is that, throughout this painful period, his faith in Islam wasn't shaken a bit, and he remained undaunted and strong, praying to Allah for help.

His innocence and perseverance paid off. A year later, the same magazine published an article on him with a positive spin. The lesson learned: his new faith was sufficient enough to sail him through the storms of life, however devastating they may be.

César remembers that the political situation in his country then also provided a ripe setting for such witch-hunting by the media. The World Trade Center attacks, and the more recent November 2015 Paris attacks, claimed by fundamentalist organisations, put Muslims in a negative spotlight, creating a climate of tension and mistrust. These were followed by years of political turmoil in Brazilian politics, which witnessed a huge shift to the right after years of progressive governments under the Workers' Party. The country shifted to a more virulent form of conservatism, represented since 2019 by the government of Jair Bolsonaro.

"Religious intolerance had been growing in those years, with unjustified police operations in mosques and raids on our Muslim brothers. And when

Bolsonaro came in, it was terrible," explains César about the not-so-recent phenomenon of violent gangs using the name of Evangelism to commit crimes against members of other communities.

César's story is unique and fascinating, a story which is inextricably intertwined with Brazil's own complex social mosaic, of which the fabled *favelas* are an integral part.

A story from the *favelas*

Fast forward to September 2022.

As evening falls, the temperature drops in the countryside of São Paulo, the largest city in Latin America's largest country, Brazil. César is thoughtful, easily identifiable in his *Abaya* that wraps his big frame in a jacket of the same colour as his long, grey beard. Through a thick pair of glasses, his eyes scan the people around him, and he uncrosses his arms to keep his *Taqiyah*[1] in place.

Today, he has substituted the hustle and bustle of the city for the serene atmosphere of a wooden cottage surrounded by trees. He frequents this camp to participate in activities aimed at teenagers coming from vulnerable backgrounds, where teachings of Islam are mixed with capoeira trainings. Capoeira is one of the most popular martial arts in Brazil that combines acrobatics, agile dance movements and different body postures, imitating (touchless) a physical contact fight.

As his frown relaxes, so do his hands. Expressive, they emphasise his words as if he was rapping, an ode to the not-so- distant past of this new Brazilian Muslim before he devoted himself entirely to Islam.

---

1   *Abaya* and *Taqiyah* are traditional garments commonly worn by Muslim men in the Arab region. The Abaya is a long robe and the Taqiyah is a short, rounded hat usually worn during the five daily prayers.

As a rapper, his lyrics, perceptive and full of social condemnation, reached the hearts of a wide audience who regarded him as a reference and a leader in the fight against the inequalities and violence ravaging *favelas*, the Brazilian name for the immense shanty towns on the outskirts of big cities, where César was raised.

His progressive path to conversion made him substitute the microphone for the Quran and a mosque. "Islam gave me a second chance, and I was reborn," he says. He took the teachings of the Quran as a guide for his actions, and devoted his life to abiding by them. "My mind found tranquility and I gave up my bad habits like smoking and drinking."

He quotes from Prophet Muhammed, peace be upon him, who said: 'None of you truly believes until he loves for his brother what he loves for himself'. This *hadith²*, which intimately touched César's soul, shows the true nature of Islam as a social organising force laying the foundations of compassion and mutual assistance in a community.

"For me, it implies that you need to find inner peace and reach a state of self-acceptance in order to be capable of helping others. Islam gave me purpose, a reason, a strength to enhance my advocacy work towards social development. Once I felt myself at peace and understood the right path to follow, my contribution and solidarity actions gained ascendancy," he affirms. In a broader sense, César's journey to Islam is a reflection of the favelas' struggle to find a place in the world, and the fight to make their voices heard. The favelas form an essential part of César's own identity and he refers to them often as people who have been constantly denied opportunities of social mobility. In such an impoverished context, Islam emerges as a communal force conducive to the dissemination of knowledge and refined values.

---

2   According to the Islamic tradition, a *Hadith* is a saying to the Prophet Muhammad.

Tough childhood and Malcolm X influence

César was born in 1972, in the middle of Brazil's 'Years of Lead', the darkest period of the military dictatorship which lasted from 1964 till 1985. Poverty on the outskirts of São Paulo, the most populous city and the country's economic and cultural backbone, ripped away his childhood, and, by the age of nine, he was already following his father to work in the narrow streets of the periphery.

As a child, during weekends, he went with his parents to the Evangelical Church, a branch of Christian Protestantism fervently growing in Latin America, and during the week he would attend along with his grandmother the *camdomblé'* rituals, one of the most widely practised Afro-Brazilian cults, a result of the syncretism of several religions brought by African slaves during the 19th century. This religious diversity always attracted his attention and piqued his curiosity as a kid.

César was a teenager when he encountered Islam for the first time. While working as an office boy in a company (it was a common job for many favela youth), he met Ibrahim, a Muslim Arab co-worker who did not celebrate Christmas, who didn't drink alcohol. César became curious about his breaks to pray during office hours. "I had never heard about Islam before or what it was to be a Muslim," he admits.

César's admission is a reality that would be shared by the vast majority of Brazilians who had no encounters with Islamic culture and for whom access to Islam is an arduous quest. The only official data on the numbers of Muslims in Brazil, dating back to 2010, estimate their population at 35,000, which, in comparison to the Brazilian population at the time (196 million), constitutes less than 0.02 per cent. In a country with the greatest number of Catholics in the world, Islam's visibility was very limited.

César reminisces that at the time he met Ibrahim, in the mid 1980's, the iron fist of dictatorship which Brazil was experiencing was giving rise to a new kind of expression of freedom – protests through music. The rhythms of music started to fill the streets, and in the squares of São Paulo's outskirts, the soul of what would later become Brazilian hip hop began to take birth. To bypass censorship, raging lyrics of protest were added to the Samba[3] tempo, which would subsequently convert into rap, as protests against the miserable inequality that would condemn the *favelados* to a life of mere survival.

Hip hop was a lifeline, a philosophy, and a medium to explain the sordid social realities during those decades, when levels of violence skyrocketed in Brazil to the point that in some favelas, the number of homicides exceeded that in war zones. Singing turned the feeling of fear and the need for revenge into an art and activism, proclaiming what was once silenced.

The life of hip hop and the lack of opportunities dragged César to prison for being involved in a minor drug trafficking offence. He was only 14 years old when he was taken to a minors' custody centre, the same centre where he now organises programmes aimed at facilitating the social integration of kids involved in legal troubles. At 20, he was again imprisoned. Deprived of freedom and dignity, he paused and deeply reflected about his life and future, and about the terrible path it was taking.

In that moment, he would read a life-changing book. César pauses and reaches inside his bag to extricate the worn pages of his amulet, *Raíces Negras* , a translation of *Roots* by Alex Haley.

---

3   Brazil's folk and festive dance, with a fast and joyful rhythm. According to Bruno Lopes, analyst, "Samba is the soul of Brazil".

He had read voraciously about Malcolm X, the Afro-American leader who turned into a symbol against racism in the United States, who converted to Islam at the end of his life. César says his first contact with Islam was through Malcolm X's autobiography. "Most rappers had Malcolm X as a reference, but his religiousness usually went unnoticed," he added.

Books were rare to find in the favelas and this one came into his hands at a time when he was looking to cement his social struggle with theoretical content. He had heard about Malcolm X before, about his legacy, and had become a hero to him, but after reading the autobiography he began to wonder for the first time about the path towards the faith his idol had chosen.

"That book changed me; it changed my mentality, and the way I saw the world and it was the beginning of my approach to Islam," says César.

The seed had been sown, but there was still a long path ahead before conversion.

Twin Tower attacks

"I was on my way to a concert when the news of the attacks reached me. I heard so many insults, accusations against the Muslim community and false information to discredit Islam that I decided to step forward and defend it," he says.

It was a time when his rap career was bringing him fame — though he avoids calling himself 'famous' and prefers 'respected' – and also brought him a living exclusively from music. It was during the search for new sounds and rhythms for his music that he, once more, encountered Islam – through *aadhan,* the five- times-daily call to Muslim prayer from mosques.

He says he was deeply moved by *aadhan,* by its soul-stirring, sonorous rhythm. This prompted a renewed interest in Islam, and he combed through Arabic words to nurture his music and even ended up founding a hip hop group named "Jihad Brasil", which was tattooed on his forearm.

"I was very interested in the historical meaning of some important words in Islam. The very name of the religion is related to 'salam', which means peace in Arabic. Another emerging concept at that time in the press, with a strong negative overtone, was 'Jihad', which of course does not mean what many media outlets have said. Jihad means effort, the personal struggle of someone to become a better self," says César.

Feeling inwardly a Muslim but without having declared the *shahadah*, he gave expression to his faith through the lyrics for an album called 'Fragments of a Muslim', which are mixed with faith, the teachings of the Quran and the rhythms of rap as a tool for social transformation, fraught with combative verses criticising the United States' military actions in the Middle East as well as Brazil's inequality.

> *There is no exclusivity in front of Allah, His goodness is infinite...*
> *Contrary to what many people say, Islam does not preach destruction,*
> *but the union, the construction of a single identity,*
> *There is not another path for mankind but love and freedom (goodness!)*
> *There are questions that cannot be silenced in our innermost being,*
> *What is our legacy?*
> César Kaab Abdul

While trying to learn more about Islam, he established contact, through Messenger chat, with an Egyptian Muslim preacher with Brazilian roots who instructed him and sent him books. One book that deeply influenced him was

The Meadows of the Righteous or *Riyad as-Salihin,* written by Al-Nawawi from Damascus (1277–1233), which was also the first Islamic book César read. It's a compilation of verses from the Quran supplemented by the prophet's sayings.

"I used to be very radical on Islam's cultural and political aspects … but then I began to understand its true nature," he says. Although he already had more than a basic knowledge of the religion, through the book, he was astonished to discover Surahs (verses in the Quran) that were dedicated to equality among all human beings regardless of race, gender or status, where he clearly saw his life's long struggle reflected. Teachings regarding the concept of unity resonated profoundly with him as he read verses referring to equality and fairness of Allah in His treatment of His servants, who are only ranked according to their *taqwa,* or piety, and nothing else.

César was also deeply touched by, and fondly remembers, a sermon delivered by Prophet Muhammad, (PBUH), about the unifying and pacifying message of Islam, which he considers as two qualities that brought him closer to this historical and religious figure. Said sermon was delivered during the annual rites of Hajj in Makkah, and it is known as the Prophet's Last Sermon:

"All mankind is from Adam and Eve, an Arab has no superiority over a non-Arab nor a non-Arab has any superiority over an Arab; also a White has no superiority over a Black nor a Black has any superiority over a White except by piety and good action. Learn that every Muslim is a brother to every Muslim and that the Muslims constitute one brotherhood. Nothing shall be legitimate to a Muslim which belongs to a fellow Muslim unless it was given freely and willingly."

Racism and discrimination are deeply rooted in Brazilian society, so it was not surprising that these words had a magical impact on César. In fact, Brazil received the largest number of African slaves in Latin America and was, for centuries, one of the main ports for human trafficking to North America.

Vivo

César explains he was not expecting faith or religion to become part of his life, but Islam came across naturally, revealing what he considered as truth.

"Raised in a country deeply rooted in Catholicism, I have often felt religion as a punitive burden, as complex rituals where access to Divinity was necessarily mediated. Contrary to what had occurred to me with politics, for which earlier I had sought answers in books, I wasn't looking for any answers on matters pertaining to religion because I didn't have questions, not even the intention to embrace any faith. I came across Islam by chance, or Islam came across to me, through people and stories that naturally guided me to what I now consider true," he says.

"Islam is love and its definition of God matched precisely with my thoughts and feelings. I want to worship God as a complete and unique entity. I feel committed to God, not to a man. I wanted to embrace Islam and feel Him in His totality, as a whole, to communicate with Him. I eventually assimilated Islam's teachings and prayers that naturally became a part of my daily life. I didn't regard it as a change at all but as a slow, natural process." When asked which aspects of Islam attracted him, he answers: "The way of life preached by Islam (the relation among Muslims and the respect to nature), the life of the Prophet, peace be upon him, and the sacred - the Unity and Completeness of God." César's journey to truth lasted around a decade - from the late 80s/early 90s until 2001, when he publicly acknowledged himself as a Muslim, though the actual declaration of *shahadah* took a little longer and happened in 2005.

His 'guardian angel', as César calls Ibrahim, encouraged him to give up his bad habits like smoking, dating and drinking. The two men forged an unforgettable connection. "He was so helpful to me, he knew what was best for me. My life had been insane and I stopped," says César with gratitude.

So, how did he feel at the time of taking his shahada? "Vivo," he says joyously, lengthening the two syllables of the Portuguese word 'alive'. "I have no other word for that moment but my feeling of being alive." César refers to a general lack of resources and information on Islam when he started his journey, since the Arab Muslim population kept their traditions close to themselves and translations into Portuguese on Islam were difficult to find. Ibrahim explained to him the differences between Sunni and Shia, the five pillars of Islam, significant aspects of the prayer and some Arabic pronunciations. Ibrahim told César, for example, that tattoos were banned in the Islamic tradition.

After conversion, César was able to procure a Portuguese translation of the Quran. After a childhood where different religions bustled around him, he found himself enthralled by one of the most charming and paramount precepts of the Quran – the concept of *tawhid*, which refers to the Unity and Oneness of God. "These are powerful words to sum up the Islamic faith," he adds, and cites a verse that touched his heart:

"Allah! There is no god 'worthy of worship' except Him, the Ever-Living, All-Sustaining. Neither drowsiness nor sleep overtakes Him. To Him belongs whatever is in the heavens and whatever is on the earth. Who could possibly intercede with Him without His permission? He 'fully' knows what is ahead of them and what is behind them, but no one can grasp any of His knowledge— except what He wills 'to reveal'. His throne encompasses the heavens and the earth, and the preservation of both does not tire Him. For He is the Most High, the Greatest. " - Quran 2:255

With more and more social projects around culture, César decided it was time to leave the hip hop scene and clear his mind to carry out the projects he was really passionate about.

First mosque in the slums of São Paulo

As César continues his narration, dates intermingle in his memory and generous laughs burst out at intervals, revealing the rich story of a life nourished by faith.

So, being socially active, the acceptance of Islam for him was not a personal affair, but a mission he had to take forward.

Devoted to the firm conviction of the need to bring Islam to all parts of the favela, he opened up what he called a *musalla* [4] in his own home, a room without windows dressed with a single tapestry where friends and curious acquaintances were invited to discuss religion. Together with other fellow converts, he began to go to other neighbourhoods, handing out leaflets with information to raise awareness of Islam.

Lack of books was soon an obstacle hindering the progress of this incipient Muslim community in São Paulo, and a collection was organised with such success that César was able to start the first library in a favela in Brazil.

An abandoned space was rehabilitated and filled with shelves containing books not only on religion but on history, poetry and biographies of leading figures in the struggle for human rights. The space was named Zumaluma, a mixture of syllables combining the names of Zumbi dos Palmares[5], Malcolm-X, Martin Luther King and Nelson Mandela.

---

4   A *musallah* is a space for prayer. It derives from the Arabic verb "to pray", as it is used primarily for prayer in Islam.

5   Born in 1655, Zumbi dos Palmares was the main representative of black resis- tance to slavery in colonial Brazil. He is known as the last leader of Quilombo dos Palmares, a free community formed by fugitive slaves. Dos Palmares fought against Portuguese troops until his death in 1695, betrayed by a former slave.

The achievement of this milestone increased César's fame in the city, where he was already beginning to be known as the Muslim rapper. He tirelessly continued his work.

And several years of constant work and commitment bore bigger fruit. Zumaluma achieved success and recognition, luring lots of people for whom the *musalla*, a cubicle that barely held a dozen worshippers, soon became insufficient. It was during the search for a wider space that César's crowning achievement was born – the first mosque erected in the slums of São Paulo.

The mosque was named after Sumayyah bint El Khayyat, Islam's first female martyr. Among the first to embrace Islam, she was tortured to death in Makkah when she refused to leave the faith preached by Prophet Muhammad, peace be upon him.

César says he chose the name to show that the idea that women are oppressed in Islam is only a prejudice. "Muslim women are neither oppressed nor submissive. In addition, how is it possible for people to think that a veiled Christian woman is a saint, but if she is a Muslim, she is a terrorist?" he asks.

Established in the favela 'Cultura Física', where he was born and brought up, the mosque's construction was financed through international support and donations. César later built up a second floor where, until a few years ago, he lived with his wife and four children.

Wife's death

Like the rest of the world, 2020 was a devastating year for Brazil and for César due to Covid-19. He says the country's high population density and the insistent denial of President Jair Bolsonaro's government caused a high number of fatalities.

César's eyes get blurry as he remembers his Week of Sorrow during which he lost his wife —his loyal and loving companion for 37 years who accepted his conversion and embraced Islam herself – and his mother-in-law and his uncle.

Referring to her by an affectionate nickname, he points to a spot in the middle of the forest where the walls of a well can hardly be distinguished. In the absence of Muslim cemeteries in São Paulo, he built it, and fruit trees were planted as a tribute to her life.

On this occasion, César again found comfort in the life of Prophet Muhammad (PBUH), who lost his beloved wife Khadijah, and soon after that his uncle and guardian Abu Talib, in a year that was later named 'Year of Sorrow'.

"Our life as Muslims is a reflection of the life of the Prophet, everything we live and everything that happens to us, he has gone through a similar situation. The Prophet teaches us that life is a continuity, and we must accept the will of Allah with gratitude," he says.

There is an expression in Latin America that illustrates César's energy and enthusiasm - *Vida loca*. It refers to a hectic lifestyle, anxious to squeeze every moment to the maximum intensity, because in the most violent favelas, unfortunately, people don't know if they will wake up the next day.

In such an immense and unequal country as Brazil, where government institutions do not have any influence or even presence in the daily life of the country's most impoverished areas, Sumayyah Bint Khayyat's mosque not only serves as a place of prayer and *Dawah* — the dissemination of Islam — but it also houses a pharmacy and a medical centre. Food banks and basic services are offered for poor people, and it played a key role during the Covid-19 pandemic by distributing food and other essential items.

Islam in Brazil

Islam's first existence in Brazil dates back to the country's foundation by Portuguese colonisers, amongst whom were Moriscos. Moriscos were former Muslims and their descendants whom the Roman Catholic church and the Spanish Crown commanded to convert to Christianity or face compulsory exile after Spain outlawed the open practice of Islam by its sizeable Muslim population in the early 16th century.

However, numbers of Muslims dramatically increased in Brazil in the 18th century due to the importation of African Muslim slaves, who are still known as *malés* and who played a crucial role when they organised the first revolt against slavery called 'The Revolt of the Malés'.

"That uprising reveals the fighting spirit of Islam. We do live under a different system now, but if you are born in the favela, you have already lost. From this starting point, it depends on our strength to change that reality. Malcolm X's teachings were the first tool I found to understand a context in which social roles were so determined, in which Black people and *favelados* were the last pieces in a chain of power that oppressed us," says César. "It is in this background where God comes in as our only and real hope. The Islamic religion, because of its history based on the Prophet (PBUH), gives us the force, the capacity to aim for a change, to fight for a life less unequal where we all have a place."

Also, if the 9/11 events had prompted César to delve deep into Islam, he wasn't alone. The number of conversions to Islam increased visibly after 2001 in certain Muslim communities in Brazil, predominantly established by Arab immigrants from the Middle East who arrived in the 1970s.

Different factors were responsible for this phenomenon, which also includes the positive influence of the Brazilian soap opera 'El Clon' broadcast on television at the time, which portayed a positive image of an Arab family, although it was also crammed with stereotypes and clichés about Islam and Muslims. However, it presented Islam from a friendly and familiar point of view.

Simultaneous to the uplifting effect of the television series, the 9/11 attacks also brought Islam to the attention of Brazilian anti- capitalism movements who blamed the United States' economic model for causing fierce social injustice and stratification. César, in fact, sparked a controversy when he attended a live television interview wearing a T-shirt with a portrait of George W. Bush facing Osama Bin Laden and the slogan: Who are the terrorists?

An additional factor helping the spread of Islam was the surge of Internet. Although still very precarious and difficult to access in the poorest areas of Brazil, connectivity allowed an emerging democratisation of information and communications at a time when "if there were hardly any books in the favelas, imagine how difficult it was to find a Quran in Portuguese. It was a wild goose chase," César states.

César is particularly focused on youth. "Despite the fact that I am getting older, I have always felt very close to the youth. Time goes by but the situation remains the same. I feel that from my position I have the obligation to pass on what I have learned and, most importantly, to give them a tool to express themselves, to let the world know who they are and what do they have to contribute for a better society."

Some of his hip hop colleagues followed his example and converted to Islam. One of the fruits of his work was the conversion of Kareem Malik Abdul, a master of capoeira, a combination of dance and martial art created by African slaves during the slavery era in Brazil (1500-1888).

"There is a socio-cultural and political positioning that involves all aspects of life in Brazil, and that, of course, also affects religion.

We should not have to defend ourselves because we are human beings like everyone else. But part of my work has been and will be to break that shell, to continue to advocate for Islam as a unifying and humanitarian force, and to continue to advocate for faith as a transforming force for those who have nothing," César says.

13

The path to Islam via Marxism, atheism, evangelical Christianity, Catholicism, and Islamophobia

———◆◆◆◆◆———

Paul Williams – British vlogger and former civil servant

———◆◆◆◆◆———

Paul's journey to truth can be aptly described as an intellectual experience that stands out both for its erudition and precision; it was slow and winding, scholarly and rational, rather than sudden and emotional. He took his *shahadah* in Regent's Park Mosque in London, the same mosque he had once wished wasn't there.

ON A mundane day, Paul Williams walked into Regent's Park Mosque, London's biggest mosque, in measured, cautious steps, his mind aflutter with curiosity. Once an Islamophobe 'at heart', as he himself admits, he didn't like a mosque standing so majestically at Regent's Park, one of Lon- don's major parks. His Islamophobia wasn't surprising, consider- ing the sustained, systematic anti-Islamic fare being dished out by the mainstream media.

He walked through the front door without any warning, to talk to Muslims to find out if Islam really was the danger to Western civilisation and civilised values that he suspected it to be. "I know this sounds preposterous now but that's where I was at. And a lot of people are still in that position now," he says.

As soon as he entered, he was spotted like a fish out of water; he saw a bookshop inside and was immediately attracted by it. Someone went on to buy him some books and that helped. More intrigued, he started attending the Islamic circle on Saturdays which was founded by Yusuf Islam in 1977. Later, he even spoke there several times – non-Muslims could go and talk to people and engage with Muslims in debate to test each other's positions. "And I did push back against what I was being told; I was not totally accepting," he says.

Talking about the roots of his Islamophobia, Paul says: "As you know, I live here in Maida Vale and nearby is the famous Edgware Road which, over the years, became more Arabic. This phenomenon progressed more and more and for me that was problematic. For some reason, I then identified 'Arabic' with 'Islam' and of course that's naive because a lot of Lebanese are Christians but that kind of nuance didn't really occur to me. So, I became quite Islamophobic but not really publicly, rather privately in my mind."

It was his early enquiry period, and the mosque visit would later turn out to be a giant step in his relentless quest for truth.

Paul's journey to Islam can be aptly described as an intellectual experience that stands out both for its erudition and precision; it was slow and winding, scholarly and rational, rather than sudden and emotional. In other words, he experienced no 'Road to Damascus' moment that can grab a reader's attention when he converted in his mid-40s, and no dramatic, revelatory moment. If you meet this unassuming, bespectacled, 58-year-old White man in the street, this wouldn't surprise you in the least.

But there is a strikingly remarkable aspect to his journey – his winding path to Islam has traversed a large swathe, including Marxism, atheism, evangelical Christianity, Catholicism and Islamophobia, making the final discovery of truth an intellectually and spiritually fulfilling experience.

In all this, he was helped by his love of books which led him to a study of the Quran and the life of the Prophet Muhammad (PBUH), which did more than anything else to convince him of the truth.

An adopted child

Paul Williams was an adopted child who was brought up in a middle-class family in the town of Leigh-on-Sea by the coast in south east England. His family was nominally Christian but secular in practice, like so many British people these days. Religion was a topic that was rarely, if ever, discussed at home.

Growing up, Paul didn't even believe in God, but this was mainly down to ignorance rather than conviction because he had no knowledge about faith and hadn't even read the Bible. And those who know this intelligent man will be surprised to discover that he was a poor student who left school without any A levels, although, paradoxically, he was intensely interested in academic matters in his private time, as we shall discover.

At the age of 17, Paul left sleepy Leigh-on-Sea for the bright lights of London. Suddenly, he was exposed to people from all over the world and new ideas. And, in a life during which he would adopt many different ideologies, his first was Marxism. And, of course, the premise of Marxism is communism which is based on atheism.

But all that was to change when Paul had a spiritual experience in his early 20s. Out of curiosity, he popped into a local church and had what he calls a 'religious experience'. He struggles to put this into words, but says it was totally unexpected and he felt the 'love of God' very strongly.

This experience prompted a journey into Christianity which was to last decades. He read the Bible and sampled the Church of England, the main Protestant church of the United Kingdom which is the country's largest Christian denomination. But he couldn't relate to its stuffiness and so gravitated towards Evangelical Christianity which emphasises individual experiences of personal conversion, the authority of the Bible as God's revelation to humanity, and spreading the Christian message. In a nutshell, Evangelism was more friendly, welcoming, and had more fellowship than the Church of England. So, Paul became a born again Christian.

Almost overnight his world changed. He now felt he lived in a moral universe as opposed to a material one, and had been given a belief in God as a gift. The Bible became a precious item for him and his belief in the Almighty was profound. He eventually went onto study theology at the University of London before changing Christian denomination once more and becoming a Catholic – the world's largest Christian denomination and the UK's second biggest.

By now, Paul was in his early 30s and working as a civil servant, although he got no pleasure out of it. He was working to pay the billes and to live, he was bored stiff, but it was a necessary evil to finance the rest of his life, the part which fulfilled him.

"Remember I was a traditional Catholic - not like Pope Francis who is quite progressive and liberal in some aspects – but a conservative one. So, Islam was something to be feared as it was a competitor on the world stage and a competitor here in England, which it still is. And I thought it was a threat because Islam was obviously dangerous and potentially violent."

Yet there were some things about Christianity which just didn't satisfy Paul. He was aware that some of the most fundamental teachings of the Bible – such as the divinity of Jesus – were actually predicated on texts in the Gospel of John which is the last of the Gospels and the most ahistorical. He eventually came to believe that John was a "theologised" account of the life of Jesus; a second-generation interpretation of his teachings rather than a factual one.

Another issue for him was the clear implication in the Bible that the world would soon end. It was clear to him that the early Christians believed they were living in the end times, but the problem is the world didn't end. And issues such as these would soon incapacitate Paul's faith in Christianity, although his belief in God was undiminished.

Nevertheless, at this point in his life Paul had many of the same perceptions of Islam that an average Briton would have today, fuelled by ignorance and the propaganda of the mainstream media. Islam is violent; Islam oppresses women; Islam leads to terrorism. You get the picture. But even though Paul hadn't gone anywhere near a Quran or the life of the Prophet at this stage, he still had questions running through his head.

"I began to question," he says. "I said to myself maybe I should look into this thing called Islam because I knew the media could misrepresent faith because it misrepresented Christian views. So I decided I would get off my backside and talk to some Muslims." That's when he visited the mosque.

The 9/11 attacks had just happened and anti-Islam sentiment was at its height in the West. Paul says that, like most Brits, he still had misgivings about Islam but he spoke to Yusuf Islam and what he said reassured him. Paul was far from star struck at Yusuf Islam's celebrity, unlike many others, but he trusted him. And about a year and half later, when he was in his mid-40s, he testified that there is no God but God and Muhammad is His Messenger.

Shahadah in Regent's Park Mosque

Paul took his *shahadah* in Regent's Park Mosque, the same mosque he had once wished wasn't there. He already believed in the oneness of God and Muhammad as the seal of the prophets, but a simple ceremony in front of two witnesses officialised it. It wasn't a huge emotional thing, but he was glad to get it done.

"I must stress that my conversion to Islam is not interesting," he says. "It was purely internal. I didn't have any conversion experience like I did when I became a Christian - it was partly intellectual and partly spiritual but in a very quiet way which developed over time. People ask me about my conversion and I feel embarrassed because I don't have anything startling to say.

"I was given a copy of Yusuf Ali's translation of the Quran. I still have it. I still use it. It's very precious to me. I found his translation amazing - for all the reasons people don't like it, I liked it. He uses archaic English which is a problem for some people but because I love Shakespeare and I love poetry, it's lovely. Also the commentary – he references Shakespeare and Longfellow and other poets and for me that's a great point of connection between my own cultural past and Islam. Yusuf Ali was a man who inhabited both worlds. He lived in the UK and died here in London, destitute, which is an extraordinary scandal – that a man of such   phenomenal talents and genius should die in such circumstances. I still don't quite understand that. But I was so compelled by the meaning of the Quran and his commentary."

Another reason for conversion was discovering someone who, in the West, certainly in his early years, hardly anyone knew anything about. This unknown figure, called Muhammad (PBUH), he discovered principally through the biography by Martin Lings, titled *Muhammad: His Life Based on the Earliest Sources*.

Like Yusuf Ali, Paul considers Martin another master of the English language.

"The Prophet's life is just extraordinary - we talk about Alexander the Great in the West, who was undoubtedly a great man, the Macedonian general who conquered the world. But Muhammad's life is on another level entirely. He was, from a secular point of view, a genius. He was unsurpassingly brilliant as a general, as a father, as a statesman, as a prophet; in every area, he excelled. Alexander the Great was a great general, I concede, but so was Muhammad and many, many other things, too. There is this extraordinary multi-genius level and we know nothing about this individual in the West! He combined so many brilliances, so it was an incredible surprise. His life is extraordinary; even now it still impresses me hugely, but I understand now he was a prophet."

Paul also mentions Charles le Gai Eaton, a British diplomat, writer, historian, and Sufi scholar, as a major influence in his journey to Islam. He calls him the "grandfather of British Islam" and says his books *Islam and the Destiny of Man* and *Remembering God* helped him on his path. Gai Eaton had an extraordinary ability to communicate Islam to a western audience, Paul says.

Interestingly, Paul says conversion didn't bring about a dramatic change in his lifestyle because he was already leading an Islamic life in many ways.

He just continued as normal in terms of his personal behaviour (he jokingly says he wasn't a murderer or a fornicator anyway), but there were a few new things. He stopped drinking completely, and going to the pub, and now thinks drinking is like some alien thing other people do. Fasting was a challenge as well and because he didn't have a wife or children, he had to face it alone, whereas Ramadan is something most Muslims share with family.

Another change in Paul was his political perspectives. On issues such as the Arab-Israeli conflict, for example, he focused more on the Palestinian perspective. And he says that Islam helped him understand today's world better and he now has a deeper understanding of events which were simply missing from western discourse. However, while most of his non-Muslim friends were accepting of his conversion, not everybody was.

"I did still have Christian friends and I told them about my *shahada*. I remember one close Christian friend of mine, who is a very respected teacher of Religious Education in London, said to me - and we were close as friends – 'that's it Paul, I'll never speak to you again.' I was devastated because we shared a lot in common intellectually, and suddenly to be cut off like that because he found Islam unacceptable was quite a shock."

Paul's adoptive father had passed away at this point and he had lost touch with his sister. He didn't tell his mother that he'd converted and hasn't to this day. It's just not a conversation that they would have, says Paul, as she isn't the kind of person you would be comfortable having a conversation about religion with. She probably does know that he's a Muslim by now, but it's unlikely to ever be spoken about.

Later on, Paul would track down his biological mother through a detective agency. Believe it or not, she was a Christian missionary and his first conversation with her was when she was in the Zambian bush. She accepted that Paul was a Muslim even though she probably didn't like it, but she was happy to rediscover her son and wasn't about to let his 'Muslimness' get in the way of their reunion. Paul would go onto have a good relationship with her, which he is grateful for, until she died a few years ago from brain cancer.

YouTube channel: Blogging Theology

Paul's quest didn't end with his conversion, and continued at a higher level. He believes truth is too precious to be kept hidden inside one's heart; its beauty and value lie in disseminating it for the benefit of those who may not have undertaken the same journey for whatever reasons.

He started a YouTube channel called 'Blogging Theology', both to learn and teach, which has since become a hit.

In fact, Paul is far more comfortable talking about his work than about himself, and given the success of 'Blogging Theology', he's got a lot to be proud about. Since it began in November 2020, it has racked up millions of views and has over 174,000 subscribers. He's also making an impact on Twitter with around 105,000 followers and counting. And his viral 'No Design' memes on Twitter have targeted hard-core atheism in a uniquely visceral way.

"Most atheists are not like the author Richard Dawkins, they don't adhere to a hardcore position," he says. "They have a lively faith in the afterlife, in angels, jinn or demons. So, I'm very careful when I use this term to describe people… Real atheism is a mental illness, a spiritual sickness, it needs to be treated and cured. If you don't appreciate the faith that should naturally come from the soul then something has gone wrong. It's not normative, it's a disorder. Atheism is a problem and belief is the cure."

But recently it is his campaign against hard-core atheism on Twitter that has made waves. It's now one of the main things he is associated with, which is ironic because it's one of the only polemical things he has done.

"This started with me just posting a few things on Twitter which turned into the hashtag 'No Design', and the meme with two eyes looking up which is my way of saying: What do you mean the world is not designed? Of course, it's designed! And accompanied underneath the eyes there are some extraordinary pictures of God's creation. And what's particularly great these days with photography, you get the most extraordinary clear, detailed photographs from the most obscure places on the planet and there's an abundance of such images.

"So, the point is instead of going with a frontal attack against an atheist and saying: 'you *kaafir*, you disbeliever' which doesn't always work, I simply demonstrate in a very Quranic way the signs of God's creation in both the verses of the Quran and the universe itself, which are signs pointing to the Creator. This does two things - it reminds atheists of these very obvious signs and the createdness of the universe, if they would but see it, but also it boosts the *iman* (faith) of Muslims. We are marvelling at God's creation, but it's also a way of vividly refuting the idea that this universe is without purpose, without design and without meaning or direction and intelligence in any way. This is about engaging the *fitra* of atheists – their natural sense of right and wrong – but ultimately, it's up to God, He is the One who turns hearts, but at least there is this constant invitation to reflect."

Atheism in Britain

Polls have demonstrated that Great Britain is one of the most atheistic places on earth. In 2019, the British Social Attitudes Survey found that the number of people who didn't believe in God had more than doubled compared to the past two decades.

Twenty-six per cent of Brits said that they didn't believe in God, 18 percent were agnostic, and only 19 percent of the public was absolutely certain of God's existence. The survey also highlighted a continued religious decline in Britain - 52 percent of people said they didn't belong to a religion, up from 31 percent in 1983 when the survey was first carried out. And whereas religious affiliation had slightly grown across some non-Christian religions, it had decreased across most Christian denominations. The sharpest drop occurred within the Church of England.

But Paul begs to differ with the notion that Britain is on an inexorable slope towards ungodliness. He says studies have shown that hard-core atheism is in fact very rare, and people who describe themselves as atheists believe in the supernatural, or life after death, or angels and demons.

"Most people in Britain right now are not affiliated to any official religion but that's far from saying they are atheists; they could have unofficial spiritual awareness which is not categorisable in any doctrinal form. So, we are not talking about real atheism, we are talking about the secularisation of religion into the private realm because churches have failed and are failing catastrophically in the entire West of Europe and in America too now. Eastern Europe and Russia are very different though.

"This is a big opportunity for Muslims, because many people are already halfway there, many already believe much of what Muslims believe so I wouldn't call them atheists. Real atheists are a tiny minority in the population and other research has shown they are declining globally in percentage. It's true that secularism is growing, but actual hard-core atheism isn't."

Paul speaks about the circumstances that led to starting his 'Blogging Theology' channel.

"Covid was the context in November 2020 we found ourselves in in Great Britain," he explains. "We were in a state of severe lockdown: I remember walking through the streets of the West End of London and it was like a post-apocalyptic scene; there were no human beings. It was unbelievable. Like many people, I was at home on my own a lot and I also had a bit of money so I bought the latest MacBook Pro. This was the start of my tech journey."

At the time, Paul wasn't really a public person apart from a little notoriety at Speakers' Corner in Hyde Park, London - a traditional site for public speeches and debates since the mid 1800s. Speakers' Corner has become world famous and there is a considerable audience for the debates, mainly between Christians and Muslims, which take place there.

Paul used to visit Speakers' Corner to engage Christians in debate about who Jesus was, about the Bible, and about topics such as salvation. And he says he had some genuinely illuminating conversations there, especially when the cameras weren't rolling. But, he adds, the advent of smartphones has changed the dynamic with many people playing up to the cameras. Paul says Speakers' Corner has now become a toxic place with a lot of aggression and shouting – the antithesis of what he is all about.

"So, apart from a little engagement at Speakers' Corner as a Muslim, I wasn't really in the limelight. My way of communicating with the world was to make a video or two, do a book review, or give my opinion on Christianity, so I started this channel called 'Blogging Theology'. In the first few weeks I got ten or 20 subscribers and I thought 'cool'. Then, in January 2021, something changed - the stats and subscriptions went viral; in fact, that's an understatement. Suddenly I found myself acquiring two to three thousand subscribers every 48 hours. All organic, no advertising. And this went on for weeks and months. Someone then said to me 'you've got to monetise this' and I didn't even know what that meant or that I could make money out of it."

"At the time my success was a great mystery," he says. "I thought to myself: 'what's happening here, because I wasn't looking for this but it was happening anyway and I have no plan, trajectory or agenda at all?' A friend of mine - a doctor here in London - said 'what's your unique selling point?' He then listed them and, embarrassingly, one of them was being a white Muslim. So, I had to kind of swallow my pride a bit because I know that's one of the reasons, even if it's not the only one. It was an eye opener."

But White privilege only goes so far - the content still has to be great, otherwise people won't keep watching and new people won't keep joining. And a cursory glance at 'Blogging Theology' and its prolific, diverse, and educational output would leave one in no doubt about the effort which has gone into its production. "I think what people like is that I invite some very high level people onto the channel, experts in their field from various universities in the world to teach me as a viewer (because I see myself as a viewer) about their given area of expertise. I do engage them in conversation but I'm not there to interrogate them or refute them or do *daw'ah* to them if they're not Muslim, not directly anyway. So, it's a safe space for these people to come on and share their expertise."

Some of his most high-profile guests have included Sheikh Abdul Hakim Murad from the University of Cambridge, the Muslim public speaker Hamza Tzortzis, and Professor Jonathan Brown from the Yaqeen Institute in the USA. The format is usually a Q&A, with Paul letting his guests speak at length without too much interruption. He wouldn't call it highbrow, he says, but viewers will have a learning experience. Recent videos have included a four-hour long interview on how Muslims should deal with LGBTQ issues, which he says should have sunk but went viral. Other videos include a discussion on the concept of the caliphate in Islam and the French presidential elections.

The content of 'Blogging Theology' is mainly academic with a sprinkling of politics. The situation in France – where Muslim organisations are being shut down – particularly irks him as he lives in the country for part of the year. Most of his guests are Muslims and the second highest number would be Christians. Paul says he hasn't invited on enough Jewish guests and when he does so he avoids conversations about Palestine-Israel. He says he has very strong views on that issue, but so would his Jewish guests and he doesn't want the conversation to 'crash and burn'.

God is absolutely in control

How does Paul see the future of Islam and Muslims in the UK?

"My fundamental view is that I am extremely optimistic about the future. Why? Because it's an article of faith, it's there in our Aqeedah – God is absolutely in control and nothing happens outside of His will. So, what's there to worry about? We are not living in a chaotic universe that is beyond the control of the Creator. In some way that I cannot perceive, His purpose and will is unfolding through history and whatever injustices remain in our current situation will be addressed on the Day of Judgement when all wrongs will be righted and justice will be done. So, on a macro level, I'm not worried at all because I know He is in control, but, on a micro level, of course I am human and there are things I worry and stress about. But Islam is an optimistic faith, the Prophet taught us to be hopeful and optimistic, but don't ask me to make sense of this because things are looking very bad on another level as well."

Finally, what would Paul say to his non-Muslim previous self, the Islamophobe, the atheist, the man he has long since left behind, but who still exists in great numbers in the UK?

"To the non-Muslims who don't like all these mosques being built,

I say go back to churches, fill them up again and go and have babies. If you really are that concerned, make the alternative happen. But you can't not go to church and then complain about the decline of Christianity; you can't not have babies and then complain about the shrinking indigenous White population. Most of the Muslims I talk to are very happy to see a vibrant Christian faith in this country because some religion is better than none. These are People of the Book after all. This is preferable to secularism, but I don't think it's going to happen. I think we are going to find that Muslims will be the only group left in Europe in a pretty short time who witness to Abrahamic faith in its purity. The pulse of monotheism has moved from the Judeo-Christian realm to the Islamic realm and, in Europe, the only people that have that faith publicly expressed in its purity are Muslims.

"So, the role of Muslims in Europe in the future is to bear witness to the Abrahamic faith in terms of the purity of *tawhid* and morally; bearing witness to forms of life which are wholesome and godly and that will hopefully attract the rest of the population who have lost faith. Islam is the faith of Abraham, although Muhammad is the seal of the prophets. But there are a whole host of prophets, most of whom Christians accept, so they will be bearing witness to their own prophets, and Muslims are reminding them of what they have lost."

14

'If I hadn't entered Islam at that time, I would have probably gone mad'

———◆◆◆◆◆◆———

Professor Ahmed Paul Keeler – University of Cambridge, Britain

———◆◆◆◆◆◆———

During preparations for the World Festival of Islam, Professor Ahmed Keeler had access to some of the greatest Muslim scholars, artists and musicians on the planet. And it was by sharing food with them and by becoming their friends that he experienced Islam first-hand and, as he puts it, he "had no alternative but to become Muslim."

ACOMBINATION of personal and professional failures led to Ahmed Paul Keeler suffering a nervous breakdown in the late 1980s and his subsequent admittance to amental asylum.

Later, writing in his autobiography, Keeler says the power of prayer saw him through this turbulent and traumatic period.

He writes: "In the wreckage that my life had become the only thing that preserved me were my prayers which I performed on time. That was all I had left which sustained me and gave me comfort."

Prof. Keeler's journey is an inspiration for everyone navigating through the tortuous terrain of life.

World Festival of Islam in 1976

Paul Keeler is best known for organising the World Festival of Islam in 1976 - perhaps the most significant cultural event on Islam ever held in the West. In the spring of that year, Queen Elizabeth II opened the festival in London. Thirty-two Muslim nations accumulated 6,000 objects of art from 250 public and private collections in 30 different countries. One hundred and sixty-two lectures on different aspects of Islamic culture were organised, as well as 50 days of academic seminars involving scores of world-renowned scholars.

Institutes involved included the world-famous British Museum and British Library, the Victoria and Albert Museum, the Hayward Gallery, the Science Museum, and many more. Aside from London, British cities such as Manchester, Sheffield and Durham took part in the festival, as did the universities of Oxford and Cambridge. And the BBC made a well-received film series.

Six months before the festival opened, Paul became a Muslim at the age of 33 and took the name "Ahmed." A year later his wife, Annabel, would embrace Islam too.

Unlike today, at the time not much was known about Islam in the West. Given the tumultuous political events of the last few decades – such as 9/11 and the Western invasions and occupations of Iraq and Afghanistan, as well as the huge mainstream media coverage of Islam and Muslims (mainly negative) – everyone seems to have an opinion on the subject. But back in 1976 Islam was not considered to be the threat and challenge to the West that it is today. The Islamic world was just emerging from centuries of European colonisation and subjugation, and Muslim minorities in the West had yet to gain the confidence to express themselves fully as citizens.

"No one knew anything about Islam then," Paul says. "In people's minds it was the Arabs, the Turks and the Persians, not Islamic civilisation. There were four years of preparation for the festival. During that time, I had access to everything - all the scholars, the artists, I was completely surrounded by *Dar al Islam* (House of Islam).

"There was a huge investment in the festival by British institutions and the Gulf countries which topped the money up so that we could do something really special. It was so educational; it was a miracle. It was seeing the world of Islam directly, not just through the eyes of the West. My whole idea was to see the world of Islam through the Islamic perspective, the Islamic aesthetic. We were seeking to understand the civilisation in its own terms. The whole festival was unique. The main exhibition was three months, but some of it went on for a year and a half.

"The people who I became very close to during the festival and the preparations for it were the Muslim scholars and academics Titus Burkhardt, Syed Hossein Nasr, Yusuf Ibish and Sidi Ismail. I had reached that point where all my friends, all my interests, all my love in terms of the arts and the culture that I was promoting was to be found in the world of Islam. So, if

I hadn't entered Islam at that time, I would have probably gone mad. It just happened naturally - I was with these friends when I entered Islam in London.

"In those days it wasn't such a big issue if you converted to Islam. The memory of the Crusades was a long time ago and there was even a sort of romanticism to it. Of course, there was the 'Pakistani-bashing' which was going on in the UK at the time and the mass immigration controversy which had begun to bubble, but it wasn't associated with Islam. It was a race thing rather than about religion.

"There are many ways into Islam. There are people from road sweepers to aristocrats who come into Islam. Old and young.   I love the Muslim community in this country, so many people have come from the subcontinent and I've met so many beautiful people. Now, where I live in Cambridge, I'm meeting so many Muslim students and they are morally intact, the community here is very beautiful."

Food, friendship and beauty

Paul Keeler said he entered Islam through "food, friendship and beauty." At that point he hadn't even read the Quran or studied the life of the Prophet Muhammad (PBUH) in depth – two of the more common ways non-Muslims enter Islam. Yet, over a seven- year-period when he was organising the World Festival of Islam, he had become convinced of the truth of this religion simply by being around Muslims and Islamic culture.

During preparations for the World Festival of Islam, Keeler had access to some of the greatest Muslim scholars, artists and musicians on the planet. And it was by sharing food with them and by becoming their friends that he experienced Islam first-hand and, as he puts it, he "had no alternative but to become Muslim."

He says: "I was promoting the world of Islam through the festival and it got to the point where if I hadn't entered Islam at that time, I would have probably gone mad. So, it just happened naturally. I was with these friends I had made when I entered Islam in London and, unlike many other converts, I had no major misgivings about Islam before I converted. I hadn't even read the Quran or studied the life of the Prophet.

"I came to Islam because I just loved that world. It all made sense to me. And I also saw the modern world for what it was – corrupted and out of balance. I saw modern art and culture, in particular, as something which was so full of angst and chaos and when I compared that to the world of Islam it was the opposite. I was just so in love with Islamic culture."

And in the 47 years since he converted, and through the many trials and tribulations of his life, the beauty and balance that he discovered in Islam in the 1970s has cemented in his mind whilst the chaos that the modern Western lifestyle represents has increased.

Early years

Ahmed Paul Keeler was born in 1942 and grew up in an affluent family in Windsor, near London, in the post war period. As a child, he was deeply in love with the Anglican church (Britain's main form of Protestant Christianity) and its rituals, as well as the stories of the prophets in the Bible, especially Jesus. He took it for granted that God existed and it was assumed that he would become a priest in the Church of England. But his later schooling taught him to love music, theatre and acting, which made him forget any thoughts of the priesthood.

At the age of ten, he was sent off to an austere English boarding school which prepared its pupils to effectively rule the British Empire (which at one point ruled a third of the whole world).

Pupils were given the sense that it was something special to be an Englishman; they were the great civilisers of the world, the conquerors and innovators. They were taught a sense of superiority and responsibility – it was the White man's burden to benefit the world. After all, Britain had just won the Second World War. Little did they know that Britain would be burdened by the debts accrued during the war, forcing them to relinquish their great empire and their preeminent position in the world.

At the age of 18, Paul had his first experience of the Muslim world when he took a trip across Europe to Turkey with a friend. This was the period when the Arab-Israeli conflict was raging and Paul distinctly remembers being on the side of the Israelis at the time. He also says that he would have been on the side of the Christians during the Crusades.

"I went there with a schoolfriend after we left school," he says. "And I sent back postcards to my parents as we went along the journey. I remember saying the most wonderful things about the Turks and about how they were such lovely people, but it's a pity they have this stupid religion - Islam. Of course, that was coming from pure ignorance and our education which considered Christianity superior and Islam backwards."

Soon after finishing school, Paul opened an art gallery in London with major financial backing from his wealthy father. The 1960s was a period when the West was questioning the traditional foundations of its society, which was based on Christianity and Empire. Modernity was taking over and Britain's history and role in the world was being questioned. Paul felt that he had been lied to by his teachers, and re-educated himself about political events like the Vietnam War (which was deeply unpopular amongst the Western masses) and, eventually, Islam.

A counterculture was emerging and Paul Keeler was living it; he even grew his hair long and became a hippie. He also set up a commune in his house which the police eventually closed down on trumped-up drugs charges. This led to a court case, and he was eventually acquitted. Meanwhile, his art gallery business had failed and he was in huge debt. His father refused to continue bankrolling a lost financial cause and Paul experienced the failure keenly – for the only time in his life he even contemplated suicide.

It was around the time of this lowest ebb that the turning point in Paul Keeler's life came - he met the Indian musician Mahmud Mirza who became his door to Islam. It was Mirza who introduced him to the world of Islamic culture where architecture, art, literature and music exists to glorify God.

Ustad Mahmud Mirza

As he writes in his book *Reflections of an English Muslim*: "Ustad Mahmud Mirza rescued me from the chaos of the sixties and set me on my life's quest. I was introduced to a master musician who came from a tradition that had flourished in the Muslim courts of Northern India for more than half a millennium and was still fully alive. The form was a perfect example of Mizan where the balance between the various notes of the Raga had to be maintained until their final resolution, bringing about a profound state of peace…

"I had not been seeking a religion. It was through the masters of the traditional arts that my soul had been opened to the beauty, truth and goodness of Islam. The first of these traditional masters was Ustad Mahmud Mirza, who, through his music, revealed to me the oceanic depth of a living tradition, compared to which the modern forms of art that I had been immersed in during the sixties were like stagnant pools. For nearly fifty years I have witnessed the glorious unfolding of Mahmud's music, as he remained true to his tradition, when all around him was being transformed into a frenzied, celebrity-driven form of entertainment."

Paul Keeler expands on these thoughts when he tells us: "I was introduced to Islam through the traditional arts. North Indian classical music is the music of the Mughal courts; this is highly sophisticated and the most refined court music. It is a Muslim art form. The Hindus of course have claimed it now and Ravi Shankar has become its most famous exponent, but even he learned it from a Muslim. It perfectly manifests the Muslim aesthetic - it's perfect, it's an incredible form. I believe it's the highest form of music and I had the privilege of meeting a master who became my friend.

"So how did I come into Islam? To begin with it was Mahmud and the music. He started quietly introducing me to the world of Islam in terms of its culture. He never pushed me to convert, which these masters don't. As a man he was normal, but someone who had a deep character and who wasn't going to be corrupted by what happened to Indian music which has been totally commercialised. This is a contemplative form, there is no ego in it. The masters know where it comes from [from God]."

Paul adds that Mahmud Mirza had a stabilising effect on his turbulent life. "He wanted me to get back to normality. So, I got my hair cut and I started to behave normally. I got back with my family, mended my relationship with my parents. My life was like a stormy sea and he took me off the ship and put me on solid ground. And this was the world of Islam which is what he inhabits. In Islam, the great sheikhs are ordinary people, they could be shoemakers. So that year (1966) was just wonderful because I began to organise his concerts. I was experiencing something completely new. It was a new world that was opening up step by step."

Series of professional failures

The World Festival of Islam was undoubtedly the highlight of Paul Keeler's working life but, surprisingly, what was to follow were a series of repeated professional failures. His attempts at mounting further festivals on Islam to rival the World Festival failed, as did other professional projects. In part this was probably because Islam had begun to get a bad name in the mainstream media and the funding for positive projects on Islam had dried up. Consequently, Paul began to experience many financial difficulties and, in 1997, was declared bankrupt.

From a spiritual point of view, he also experienced disappointments. Not because of Islam, but because of some of the people who professed to practise it. He eventually realised that a Sufi group that he had gotten involved with was in fact a cult whose senior members held esoteric beliefs incompatible with mainstream Islam. And it was a combination of these personal and professional failures which led to a nervous breakdown in the late 1980s and his subsequent admittance to a mental asylum.

In his autobiography he writes: "In the wreckage that my life had become the only thing that preserved me were my prayers which I performed on time. That was all I had left which sustained me and gave me comfort. In time my manic state dissipated but depression settled in. I became acutely aware of

the incredibly narrow band of normality allowed in our modern secular world. When the reality of the spiritual realm is nullified, the soul is severely restricted and terrible suffering ensues. The vastness of the soul that can encompass the ecstasy of inspiration and illumination, and suffer the terrors of the dark night of the soul, is denied, and such experiences are turned into pathologies." Eventually, Paul recovered. The years passed by and, at the age of 70, when he and his family had moved to the university town of Cambridge, he considered himself a failure on all fronts, although those close to him certainly did not. But then he began to write for the first time in his life, at the urging of a friend, even though he felt no particular aptitude for it. And through his writing he started to make sense of his life and realised why even his many failures were part of the bigger picture.

"My friends told me 'you have not failed because your projects have engaged so many people, you have brought so many people together and your ideas have percolated to so many people and they have affected their lives.' The 1976 festival was of huge importance to the whole generation which came after and this is not something I was aware of. So, what became clear to me was that Almighty Allah had taken me on a path and these projects had to fail.

"The last ten years have been wonderful because, when I was 70, I genuinely believed I was a failure. In many ways the last ten years have been the happiest years of my life. I had no thought of writing but a friend forced me into it. This led to a lecture series on something called the Mizan Thesis which I had developed and then all the pieces fell into place, and I realised that all these projects that had failed provided me with a piece of the puzzle which ended up here."

Central to Paul's thought now is an idea he has developed from Islam called the 'Mizan Thesis'. In a nutshell, this is a comparison between the West and the Islamic world which concludes that the West has become out of balance with man's natural nature whereas Islam holds the keys to a world which is at ease with itself. "In the West you have the Christian world, the civilised world and the modern world. Whereas Islam is one civilisation. In the West you have extreme spirituality with cathedrals trying to reach the sky; you have extreme civilisation with humanism where the human being becomes everything; and then you have extreme materialism. And the problem we have is that in the West these three worlds are constantly at war with each other. On the other hand, in Islam they are integrated into one world. Why? Because the Prophet was the warrior, was the great man of knowledge and came from a merchant community.

"The amazing thing about Islam compared to other great civilisations like Rome was that Rome was held together by politics but when the empire collapsed Roman civilisation collapsed. Islamic civilisation had hundreds of dynasties which came and went, but what maintained was the structure of the world of the sharia, the culture and the art. The Mizan was a situation when everything was in balance.

"The *mizan* principle is a universal principle. If things are not in balance that means they are out of order. If that tiny thing in your ear goes wrong you can't stand up; the same if your organs start going wrong or if your mind is unbalanced. Everything is regulated by this balance. Human beings have an innate understanding of scale and we know if something is out of scale; everything in nature has its scale and everything in human existence is subject to mizan and justice. If justice is broken there is disorder. The *mizan* is most perfectly manifested in Islam. Through *mizan* you can understand why we have arrived at this point of chaos and crisis in the modern world – through the breaking of the balance. By abandoning the concept of progress and returning to the *mizan*, you can see the world afresh."

That said, through his extensive travels through the Muslim world, Paul also realises that the Muslim world itself has been affected by Western modernity and has itself gone out of balance. "Through travel I have experienced a great change in the Muslim world. What has saddened me is how it is all becoming the same place - the same airport, the same hotel, the same food in the hotels. I went to Makkah when the old city was still there but now they have buildings which are taller than the Kaaba. That said, there are many places in the Muslim world which still exist and retain their individuality while being part on Islamic civlisation."

Pilgrimage to Makkah

Shortly after he converted, Paul would make the pilgrimage to Makkah which is incumbent on every Muslim who is physically and financially able to do so once in their lifetimes. As he explains in his book *A Life's Journey*, the pilgrimage had a profound impact on the new Muslim.

First of all, as someone who came from a society riven by racial, class and nationalist prejudices, he was deeply affected by the universality of Islamic civilisation, where all races and the rich and poor were equal before God. This forced his prejudices to melt way. He also describes the profound emotions of seeing the House of God – the Kaaba – for the first time.

"We approached the Kaaba. Nothing had prepared me for this moment. It was as if I had never seen it before, and yet I had seen it in hundreds of photographs and films. As the pilgrimage unfolded so the presence of the Kaaba increased. The culmination of our visit was reached when we were allowed to enter the sacred edifice and pray in any direction. I felt certain then that this was the sacred centre of our world."

As for other details of Paul's own spiritual and private life, he is more reluctant to expand. He says that he is essentially a private person and those details are for him alone and God. This seems to be in harmony with the Islamic ideal – we have no need to put our entire lives on social media and our successes and failures need not be shared by the whole world. So, at the age of 80, Ahmed Paul Keeler seems more in balance now than at any time of his life, having put all the pieces of the puzzle together.

Perhaps he has attained Mizan.

15

'My road from Rome to Makkah'

—•♦♦♦♦•—

Dr Sabrina Lei – Italian philosopher and author

—•♦♦♦♦•—

Dr Sabrina Lei was no ordinary seeker. An author, philosopher and scholar, her story stands out for a simple reason: the wide spectrum of her intellectual pursuits, which lend a certain poignancy, depth and intensity to her spiritual journey that's seldom seen in others.

URING Ramadan of 2009, Dr Sabrina Lei woke up in the wee
hours at her home in Rome in Italy for *suhoor*, the pre-dawn meal Muslims
take before fasting. She wasn't a Muslim yet, but that didn't diminish her
fervour. She was on a journey of self-discovery, an exploration of her spiritual
self that demanded answers to deeper questions about the purpose of life
and death.

As the long day wore on, she felt the pangs of fatigue, but a quiet
transformation was underway within her. She visited local mosques and felt
an intense calm; observed the faithful performing Friday and other prayers.
She didn't participate in the prayers, but participated in the joy of those who
experienced the certainty of faith. She spent the day reading and exploring
matters of faith and philosophy.

Not only did she fast during that Ramadan, but during two previous
Ramadan.

Why would a seeker fast for three consecutive years before conversion,
a religious obligation which is considered one of the toughest among all
Islamic practices?

But then Dr Sabrina Lei was no ordinary seeker. An Italian author,
philosopher and scholar, her story stands out for a simple reason: the wide
spectrum of her intellectual pursuits, which lend a certain poignancy, depth
and intensity to her spiritual journey that's seldom seen in others. She is
deeply interested in philosophy, history, European classical languages, and
literature, and most notably she is an expert in two European languages –
classical Latin and Greek. Through these languages, she mastered ancient
Greek and Latin philosophy, and was trained in Biblical studies.

So, she approached Islam from multiple angles, with the precision of an
alchemist, applying rigorous methodologies of philosophy and comparative
studies – more like an academic experiment than a religious exploration
which gave a certainty and uniqueness to her findings.

Dr Sabrina prefers to call her journey, and aptly too, 'My Road from Rome to Makkah'. The eloquent symbolism won't be missed – it's the journey from the spiritual centre of one religion to that of another.

Roots in southern Italian nobility

Dr Sabrina, who now lives in Rome, was born in 1977 in Latina, the capital of Lazio province in central Italy. Her family, which has roots in southern Italian nobility, was of Catholic origin, and some of her ancestors served the Roman Catholic Church as high-ranking officials; however, the influence of religion in the family started waning, in keeping with a general dwindling of religious faith in the country in the post-Second World War era.

"My parents, though morally and ethically upright, have never been religious in its traditional sense. In spite of this, from childhood, I felt very religious and spiritual; however, though I revered Jesus from the bottom of my heart, I did not worship him or perceive him to be God. A pristine faith in one God dwelt in my heart, and remained etched there at very a young age," she says, pointing out the central reason that led her to Islam.

It was an innate, inborn longing to worship only one God. She believes this must have helped her grasp the monotheistic creed (*tawhid*) taught by Islam, which she encountered many years later.

When she was eight, her parents arranged regular private tuition for her in Latin and Greek. In addition, she also studied Greek and Latin philosophy. During those years, she also received training in Biblical studies and its interpretation, and all of these studies gave her a thorough grounding in the religious, cultural, literary and historical foundations of Europe in a fairly good way, giving her the intellectual and linguistic tools to interpret the works of some of the best Greek and Latin philosophers such as Plato, Aristotle, Homer, and so on.

Later, she translated some of the surviving poems of two of the sixth-century BC Greek poets, Alcaeus of Mytilene and Sappho, into Italian and won a number of regional and national prizes instituted for young classicists. She also studied French, German and English literature and some of the classic works in these languages in their Italian translations. While doing an MA in philosophy, she specialised in the philosophy of Ludwig Wittgenstein from Sapienza University of Rome, one of the oldest European universities founded in 1303, later obtaining a PhD in ancient Greek philosophy from a noted Vatican-affiliated university.

With such an erudite background, the religious issues she grappled with weren't new, as she had already addressed them as a philosophy student. If at all, her knowledge of philosophy helped her delve deep into Islamic philosophy; the comparisons were easy and, when she found the answers, she was able to test their authenticity and purity against the rigorous standards of philosophy.

So, how did it all begin?

Her interactions with Muslims as a child and adult weren't sufficient enough to spark any curiosity about their faith. In fact, she didn't have significant interaction with Muslims; one of her first distinct memories in this regard was seeing a large number of Arab immigrants, perhaps from Morocco, offering Friday prayers by the side of a public square in Latina. She was 12 or 13 years old, and she didn't feel anything strange or unnatural.

She also remembers an Arab Muslim family, neighbours in Latina she interacted with very respectfully. "I was able to discern certain attractive personal and spiritual rhythms in the life of this family," she reminisces.

Dr Sabrina considers her impression of Islam before her journey to be neutral, not coloured by the virulent Islamophobia that existed in the West. This was due to her own psychological openness to diverse cultures and religions, and also, as a person deeply interested in philosophy, she knew religions from their first sources rather than extraneous elements, and was easily able to see through the connivances and machinations of the media.

Balance between piety and practice

She started studying Islam seriously after the completion of her PhD in 2006; it was not a process that she started with an intension of leaving Catholicism and embracing Islam, but rather an unconscious journey while she was still a practising Roman Catholic.

"Christianity, of course, offered me certain valid ethical and moral principles. The Catholic priests and nuns who taught me were devoted and sincere; however, I gradually felt the pressing urge for finding a path that could show me how to lead my life in its fullness by adequately responding to the longings of my body and soul," she says.

"I studied Christianity, its history, theology, its holy books, very thoroughly. This study almost impelled me to search for a way of life that was more genuinely rooted in the messages of all prophets mentioned in the Bible. And, without being completely aware of it, I was searching for a deeper relation with God, without any intermediary figures presiding over my relation with Him, and to find a direct way of worshipping Him alone, as worshiping God alone had been part of my own religious consciousness, even at the early years of my life."

So, this irresistible urge to pray to one God, and find a faith that encapsulated the messages of all prophets mentioned in the Bible, was the primary reason that led her to Islam. For her, Islam was the only universal religion that contained within its essence the messages of all true Biblical Prophets, especially the pure and unadulterated monotheistic faith taught by Abraham, the central figure in Islam, Christianity and Judaism.

She felt a connection. Over the years, as she delved deep into the Quran, the life of the Prophet (peace be upon him), Islamic history, Islamic philosophy and Islam's popularly unacknowledged contributions to the West's own scientific, cultural and civilizational awakenings, she arrived at the realisation that Islam had always been part of her deeper self and was not an alien philosophy.

Another factor was the balance she found in the religion, a balance between piety and practice, which doesn't confine one to a world of solitude and renunciation. "I encountered a way of life that could help me to achieve the balance between life in this world and the hereafter. My sincere belief is that Islam has taught me that achieving such a balance is possible. I also found, after years of these studies, this religion consoled my deeper self which had an unconscious resistance to worshipping anything other than God even when I was a practising Catholic," Dr Sabrina explains.

Among the books that influenced her was South Asian poet- philosopher Muhammad Iqbal's philosophical masterpiece *The Reconstruction of Religious Thought in Islam*. She later translated the book into Italian, and over the years, this translation has been widely read and accepted as a modern Muslim philosophical classic by academics and scholars in Italy.

Dr Sabrina explains that Iqbal's approach to religion and philosophical thoughts was very fascinating. He did not see any fundamental conflict between Western thought and some of the key philosophical teachings of

Islam, and presented Islam as a dynamic force that uplifts both individuals and the society to a higher and refined religious, social and political sphere through its faith and institutions. Iqbal argued that Islam bridges the gap between the genuine spiritual and material longings of human self and offers a way of life and thought process in which there is no conflict between our life in this world and the one to come in the hereafter.

The book enhanced her interest in Islam. Later, she read biographies of Prophet Muhammad (PBUH) written by both Muslim and non-Muslim writers, along with various translations of the Quran. She closely studied Sahih Al-Bukhari and Sahih Muslim, which are the sayings of the prophet, and also the works of classical and modern scholars of Islam, as well as delving deep into Islamic history and culture.

However, her studies of the Quran and the Hadith of the Prophet opened a new world of knowledge.

She learned more from the Quran than an average Westerner.
There is a reason.

Her deeper engagement with the holy book started after getting a fairly good insight into Islam, its history, its worldview, its civilisation, etc. This early intellectual engagement had given her certain solid ideas about the Quran, like the history of its revelation, its content and style, etc. In other words, as she began to study the Quran, she already had preliminary insights into the holy book. Many Westerners tend to approach the holy book in the light of their experiences with the Old Testament and Christian Bible; both of which, in their current form, in spite their original status as divine revelations, are very different from the Quran.

Dr Sabrina explains that the Jewish and Christian scriptures, in varying degrees, are narrational, linear and biographical in their style, mainly recapturing the histories and legends of their communities and prophets, though the Old Testament has books of law and wisdom within its purview. The Quran, however, in its contents, literary style, arrangements and length of its chapters, verses and the diverse ways in which certain crucial themes are presented, stressed and repeated, comes across as a very unique book of revelation; in short, the Quran is *sui generis*.

So, obviously, when Westerners of Judeo-Christian affiliation approach the Quran, expecting to find the familiar style of their scriptures in it, especially without any overall understanding of the nature of the Prophet's mission and the history of the revelation, they find it daunting to understand its message. Also, the image of the Quran as an incomprehensible book, created and projected by a very dominant section of polemical Orientalists, also plays a very negative role in creating the barrier between an average Westerner and this holy book.

There were other factors.

Muhammad Iqbal's insight

The most attractive and inspiring fact about the Quran, she says, is the way it presents Allah. "A clue to this special aspect I got from Muhammad Iqbal's observation in his book where he says, 'The main purpose of the Quran is to awaken in man the higher consciousness of his manifold relations with God and the universe'. In fact, Muhammad Iqbal offers some very original reflections on the theme of the Quran, especially the way he presents God, connecting God, man and universe, along the concept of destiny, the nature of the time, etc," she says.

She puts it more emphatically: "Neither in Old Testament nor in the Christian Bible or in any other religious books that I know have I seen such an eloquent, yet brief and deep statement about God. It was a truly life-changing experience for me to ponder over this aspect of the Quran."

God's glory, majesty, power, knowledge, and His control over everything, including the heavens and the earth are eloquently enunciated in the famous verse called *Ayatul Kursi* (Quran 2:255). However, is Allah a distant entity who has almost left man alone, so distant and separated from him? This is an argument certain Orientalist and Christian theologians make, presenting as a skewed concept of God in Islam. However, the Quranic answer is an absolute no. The Quran says that Allah is closer to one than one's own jugular vein. He knows one's innermost thoughts.

"It was We Who created man, and We know what dark suggestions his soul makes to him: for We are nearer to him than (his) jugular vein." (Quran 50:16, Qaf)

And Allah is very close to us and He answers the prayers of those who call him sincerely.

She says no other known religious book has offered such a comprehensive and convincing picture of God as the loving, ever- caring and just God Who does not allow to go in vain the good deed of any human being, whether by man or woman (3:195, Al-Imran). And, in spite of this closeness of God to man, God is One, with no partners whatsoever in His existence, attributes and actions.

Compared to the sin-laden approach of Christian theology, 'with an extremely unclear, mysterious, ambiguous image of God' rooted in Christological controversies and the Old Testament's almost tribalistic concept of God, excessively interested in the destinies of the children of Israel alone, Allah exhorts even the worst sinners not to lose their hope in His boundless mercy.

"This is one of the most crucial messages of the Quran that convinced me without any doubt that the Quran is the word of God and Prophet Muhammad (PBUH), the bearer of the Quranic message from Allah, is the Messenger of Allah."

She also found the Quranic approach to human nature immensely uplifting, bold in comparison to the Biblical approach to man as a sin-laden, fallen 'being'. The Quran says that Allah has created man in the purest form (Quran 95:4, At-Tin), without the burden of any original sin attached to him. Allah forgave both Adam and his wife, as they repented after they ate the forbidden fruit from the tree that God warned them not to approach. Interestingly, unlike the Old Testament that tells us that it was Eve, his wife, who instigated Adam to approach the forbidden tree and eat the fruit, influenced by the whispering of Satan, and thus blaming the woman, causing the original sin and subsequent sins, the Quran makes it clear that both Adam and his wife were equally responsible for their disobedience.

As there is no original sin, man can redeem himself, without the need to believe in any redeemer who was supposed to have died for him to atone for the sin. The Quran teaches that there has never been any gap between God and man, as He is his caring Lord, who not only forgave the primordial sin committed by Adam, but also sent prophets throughout the ages offering His guidance, culminating in the mission of Prophet Muhammad (PBUH).

"In addition to all this, the importance the Quran gives to human reason, constantly asking man to think about the various creations of Allah, including man, the wondrous world phenomena around him, the historical events of mankind, is something that deeply impressed me. The Quran also asks us to reflect on its own unique quality as the inimitable text, revealed by God.

"As someone who studied the New Testament of Christians in its original Greek, I found this strong appeal to human reason as something divine. In the New Testament, I found it not properly stressed at all, and instead its stress is on the inexplicable mystery of   faith rooted in the veiled life of Jesus, its vicissitudes and meanings," she emphasises.

At the end of it, she was fully convinced that it was the   final revelation - the last revelation from God given to Prophet Muhammad (PBUH) as the completion of the revelations carried by other prophets, especially those Biblical Prophets.

Beauty of the Prophet's personality

What did she learn from her extensive studies about the life of the Prophet (PBUH)?

"It is the beauty of the Prophet's personality manifested in some of the finest human qualities such as forgiveness, empathy, justice, truthfulness and generosity that I found immensely attractive. All these and so many other human qualities, in their fullness, were visible in his life. And none other than God testifies this fact, as the Quran stresses this aspect of the Prophet's life," she says.

"And thou (standest) on an exalted standard of character." (Quran Al-Qalam, 68:4)

She found one incident especially telling. As the Prophet received the first revelation of the Quran and the weight of the revelation and thought of the supreme responsibility of the prophecy seemed to have shattered him, he rushed towards his beloved wife Khadijah. The consoling and deeply appreciative words of Khadijah amply prove the exemplary nature and the character of the Prophet. Khadijah said: "God will never forsake you, (as) you fulfil the duties of the kinship, support the weak, help the destitute, generous towards a guest and help those in genuine need."

In another incident, as Makkah was being conquered by   the Prophet, those who had persecuted the Prophet and his companions, killed a large number of them, and forced them to leave their own homeland, now stood in front of him, defeated and humiliated, in an utterly despondent and desperate situation, literally pleading for the mercy of the Prophet.

The Prophet then asked them what they thought of him. And they replied: "We say well, and we think well: a noble and generous brother, son of a noble and generous brother." And the Prophet simply replied, quoting Prophet Joseph (peace be upon him): "Verily, I say as my brother Joseph said: This day let no reproach be (cast) on you: God will forgive you, and He is the Most Merciful of those who show mercy!" (Quran 12:92, Yusuf) Only a person who attained the highest level of human enlightenment, with all its beautiful human qualities in their fullness and fineness, would be able to treat his worst enemies in such an exemplary way.

"Another aspect of the Prophet's life that I found deeply fascinating, coming from a Christian background where holy persons and religious teachers are made to be models of complete asceticism and world denial, is that the Prophet (PBUH) presented before the world an exceptionally exemplary model of life in which one can be truly religious, immensely spiritual and devoted to God, without denying any of the genuine pleasures of this world by leading life in its fullness, fulfilling one's responsibility towards one's family, the society and the people around."

Another extremely fascinating aspect of the Prophet's life she found touching was his care of animals and birds. "I grew up with so many pets like cats, rabbits, etc. And I love animals, birds and nature; of course, this, I see as an extension of my love and care for God's creations."

The Prophet narrated how Allah thanked and forgave a man who gave water to a dog suffering from extreme thirst in a hot desert. As the Companions heard this story, they asked:

"O Messenger of Allah! Is there a reward for us in serving the animals?" "Yes, there is reward for any animate being." He also said: "A woman was punished and was put in the hell because of a cat which she detained till it died of hunger."

The Prophet (PBUH) also prohibited using animals and birds for target practice.

In addition to all these, there was another reason for her conversion. It was her deeply spiritual experiences, she asserts, adding one must go through these experiences oneself, which are intensely personal and subjective and incommunicable.

There is also the contribution of Islam to human civilisation. She reiterates with the knowledge of a scholar that the Prophet and his companions created the glorious Muslim civilisation which contributed more than any other known civilisations to the religious, spiritual, moral, political and scientific development of our collective human civilisation.

It was, finally, in the middle of Ramadan in 2009, that she was fully convinced of the splendid reality of Islam and took the *shahadah*, a solemn culmination of a journey that started in 2006. The *shahadah* echoed in her heart even before she formally declared it; so it was just a matter of pronouncing it, and she did it in front of a Muslim, a highly spiritual and knowledgeable person who played an important role in connecting her with Islam.

"My first thought after becoming a Muslim was that I had been always a Muslim. Islam, as the Quran teaches, is human *fitrah* (the intrinsic human nature). When one embraces Islam, one simply rediscovers and consciously acknowledges one's inborn *fitrah*."

She was fasting during that Ramadan when she converted. "I had already deeply immersed myself in one of the most touching and inspiring worships of Islam that tests one's physical and spiritual endurance in a most challenging and inspiring way. I fasted for three years. And Ramadan is the month of guidance, as the Quran says.

And I was fortunate to be guided in the very month of guidance."

Parents' support

She didn't face any outright hostility or loss of friends following that life-changing decision. "My parents have been very understanding and supportive of my choice and the determination to live as a practicing Muslim. There were instances of me being invited to speak about Islam at a top university in Rome run by a Catholic institution, where, to my surprise, I was introduced as an Italian Muslim scholar-convert. Also, a noted Catholic foundation based in Milan, over three years ago, published a long conversation with me on my journey," she remarks with a sense of fulfilment.

However, there were some hostile reactions she faced, and continues to face, from certain influential clergymen, though it is not part of their public policy to ostracise converts. "However," she adds "I think the right-wing clergy is there in all religions."

On assimilation, she has a point to make. Some Western converts tend to isolate themselves from their family and original cultural settings after conversion, even when such settings are not contrary to Islamic ethics and morality. This attitude makes Islam appear a strange faith associated mainly with certain Eastern countries, not a universal religion that can be at home anywhere in the world.

"In my view, we Muslims in general, and Western Muslim converts in particular, should be wise and sensitive to the religious, cultural and social situations we live in. Muslim converts should realise that conversion is not synonymous with a conversion to Arab culture or any other dominant cultures. When we embrace Islam, we don't cease to be part of our families, as Islam clearly teaches us to maintain our family ties and even with relatives who are non-Muslim."

Her journey didn't end with the conversion, but has been continuing more rigorously at a different, higher level. She devotes most of her time to spreading the truth, and finds it an inspiring and rewarding experience both personally and spiritually. As a translator and author, she has translated, since her conversion, over 25 classics, including Abdullah Yusuf Ali's 1934 English Quran translation, and Sahih Al-Bukhari and Sahih Muslim - sayings of the Prophet (PBUH) - into Italian, as well as producing a widely read biography of the Prophet himself. She has also authored a number of other books on Islamic studies, philosophy, medieval studies, comparative religious studies, and is currently working on a critical study of the first Latin translation of the Quran produced in 1143.

"It is not an exaggeration to say that Islam and my life as a Muslim have played a key role in inspiring me to produce all these books, as they are enabled by my faith, as a way of making it very lively and robust in my efforts to actualise *Ihsan* (excellence) in my life and career," she says with a tinge of pride.

Dr Sabrina is also deeply involved in a project to situate Islam in Italy and Europe, as a universal religion, rooted in the oneness of God, beyond and away from all regional, tribal and communal colours. "This work is a very important one that I think every European Muslim must undertake due to various reasons. European Muslims have, like any other Muslims from any other part of the world, equal duties, responsibilities and rights. However, as European Muslims live in a very different cultural, social and political milieu, we face a different set of challenges and opportunities simultaneously."

"As an Italian and European Muslim, I am fully aware of these challenges and opportunities; so I find myself spending a great deal of my time addressing this situation. European Muslims, as it appears today, need to start a process of synthesis and concord between Islam and the European historical and cultural traditions, without losing or cutting themselves off from the bonds with the rest of the Muslim community in order to situate Islam in Europe. Islam is a universal religion and its teachings, as we Muslims believe in, can be applied in all historical epochs, geographical, social and cultural contexts."

Vicious Islamophobia

How is she able to perform such a role in the current atmosphere of a vicious strain of Islamophobia infecting the entire West? She is intensely aware of this, but is unfazed because she understands that today's Islamophobia is orchestrated, making it not a natural reaction to separate events, but part of an organised campaign supported at the highest level.

She says that, a few years ago, the Center for American Progress published "Fear, Inc.: The Roots of the Islamophobia Network in America." The report, a fine objective study, clearly showed how a number of scholars, pundits and activists comprising a tightly linked network spread misinformation and hateful propaganda about American Muslims and Islam. The report also found that seven American charitable foundations spent $42.6m between 2001 and 2009 to support the spread of anti-Muslim rhetoric in America.

"This study gives us a fairly good idea about the growing Islamophobia industry in the West. And, indeed, there are so many such foundations, think-tanks, media pundits and right-wing nationalist politicians in America and Europe who have made spreading misinformation and hatred against Islam and Muslims part of their career and public activity. And even in Scandinavian countries like Sweden, Norway and Denmark, there is a rapid growth of a very narrow and even violent nationalism, rooted in racism, religious bigotry and Islamophobia.

"One of the first things we Muslims must realise in this regard is that, in spite of virulent growth of Islamophobia industry in the West, there are so many brilliant, refined and liberal Western scholars, thinkers, influential people and foundations in the West who are vehemently challenging Islamophobia."

She says Islamophobia is growing in Italy, too, but fortunately it is not at all the mainstream phenomenon. This is because of a number of reasons. Firstly, the memory of the destruction of the country, and the cultural, social shame that fascism brought to Italy, are still alive in the national psyche, and so a majority of Italians don't want to recreate and re-live the country's xenophobic historical experience again.

Secondly, though Catholicism is no longer the official religion of Italy, and the majority of Italians are Catholic by birth, but don't follow Catholicism, culturally even now Catholicism plays a significant role in shaping the Italian national psyche. And Catholicism, since the Second Vatican Council (1962-65), has opened up to the presence of other religions, especially Islam. "Today, especially under the leadership of Pope Francis, Catholic leadership in the Vatican is actively pursuing dialogue with Islam and the Muslim world," she says.

And, finally, Italians themselves, apart from a few instances, did not have any prolonged, direct, violent colonial experiences with the Muslim world; so, historically, the Italian mind has not been adversely influenced against Islam and Muslims.

"When it comes to Italians' reactions to Islam and Muslims, from my personal experience, I see their reactions as very positive and constructive. My books, especially my biography of the Prophet (PBUH), and my studies on the spiritual and medical benefits of the *salat* (Islamic prayer), have been widely read and accepted in Italy across the religious divide. We have also got a large number of Italians willingly, after studying Islam, accepting it every year," she adds.

However, the spread of misinformation against Islam and Muslims has its adverse effects. Freedom of religion and conscience is part of any international human rights convention and the constitution of almost all modern countries. However, conversion to Islam, at a time when the right-wing nationalism and Islamophobia witness a surge, is now approached by many people as a political act or an act of betrayal of one's national heritage rather than a personal decision.

Director of Tawasul Centre

Dr Sabrina is currently the director of Tawasul International Centre for Publishing, Research and Dialogue based in Rome, a Muslim think-tank she set up, devoted to building peace and understanding across different religions and cultures in Europe and across the globe.

Tawasul stresses the idea that beyond the East and West divisions, based on the Manichean supremacist, clash of civilisation view, there is a common human destiny in which we all partake independent of our geographical, racial and religious affiliation.

Tawasul has been focusing on spreading harmony and building bridges between faiths. In this regard, it is a willing partner in a very humble way in the Vatican's dialogue with Islam and Muslims. Dr Sabrina says this open approach has been very helpful in arresting the growth of Islamophobia in Italy.

With almost 100 titles to its credit, Tawasul has also carved out its own unique place as a publishing venture in areas as diverse as the Quranic studies, Hadith translation, biography, *Fiqh,* history, theology, philosophy, and cultural studies, etc. It has also translated poems, short stories, novels, etc. from the Arab-Muslim world.

Some of its translations run into many volumes; for example, the Sahih Al-Bukhari (Prophet's sayings) book has nine volumes, with over 5,000 pages, and its Sahih Muslim (also Prophet's sayings) translation in Italian has seven volumes, with around 4,000 pages.

Dr Sabrina's voluminous and invaluable work in all these areas hasn't gone unrecognised. Recently, she won the prestigious Doha International Interfaith Award, instituted by Doha International Centre for Interfaith Dialogue (DICID).

Looking back, Dr Sabrina sees her journey to Islam as one of the greatest blessings that Allah has bestowed on her. As the Quran teaches, it is Allah who guides one to Islam, and He guides as per His will. *"It is true thou wilt not be able to guide every one whom thou lovest; but Allah guides those whom He will. And He knows best those who receive guidance."* (Quran 28:56)

"Every moment of my life, in spite of the many challenges, and tests that come with it, I experience the blessings of Islam spiritually, emotionally and intellectually. My ceaseless quest, something that started very early in my life, to understand the meaning and mysteries of my life, my relation with my creator, my relation with the world at large and other human beings seem to have been very clearly addressed by Islam, the Quran and the life examples of the Prophet (PBUH).

"A Muslim, when he remembers God in the midst of the duties of his own existence, however modest they could be, understands that every action has got an eternal value, and that the life of this world, which worries and occupies his thoughts, is also an occasion for rest and spiritual happiness."

Altogether, it has been a journey of certainties and spiritual fulfilment. Every step she takes is a progress on previous steps and for those who ask what she gained from all this, there is a one-word answer:

PEACE.

16

'You can't just pick and choose snippets of the Quran out of context – it's not a book, it's a divine revelation'

——•••◆•••——

Dr Myriam François – Franco-Irish presenter, writer and documentary filmmaker

——•••◆•••——

In the days that followed 9/11, Myriam François, then an undergraduate student at Cambridge University, found herself horrified at the hate being levelled at her Muslim friends. Later, becoming aware of her own lack of knowledge about Islam, she embarked on an intellectual journey, eventually reaching the point of *une verité incontournable* - an inescapable truth she had to face.

BEGINNING her story, Dr Myriam François makes clear she is not a fan of the 'convert narratives'. "It's very difficult to speak about faith without sounding overly earnest and I'm generally quite suspicious of how my very personal story can be interpreted for other people's agendas," she said.

When asked when she first began to take a serious interest in Islam, her thoughts trailed to her varsity days and what she described as an atmosphere of 'burgeoning tension', rife throughout Britain, including Cambridge University's campus in the aftermath of 9/11. "I genuinely could see the tensions against Muslim students rising!" she exclaimed. "It wasn't *just* a case of rhetoric – it was rhetoric that turned nasty," she continued, alluding to the subsequent spike in Islamophobic crimes.

"I felt protective of my Muslim friends," she asserted. "While on the other hand, even though I was outraged at the discrimination, that didn't necessarily mean I wasn't critical of the religion – especially as a feminist."

As conversations surrounding Islam grew more and more heated on campus, an undergraduate Myriam felt it necessary to arm herself with the knowledge to better engage in the campus debates that were becoming more frequent. "People would throw inflammatory accusations of the Quran saying things like 'It's okay to beat women' – I wanted to get to the bottom of this; I wanted to know what the Book actually says!" Thus, leading to her in-depth textual analysis of Islam's holy book.

To better understand the underlying meaning of Islam's tenets, Myriam's investigation of the Quran saw her scrutinise a series of translations. "The first English translation of the Quran I read was just so far removed from what I understood to be spirituality – I put it down after a few pages and left it." A few weeks later, however, she found herself revisiting Islam's sacred text, but through the purview of a French translation instead.

"French was the language I was educated in, so the French translation was easier for me to read in some ways, but there were still issues I was at odds with," she said. Finally, as a feminist, she then felt it would be important to hear how a woman might interpret the Quran, given the plethora of ways the text could be understood.

"With a bit of luck," said Myriam, "I was able to find an English translation written by a Pakistani female scholar." She continued: "The tone of voice, the choice of words and the compassion of her translation paled in comparison to all translations I read prior." At long last, and for want of a better word, Myriam had finally found a translation of the Quran that she could *"vibe"* with. Despite eventually finding a translation that did not feel completely skewed toward a male and often highly patriarchal worldview, Myriam also hinted at her sense of shrewdness in approaching the holy book.

"Naturally," she began, "I would have been influenced by what I saw to be double standards for men and women in Islam. And I was very militant against the hijab – my perception at the time was that it's a constraint against women and a way of hiding them. Basically, I just never understood it from the inside." Despite this scepticism, she also journeyed back to her infant years, growing up in cosmopolitan London and seeing cultural Islam through her Muslim peers.

As a child, she was always being made to feel welcome in the homes of her Muslim classmates. What especially struck her during those visits was what she described as the "clear spatial recognition of the home being a sacred area". When invited for dinner after school by her Muslim friends, Myriam vividly recalled having to leave her shoes at the door, and the clear distinction between public and private attire, especially for women. "It was like that in many Muslim homes I went to. And with that," she continued, the home is kept clean for people to pray or sit on the floor to read the Quran." These were the warm sights she observed of Islam from a young age – as such, Myriam felt an affinity to Islam, but as she grew older, aspects of Islamic culture became increasingly contentious.

"I had an attachment to Islam," she revealed. "So, by the time I got to university and things took an antagonistic turn against Muslims, I was forced to explore my own latent fears about the religion and cliches about Islam that were circling around campus."

The foundations of faith

The phrase 'ambient faith' is how Myriam recollected the religious landscape of her home growing up. The daughter of an Irish mother from County Leitrim and a French father, she described her Catholic upbringing as largely cultural. In light of this, she recalled a conversation with her father about God's existence – "Dad's advice to me was that it's probably best to believe in Him; just to be on the safe side!" she chuckled.

She further fondly remembered her days going to church always being accompanied by a selection of sweets, a few biscuits and a *cuppa*[1] up for grabs while learning about Jesus. "I think I learned a lot of very useful moral guidance lessons during that time," she said. These moral guides, alongside stories of the prophets she learned as a child, served to eventually foster a sense of familiarity as she began to learn about Islam. As such, for Myriam, given that Islam recognises the prophets and revelations that came before the Quran and Prophet Muhammad, her embracing Islam was not a rejection of her childhood faith.

"For me, becoming Muslim was more of an extension of what I already

---

1   Within the British lexicon, *cuppa* is short for a cup of tea.

believed as a Christian," she said. "I feel Islam was able to give me some clarification around things that I didn't necessarily believe before – especially to do with something like the fallibility of the Pope."

She also discussed how, although her Catholic upbringing gave her reference points about how best to live her life, she grappled with the idea of religion being something one engages with only on a Sunday. "We'd go to church on Sunday mornings, do confession, and ideally, say a prayer every night before sleeping." She continued: "So I guess, for me, Catholicism was the background mood music to my childhood, but I wasn't practising in a meaningful way." In contrast, she said, "despite not being the 'perfect' Muslim today, whatever that means, I aspire to live an ever more aligned life."

The search begins

When friction from non-Muslim students against Islam came to the fore on campus, Myriam found herself struck by her lack of knowledge. "At the time, I probably wouldn't have known much about Islam – except for the nice food and generosity I saw from my friends," she confessed.

Aside from the hostile environment that ensued following 9/11, Myriam remembered Cambridge's campus backdrop being profoundly 'hermetic' – "I stepped into an unknown world," she said. As a French, Irish, Londoner, she found herself on the fringe of the campus' exclusionary understanding of identity. She gravitated more towards a like-minded crowd of students outside of her university, with most of her friends either hailing from France or Francophone countries.

The 19th – 20th French colonial enterprise saw France's influence span over nations such as Senegal, Algeria, Mauritania, the Republic of Guinea and Mali – amongst others. Regarding the history of Islam and France, it may surprise some readers to see the Napoleonic aspiration for Franco relations with Islam. According to Christian Cherfils, Emperor Napoléon Bonaparte had hoped for a day when he would succeed in uniting:

"[…] all the wise and educated men from all countries, and establish a uniform regime based on the principles of the Quran, which alone are true and alone can lead men to happiness.[2]"

"A very good friend of mine at the time – and someone I'm still very close with today, Almamy – was of Malian-Senegalese background," said Myriam as she continued to describe how, through her friend, her knowledge of Islam being a way of life started to develop. Without directly speaking to her about his religion, her friend would, for example, discretely leave Myriam and their fellow band of friends to say his prayers.

"If we were watching a film, for example, he'd just quietly go and pray. He would never even ask for the volume to be turned down or for it to be paused." She further remembered how he and the other Muslim friends she made at university were some of the most helpful and caring people she had ever met. In seeing their devotion to saying their five daily prayers, being considerate and caring for others and being disciplined with what they consumed to lead a healthy lifestyle, Myriam deeply admired them and the framework of Islam she saw which made her friends become the best versions of themselves. "I was in awe of this *thing* that was making them conduct themselves in a way that I cannot describe as being anything short of beautiful," she beamed.

Regarding her views on the hijab while at university, Myriam highlighted how, despite living in multicultural Britain, she would have had very few encounters with veiled peers. Up until starting university, Myriam was educated in a London *Lycée*[3] where students were banned from donning

---

2   See Cherfils, C. (2005) Bonaparte et l'islam. Studley: Alcazar.

3   A *lycée* is a French public secondary school.

the veil. "Technically," she said, "since my school was within land belonging to the French embassy, it meant the school was on French territory. So, the laws of France applied once I entered the four walls of school." She continued: "When I started uni [sic] and met hijabi women who were unapologetic about their Muslim identify and their belief – it caught me by surprise!"

The more Muslim friends Myriam made, the more burning questions she had to ask. However, her questions surrounded theology – "And theology", she interposed, "is very complex." According to her, much like philosophy, matters of theology should not be cherrypicked in a decontextualised fashion. "'And kill them wherever you see them' has gotta be an Islamophobe's favourite line to use against Islam, right?" she stated sardonically. Closer to home, however, she unpacked how her era of self-study evolved from bewilderment to openness to the Quran.

As the 2001 academic year drew to a close, Myriam's studious inquisitiveness about Islam yet persisted. Said curiosity saw her at the doorstep of her local mosque. "The mosque actually wouldn't have been a very strange place to me – my friends would go there to pray, I wasn't that odd." Although a building familiar to her, hers was not a face familiar to the congregational prayer goers. "As you can imagine, when I stepped in and asked for a translation of the Quran, the people I met were more than happy to oblige!" What she ended up reading, however, surprised her – and not in a pleasant way.

Much to her dismay, the translation she was given had "harsh" undertones. Simply put by Myriam, the translation was "abominable". She especially took issue with the author's addition of asterisks next to mention of 'unbelievers' and the choice in designating 'unbelievers' as Christians and Jews.

"I remember thinking to myself, 'Did God intend for asterisks to be put in His holy book this way?'" Although initially conceding her search for answers, just weeks later she found herself immersed in the Quran once more.

While ambling through her father's expansive at-home library, Jacques A. Berque's *'Le Coran - Essai de Traduction*[4]' caught her eye. As her father was well read on a plethora of subjects, Myriam recounted not being too surprised by the copy of the Quran in his book collection. Hoping he would not notice, she picked up Berque's translation and retreated to her room to have a look.

Berque's French rendition of the Quran's translation was   20 years in the making[5], and although the language and tone were more accessible, Myriam yet found herself struggling to fully connect with the text. "Berque comes from the old school orientalist tradition," she remarked. Therefore, despite being easier to understand, the choice of language was still at times concerning and the context of the verses was also left wanting. Notwithstanding, it also troubled her that her dad's copy was printed as a humdrum paperback. "I was just beginning to get my head around the Quran being a special kind of book, in many ways it really isn't actually a book in the traditional sense," she said. "The words were more clearer to me [sic], but it was just so off-putting that there seemed to be a mismatch with sacredness of the words and the undistinguished paperback format it was presented in."

What Myriam needed was a holistic translation of the Quran, such that was translated with "compassion and heart", and would provide her with the necessary context when certain more complex verses were revealed — especially regarding matters of violence and war. As Myriam later came to

---

4   This translates as 'The Quran – A Translation Essay'.
5   Riding, A. (1995) "Jacques Berque, 85, Expert on Islam and Arabs," The New York Times, Section D, p. 21.

understand: "You can't just pick and choose snippets of the Quran out of context – it's not a book, it's divine revelations!" She continued: "For someone reading the Quran as a book, as opposed to a living revelation, naturally, certain verses will be misconstrued, including by some Muslims..." Unrelenting in her pursuit, however, Myriam's summertime remained occupied with learning more about the Quran.

On one summer's day, her quest led her to an Islamic bookshop in London's Shepherd's Bush – the place where she found a female translation of the Quran. It was through the female lens, devoid of so many of the deeply problematic assumptions of male authors who masked their own biases as neutrality, that Myriam's strong bond with the Book as a revelation began. "This makes sense!" she thought to herself. "Finally," she continued, "it felt like God was speaking to me very directly and I maintain that this is essentially the real purpose of the Quran – a direct conduit for communication with the Divine."

The voice of the Most High

Myriam speaks fondly of her blossoming relationship with Islam's holy book as being a metaphorical conversation between her and her Creator. "Sometimes things would be said that were confusing to me," she began. "The Quran does have verses that are severe, but then, as you read on, we are reassured that God's mercy always overtakes His wrath." This level of sophistication and self-awareness struck her.

"The voice that came through from the Quran wasn't speaking from this worldly plane," she remarked. "The Quran speaks from another subjectivity – the subjectivity of a Being above us all."

Against the campus charges of the Quran being an illegitimate book written by a man, Myriam was astonished at the broad discussions of natural phenomena, at times in detail, which appeared at odds with the knowledge available at that time. For instance, in the *Quran's surah al Rahman*, verses 19 to 20 state:

"Allah mixed the two seas, the salty and the sweet, that converge as far as the eye can see. [But] between them is a barrier that prevents each one of them from transgressing over the other so that the sweet remains sweet and the salty remains salty. (Quran 55:19-20)."

Today, modern science tells us that when there is a difference in salinity and density between water bodies, a surface tension is created which acts as a barrier – preventing the two bodies from mixing.

"Over 1400 years ago when the Quran was revealed, who would have known that?" pondered Myriam. More to the point, would desert dwelling nomads have known about this?

Shahadah with the Angels

"It took a while for me to be drawn to Islam as a religion, meaning a *deen* that has to be enacted, as opposed to a simple belief system," Myriam confessed. "Truly, I was attracted to the revelation and initially sidelined the body of knowledge around the Quran too much to be able to engage with the practises." When asked of the other sources she used to further her knowledge about Islam, she continued: "I was somewhat of a Quranist, you could say. I came to Islam through the Quran – not in tandem with the Hadith." She further discussed the difficulties many face in navigating the latter.

"I myself at the time was not well versed in the science of Hadith or of the Prophet's *seerah*[6] but even when you are, the hadith are clearly of a different knowledge category than the Quran." Therefore – "Because this

---

6   In Islamic theology, the *seerah* refers to the Prophetic journey of Muhammad (PBUH) – documenting his life through Prophethood.

field is challenging to access, many. Muslims find themselves relying on other people's interpretations; having to give someone else such power and authority can be deeply problematic, especially when that tradition is embedded in deeply patriarchal structures." This, she situated in the wider context of the erosion of Islamic centres of learning during the colonial era and the limited space afforded to female voices.

"It was a huge loss," began Myriam. "Not only in terms of us having centres producing contemporary and relevant Islamic knowledge, but we've also lost figures within local communities who not only know about Islam, but the context of their locality who would therefore be able to offer appropriate counsel." In losing that, "Who can you trust?" she pondered.

"The truth is, most people are seeking counsel from a sheikh on a different continent, let alone country who in all probability has no idea of the challenges of your day to day life – this is not how *fiqh* is meant to operate and because of that, we end up with all kinds of ridiculous advice being meted out."

Having subsequently studied Arabic, Myriam eventually began learning about the Hadith for herself. "A lot of my friends told me it would be more fruitful for me to learn Arabic and engage with Hadith in the Arabic language – so, I took myself to Palestine!"

During her year-long stay in Beit Hanina working for a non-governmental organisation, not only did Myriam relish learning Arabic, but she also saw the beauty of Islam being a lived religion and the community cohesion between Muslim and Christian Palestinians.

She described this time as being a "beautiful experience". In living a stone's throw away from a mosque, she joined worshippers withdrawing five times daily from the busyness of worldly affairs to go pray to their Creator. She also described becoming welcomed by the Palestinian people and rarely having to cook her own meals as she was invited almost daily to dine with neighbours and friends; true Arab and Islamic hospitality. "I have a tremendous respect for the people of Palestine and will always consider myself part Palestinian, as such, the liberation of Palestine from illegal occupation remains a deep commitment to me," she said.

Over the course of her lengthy intellectual process of learning about Islam, Myriam's journey culminated by reaching the unexpected point of, as the French say, being *'incontournable'*. "This isn't a word that exists in English, as far as I can tell," she said. Very roughly, however, *'incontournable'* can be translated as 'a thing unavoidable', you cannot get around it – it must be faced. Hers began as an endeavour to be better prepared when arguments arose on campus, and ended with a personal connection to the Divine. When met with the crossroads of either choosing to be intellectually coherent with and abide by the undeniable outcome of her findings, in line with every other decision she had made in her life prior, or suppress her belief[7] – she chose the former. "Although being coherent is not really a very human trait," she chuckled – "we're all just trying our best out here."

"I was sat at home one day, reading a booklet," she began to narrate. While reading the book, which was a small guide on how to perform *salah*, she was struck by the sentence:

"Declaring the *shahada*, in the presence of two or more witnesses, is the necessary step to embracing Islam."

Just days prior, Myriam had also read that, within Islamic theology, two angels are believed to be sat on either person's shoulder, recording their good and bad deeds. "Boom!" exclaimed Myriam, pointing at her shoulders "there were my two witnesses!

---

7   BBC, 2011. Muslim White Female. [podcast] Heart and Soul. Available at:
     <https://www.bbc.co.uk/sounds/play/p00jy6cc>

I didn't need the big celebration in the mosque – my *shahada* was a personal matter. Just me, and the unseen world."

Life after becoming a Muslim and *laïcité*[8]

After embracing Islam, she adopted Myriam in place of her birthname Émilie. "I feel very connected to Maryam, may Allah's blessings be upon her," she beamed. "The fact that the Quran dedicates a whole chapter to her name, and in many ways, she acts as a bridge between Islam and Christianity – it just speaks volumes to me!" She further detailed how the Quranic depiction of Mary's resolve in enduring hardship, alone in a remote desert, spoke to the hardships she sees women endure till this day and strengthened her belief that the Quran contains profoundly feminist teachings.

"Do we need a better encapsulation of the female state? Maryam's story of struggle in so many ways is still relatable – even today!" Although not minding whether folks call her Myriam or Émilie, she maintained that, in bearing a Muslim name, she has an established link between herself and the wider Islamic community. "Let's face it," she said, laughing, "people probably won't assume just by looking at me that I'm a Muslim. So, it is important for me to have a Muslim name that signposts my faith and connects me with my identity in my day to day interactions." Such outward signposts, however, did prove testing at times. After becoming a Muslim, Myriam began wearing a headscarf, which she regarded as a feminist act. In contrast to the normative European stance, Islam regards modesty, which extends beyond one's attire and encompasses one's conduct, as a means of achieving equality by shifting the focus from the externality to the inner substance of a person. In her native France, however, societal reactions to her wearing the hijab relegated her to no longer

---

8   The doctrine of *laïcité* informs France's system of secularism. It stipulates for

a demarcation between religious affairs and the political public sphere.

being part of the *white category*. "I soon became relegated to the second-class citizen category, and assumed to be foreign and lesser!⁹" she exclaimed as she remembered instances of being refused service in cafes and restaurants she once used to frequent freely before veiling[10].

Following from the thread of the post-Napoleonic problematisation of Islam during France's colonial era, Myriam stressed how Islam's perceptions within wider French society, continues to be a source of contention in the lives of many French Muslims. In line with the doctrine of *laïcité*, Myriam explained, "There's a huge resistance to the visibility of religion in public spaces." She continued: "And that's especially troubling for Muslims – there are no prayer spaces in French workplaces and women can't wear the hijab to school or most workplaces."

When asked whether an overhaul of *laïcité* would remedy such woes, Myriam was quick to interpose that, "The issue is not with *laïcité* – it is with remnants of France's history of being anti-clerical, anti-religious and its colonial history, which remains largely unexamined by the majority." Further, Myriam cited a survey that found French Muslims to generally support *laïcité*, recognising that the principle contains all the elements to protect the right to practise religion within society without intrusion from the state – in theory...

"*Laïcité* in and of itself is not the problem – as a doctrine, it calls for there to be no religious interference in the country's political sphere, and vice versa, and the majority of France, whether religious or not, is all for that!" Notwithstanding, provisions in the French Constitution guarantee that: "All citizens, regardless of their origin, race or religion are [to be] treated as equals

---

9   BBC, 2011. Muslim White Female. [podcast] Heart and Soul. Available at:
     <https://www.bbc.co.uk/sounds/play/p00jy6cc>

10   Ibid

before the law [with] respect [to] all religious beliefs."

Thus, for Myriam: "The issue is the way in which the French government has instrumentalised the doctrine; wielding it as a stick to goad Muslims into a narrow ideation of what it means to be *French*." Aside from politics, she further described the French as having an unspoken, and at times very clearly spoken, hierarchical understanding of who is *quote-unquote truly* French. "France continues to deny the evolving nature of national identity. From the moment it colonised West and North Africa, those communities and their history have now become part of France; its identity and history. It's about time the country made peace with that." She continued: "Despite the underlying European superiority complex of 'us' and 'them', Islam as a religion is a French religion today, whether people want to accept that or not!"

The convert/revert construct

As a Doctorate degree holder in Islamic Reform Movements in Morocco, Myriam has garnered bylines in publications such as *Time* Magazine and *The Guardian*. While from 2015 – 2017, she was to be seen on television screens worldwide as TRT's Europe Correspondent. Later, in 2019 she reported on home soil for BBC London News. A prolific documentary maker, her films on issues from the genocide in Srebrenica to Brexit, the #metoo movement and more, have aired on the BBC, Channel 4 and more.

Just this year, her new series 'France in Focus', presented and produced for Al Jazeera English, aired globally.

What is in store next for Myriam?

"I recently established my own production company, MPWR Productions and I'm directing my very first documentary film for the BBC and CBC networks. So watch this space!"

In drawing her story to a close, Myriam was asked about a blog post from almost ten years ago. Under the title *'Don't call me "convert" nor "revert" for that matter'*, she argued for the dismantling of the convert/revert paradigm – asserting it to be an exclusionary construct, especially for those who have been Muslim for a long time[11].

"For that reason, I advocate Muslims stop using the construction, stop validating it and put an end to the cult of the "convert". I converted 11 years ago. Today? I'm just Muslim thanks,[12]" she penned. Revisiting this blog entry ten years on, Myriam's position has not budged.

"I still stand by it!" she exclaimed. "All the early *ṣaḥābah*[13] were *converts* to Islam – but we don't call them that, we just refer to them as Muslim. And, more recently, Muslims who grow up in the West with cultural Islam and choose to be practicing later on in life, we don't refer to them as *converts* either." She further discussed her dislike for what she referred to as a "racialised undertone" within this concept.

"For us White Muslims, we stay converts our entire lives," she said. While on the other hand, she observed: "I feel like a lot of the time, Black and Brown Muslims aren't even afforded the support of being new Muslims when they do convert." This, in her estimation, induces "a little bit of a cultish adulation" surrounding the White convert experience, which she deemed misplaced. She argued that everyone who commits to their faith is essentially a convert and as a community, "we need to let this obsession go -

---

11   François, M. (2013) "Don't call me 'convert' nor 'revert' for that matter." http://myriamfrancoiscerrah.wordpress.com/. Her WordPress blog no longer exists.

12   Ibid.

13   The *ṣaḥābah* refers to followers of the Prophet Muhammad (PBUH) during his lifetime. As those who would have interacted with him personally, they are regarded as important sources within the field of the Prophetic hadith.

you don't need someone else to confirm the validity of your faith to you and you especially do not require a white stamp of approval. We should be looking within. "I became a Muslim when I was 21," she said. "Am I *still* going to be a convert by the time I'm 50?"

17

'The Quran stirs and moves me to this day. It's such a powerful experience!'

Alfred Wondratsch – Austrian former far-right politician

The media portrayed a negative image of Islam and Muslims that fostered abhorrence and fear, whereas Wondratsch's own Muslim friends and colleagues were very polite, gracious, and kind. "Why this discrepancy?" he asked them. "Go and read," they said. He did, and became Ali Wondratsch.

ALFRED Wondratsch worked as a paramedic. He loved his job, because it was all about helping people. The job was part of national service, which all Austrian men were required to do, either by serving in the military, or as a form of social work. Wondratsch worked in the field of emergency medical treatment in 1991-1992, and enjoyed it so much that he decided to work full time as a paramedic when his service was over.

"Sometimes I was used as a driver, sometimes a transport leader, but in both cases, you are a paramedic. The main task is to bring patients who cannot get to a hospital on their own from their place of residence to an ambulance and return [them] again after their treatment," he says.

"In addition to patient transport, there are also orders for emergencies or events such as transporting pregnant women who have already had a ruptured membrane to the destination hospital. It also happens that they no longer make it to the hospital and the baby is born in the ambulance."

In 1992, Wondratsch had an experience which had a profound impact on his life, an experience which made him realise that God had a completely different plan for him than he had drawn for himself.

On a sunny Tuesday in September 1992, 42-year-old truck driver, Emmerich Pock, who had been working for 20 years in Vienna, was racing at 100 mph along the A2 motorway towards Vienna. At the same time, 24-year-old Regina Wsseticzka was in an ambulance, being rushed from her home in Baden to a hospital in Vienna so she could give birth. Also present in the ambulance was her mother-in-law Barbara Bajlicz, 20-year-old paramedic Alfred Wondratsch, and his colleague Herbert Strusky, who were comforting the soon-to-be mother and monitoring her contractions. It soon became clear that Regina was going into labour, and the vehicle swiftly pulled over. Regina then gave birth to Thomas, a beautiful little boy, safely delivered by Wondratsch. Giving birth is stressful enough when in a hospital bed and surrounded by nurses. In the back of an ambulance, however, it is far more stressful. And when the ambulance is then parked on the hard shoulder of a major national motorway, the pressure increases further. But, tragically, the drama was still far from over, and the worst was yet to come.

"I held the baby in [my] hands. And then there was an almighty crash," says Wondratsch. Seconds before, lorry driver Emmerich momentarily dropped a delivery note and, as he bent down to retrieve it, he had swerved out of his lane, onto the hard shoulder, and straight into the parked ambulance. The lorry ripped through the left-side of the ambulance, wreaking pure havoc and sending all inside flying through the air. Miraculously, new-born baby Thomas had been hurled into a bush, and had survived. Meanwhile, young mother Regina suffered a broken jaw and a broken thigh bone. Wondratsch also sustained a broken thigh bone and severe injuries to the head, as did his colleague Herbert, who went on to suffer from epileptic fits.

"All three of us had been thrust out of the ambulance and we were lying, smashed and unconscious, on the motorway. Meanwhile the mother-in-law, Barbara, who had suffered lacerations to the face and severe bruising to the ribs, still got up, found the baby then even drove him to the hospital to be treated. It was quite incredible.

"They needed to send a medical helicopter to bring us to hospital, and my injuries were really severe. It took me a full nine months to recover. I had to learn everything again from scratch. I had to learn how to breathe, how to eat, how to speak. I very nearly died – and yet I didn't. God had saved me. And it was then that I realised that God still had something in store for me, and had wanted me to live, but I just didn't know what it was yet. It had to be revealed to me over time," Wondratsch reminisces over the traumatic incident with a sigh.

During those nine full months, Wondratsch says he did a lot of thinking about absolutely everything – about God, destiny, the purpose of life and death, and the deeper questions that roil ordinary minds. He didn't find any immediate answers, but such deep cogitations prepared his mind, like raw earth being tilled for crops, for a deep philosophical journey that finally saw him embrace Islam.

But what lends poignancy and excitement to his journey is the extraordinary path it has taken. After leaving the hospital, he joined the far-right Austrian Freedom Party, whose oxygen was Islamophobia.

That's when he discovered a disconnect – a galling disconnect between propaganda and reality.

The media portrayed a negative image of Islam and Muslims that fostered abhorrence and fear, whereas his own Muslim friends and colleagues – and he was fortunate enough to know a few of them - were very polite, gracious, and kind.

Why this gaping discrepancy, he thought.

"What is this Islam you are following?" he asked his Muslim friends out of curiosity.

"Go and read," they said.

He did.

Lurch to far-right populism

In early 2000, the European Union (EU) was extremely anxious. The Austrian Freedom Party, FPÖ, the hardline nationalist, anti-immigration party founded by an officer of Adolf Hitler's chilling SS militia, had now taken Austria by storm.

Having taken a violent lurch to far-right populism in 1986, the party secured 26.9 percent of the vote in 1999 – making it Austria's second biggest party. And then, in 2000, the unthinkable had happened. For the first time since the genocidal horrors of World War II, and the colossal suffering inflicted upon the peoples of Europe and across the world, a far-right, ultra-nationalist and anti-immigration party was now back in government – in the very same country where Adolf Hitler had been born.

Part of this anti-immigration aspect of the FPÖ was widespread, virulent Islamophobia. In the 1990s this had started as merely an attack on Islamic extremism, but it quickly morphed into an attack of supposed "Islamisation" and on the increasing number of Muslims in Austria. Before long, it even pledged to make distributing free copies of the holy Quran an illegal act.

The EU acted fast, immediately imposing sanctions upon Austria, and threatening to sever all diplomatic ties with Vienna should it fail to take action. Overnight Austria, the same country which year upon year had delighted millions of guests from across the world with its idyllic towns and villages and breath- taking, snow-capped Alpine ski-slopes, had now become a pariah state, and the world looked on with a mixture of concern and revulsion. In this disturbingly xenophobic climate, it might seem incomprehensible to many that a political member of this far- right, Islamophobic party would choose to become a Muslim.

And yet, this is exactly what happened in the case of Alfred, now 'Ali', Wondratsch.

Alfred Wondratsch was born in 1972 in the beautiful Austrian capital of Vienna to a working-class family. His father was from Steiermark, and his mother was from Vienna, together they raised him in the north-western district of Währing, named after the asteroid 'Weringia' which Austrian astronomer Johann Palisa had discovered in 1882.

Austria is a staunchly Christian country with conservative values, and most children receive Catholic indoctrination at the local school.

This was also the case for young Alfred, though at home he was raised with a more modern, liberal approach to religion. After graduating from polytechnic in 1986, Wondratsch did an apprenticeship as a car mechanic from 1987-1991. At this point, however, he felt that his connection to the church was no longer that strong.

"I decided to officially leave the Catholic church, having been kind of born into it instead of ever consciously joining it. This did not stop my belief in God but, to be honest, religion just did not really play a major role in my life. I suppose in a way it was at this point that I had really started my journey towards Islam, even though of course I had absolutely no way of knowing it at the time."

After recovering from the near-fatal accident, Wondratsch spent the next seven years working in ambulance transportation and then from 1999 as a paramedic, which he has continued throughout his career. Alongside his work as a paramedic, he began to discover that, through politics, he was also able to serve and care for people by representing them. After working as a deputy in the Social Justice Group (FSG), in 2010 he became the official spokesman for the disabled in the Action Group of Independent Freedomists (AUF). And it was this, said Wondratsch, which ultimately led to him joining the FPÖ – even if it was fully unintended.

"Many local politicians were already aware of the work I was doing on behalf of disabled people, and one who I had already known from my time doing national service officially put me down for as the 2010 candidate for the FPÖ district council in [the] Vienna district of Floridsdorf.

"I hadn't requested this – I didn't even know about it until he told me, but I just thought, right okay, well I guess I will then just take a look at it. And then I was voted in – and suddenly I was then on the social, civil protection, transport, culture commissions on behalf of this party.

"The truth was it wasn't really as though I was particularly committed to the FPÖ's politics at the time. There were some aspects which appealed to me - I used to feel quite close to the FPÖ's sense of 'homeland' because Austria has always been my home, but really, I was just interested in working with people and helping people, so I just saw this political position as an opportunity to do this."

But for others, particularly foreigners and Muslims in Austria, the FPÖ were now becoming an increasingly frightening political force and any involvement in it was no trifling matter.

Propaganda and reality

Wondratsch says the Austrian media's virulent Islamophobic agenda had caused him to originally hold a negative view of Muslims. "It was only a few months after my accident, when I was forced to suddenly take life very, very slowly. I had so much time to reflect during my recovery, and I did a lot of thinking about absolutely everything. Then, shortly after, the terrorist attacks on the World Trade Center happened and stirred up in me a lot of negative thoughts about Islam. I ended up feeling that I really didn't like Muslims.

"Now I know it was a totally false picture that was being fed to me as it was described in the media. But I had been constantly bombarded with reports and images of explosions and shoe bombers. The truth, which I now know, is that Islam is an extremely humane and peaceful religion.

"But I realise now that this is also another thing which helped me on my path towards Islam. It came because I noticed there was a clear discrepancy and contradiction between what the media was telling me about Muslims in the newspapers and on television, and the various Muslim friends and colleagues I had, and how they behaved. The media was telling me how Muslims were all about demanding death to the infidels, and how Muslims were angry and hate-filled, dangerous and frightening. Yet, the Muslims I knew a little were kind, gentle, polite, and wholly decent people. Their behaviour was really exemplary. So, I was intrigued. How could it possibly be, I wondered, that what I am being constantly told about Muslims bears absolutely no resemblance at all to the several Muslims I know?

"It was now summer 2011 and I was serving as the FPÖ district councillor in Floridsdorf, and I felt I just had to explore all of this. So, I decided I would ask the Muslims I knew if they could enlighten me a little about Islam. I just wanted a little insight into it all. Here, they all seemed to have a clear position – go and read, they said, go and read, and find out more about it. Looking back, I really admire this. They could have just started trying to convert me, or to persuade me of Islam's merits, but they didn't. And this was in direct contrast to the behaviour of the media. The Austrian media, and also the world media, to some extent, was kind of force-feeding me a perspective of Islam. But there was absolutely no coercion here on behalf of the Muslims I was talking to. There was no aggressive 'hard sell', in fact, no sell at all. They were just kind, supportive, and encouraging and I really appreciated that. I really applauded the honesty of these Muslims in telling me to go and get literature on Islam myself.

"And so I got myself five books that described the way of life in Islam in a more compact way. This is important because there was so much information out there that it would be very easy to get overwhelmed. One of the five books was by Jürgen Tödenhofer, entitled *Islam as the Enemy*. I really liked his take on it, which was basically that Islam is not the problem, rather the West's take on Islam is – and particularly how it is reported, or rather distorted, in the Western media. This really resonated with me as I had found media coverage of Islam created such a terrible picture of the religion."

It took him about a year to finish reading the books, and he was also reading parts of the holy Quran. Everything fell into place and made sense, as he realised that Islam is actually a religion of peace, and not a religion of violence and death and oppression, which is the narrative the media was peddling. Equipped with this knowledge and understanding, he felt ready to embrace Islam. He decided to visit the Islamic Centre in Vienna, where he later took his conversion.

"In July 2012, one Saturday morning, I visited the Islamic Centre. A little shyly, I asked the believers who were waiting there for midday prayer if I could look around the mosque. There were three people who received me kindly and first showed me how to achieve ritual purity through ablution *(wudu)*, which is necessary for prayer.

"It was just such an unbelievable experience. And after this prayer I felt so good that I later decided that I would officially proclaim the confession of conviction in Allah, and officially make my *Shahadah* with the Imam, Sheikh Marwan from Adana. And so I did. And then I had a moment which will stay with me forever. Not only was I spiritually filled with joy, but spiritually, and also physically, I also felt this giant weight which was lifted from me. I was so moved by this I discussed it with the Imam Sheikh Marwan and he explained that if one accepts Islam as one's religion out of conviction, all previous sins will be blotted out. So, I had all my sins washed away and had been reborn in Islam."

First Friday prayer

The week after, Wondratsch attended his first Friday prayer and didn't notice that carpets were laid out in front of the mosque because far more Muslims come to this service. So, he strutted unhindered onto the carpet in his street shoes and was immediately reprimanded, but in a friendly manner, by the director of the mosque. An Indonesian camera team who interviewed the director also noticed this, and he was asked by the Indonesian reporter to say the *Shahadah* again that Friday so that it could be filmed and shown in Indonesia. "Again, I spoke the most important words for me, and I was literally hugged and congratulated by so many believers present. People left, right, and centre were coming up to me and shaking my hand, hugging me, and they were truly delighted for me. I felt so welcomed. It was incredible," Wondratsch said with a smile brightening his face.

Following his Shahada, a month later, Wondratsch had his first Ramadan and a fellow Muslim showed him where he could find other mosques where he could break his fast. Captivated and enthralled in his new found faith and new found friends, Wondratsch immersed himself in the Quran.

"I read the Quran for the first time all the way through, and visited the Islamic Centre every free minute to learn more and more about Islam. For chapter Al-Fatiha (the mother of the Quran) it took me about 14 days to memorise it in Arabic. As a promised form of encouragement, I received a certificate from Sheikh Marwan. After that, I learned more and more. I don't really know if I had a favourite Surah, or chapter, because all parts of the Quran are so striking that they leave an impression on you."

Though feeling completely at home as a newcomer to the fold of Islam, Wondratsch still did not feel comfortable about sharing his conversion with his political colleagues at the FPÖ. But when he eventually decided to come clean about it, however, he was surprised at how the political party reacted.

"At first, I had kept it a secret, given that the party had a robust position on Islam, but when I told the party, they saw that it was actually an advantage for them. I was the first ever member of the Austrian Freedom Party to convert to Islam, so I really made a name for myself. But now I think that for them it was just a form of good publicity, so they could say: 'Look! We are not all bad people and we are not against foreigners and against Muslims. Look! We even have a Muslim amongst us!'"

Now a Muslim who was openly practising his faith, Wondratsch remained in the FPÖ, and was now forced to explain this to a perplexed Austrian media which had to grapple with the idea that the party which had spent years peddling a hard-line, anti-Muslim narrative now suddenly had a Muslim within its own ranks.

Wondratsch, too, was struggling with all of this. And by 2017, it was not just the mainstream Austrian media which wanted to know how, as a Muslim, he could ever have been associated with an Islamophobic party like the FPÖ. Now, other less prominent media also wanted to interview him. In 2017, Wondratsch did an interview with Citizenship, Education and Islam (CEAI), an initiative of the Institute for Islamic Theological Studies at the University of Vienna, where he was challenged on how he could be a member of a political organisation whose political slogans and election posters were so polarising and Islamophobic, including even calling for a "Love of homeland instead of Moroccan thieves".

Here, Wondratsch not only showed himself incapable of defending the FPÖ, rather he also revealed how he found this behaviour disturbing. "That's terrible," he said. "It hurts to read something like that," and he stressed how Islam had both opened his eyes to the wider world and changed his interests.

"I used to be a little closer to the FPÖ sense of 'homeland' than I am today. For me, Austria has always been my home. But now, as a Muslim, I see the whole world that God created as my home.

There are many things I appreciate about Austria, such as nature, history, and architecture. I also used to listen to classical music. Now, however, I listen almost exclusively to Quran recitations."

Even though he was becoming aware how confused the media was, he held out that there was no conflict between his identity as a Muslim and his role as a local FPÖ politician, even though he admitted that the official tone of the FPÖ leadership on Islam was certainly undesirable. "It must also be clearly stated," he said, "that district policy is largely different from federal policy. That is why, as a district councillor, I do not have to advocate such a mood being created at the federal political level."

And, perhaps not even realising it at the time, Wondratsch revealed here that it was now being Muslim, and not far-right politics, which was now guiding his approach to life.

"I would like to see a politics of the centre, and charity, as it is also shown in Islam. I don't believe in extremes, such as extreme right or extreme left," he said.

Wondratsch officially left the FPÖ and, within just two years, he went on to see his dream realised, as in May 2019, upon the Austrian political scene came the Social Party of Austrian Future (SPÖZ), a micro-party led by Austrian-born Hakan Gördü of Turkish descent. Describing itself as "left of centre", SPÖZ's core beliefs included everything from social ecology to minority rights and multiculturalism.

First and foremost a Muslim

Wondratsch has done many interviews about his conversion, both with Austrian mainstream press, non-mainstream media, and even Islamic media in Austria, such as the 'Imam Talk' television programme. Today, he continues to work in the profession he started at the age of 20 - as a paramedic and, after work, enjoys spending time with his wife and son. When it comes to politics, however, he says regardless of what will or will not happen with the SPÖZ, he sees his identity first and foremost as a Muslim and a servant of Almighty Allah, who he says guides the way he lives his life.

"I am convinced that there is a creator who cannot be compared to anything earthly, who is above his creation, who no man has ever seen, who tests people and will hold them accountable in the end. So, it can only be at our discretion that we do everything imaginable that pleases our creator and refrain from everything that displeases him." Wondratsch says what was absolutely overwhelming was when he heard the Quran recited in Arabic. "It still stirs and moves me to this day. It is such a powerful experience! When someone recites Quran, it has an extraordinary effect on me. By this I mean the rhythm of the recitation, and the melody. I can't describe it exactly, because it is something spiritual and hard to put into words, but suddenly my soul definitely finds a sense of nourishment, and through the contact with the Quran when praying in the mosque.

"I started learning Arabic. It is difficult because just one word can have so many meanings, but I have made progress. I can pronounce Arabic now and communicate to some degree in speaking, but I am still learning to read and write it. It is such a rich and manifold language.

"I accepted Islam as my religion at the age of 39, and this came after I had actively been researching for around a year. But really, I would have to say that my journey to Islam took all 39 years, because I think I was always actually on my way towards Islam - I was actually moving towards Islam slowly and via all sorts of twists and turns, but I just never realized this at the time.

"Looking back, it has been a real journey - but I made it, and I am so happy to have been guided by Allah. It was the best thing that has ever happened to me."

18

'Belief in Allah bestows the same security of being in your mother's arms'

Amanda Figueras – Spanish journalist and expert in interfaith dialogue

After the 2004 Spanish terrorist attacks, Figueras, a journalist working at *El Mundo,* a leading conservative newspaper in Spain, was assigned by her editor to track potential reprisals or consequences of the attacks for the Muslim population in Madrid. This was the beginning of an illuminating journey that lasted for over a decade, culminating with her embrace of Islam.

AMANDA Figueras fondly remembers her first encounter with Islam. She was a little girl visiting her Moroccan friend's house, and through a partly open door, she notices something that triggers her curiosity and excites her - her friend's parents in loose attire were chanting something in an un- familiar language and prostrating on a carpet in a rhythmic movement. Her curiosity piqued, she immersed herself in the scene for some time, imbibing its beauty and wondering what it was all about.

A little later, she learned that it was a Muslim prayer.

Several years later, her second brush with Islam was far more turbulent.

On 11 March, 2004, a dozen bombs exploded at Atocha train station, the backbone of Madrid, leaving 193 bodies under the rubble in the biggest terrorist attack in Spanish history, and one of the deadliest in Europe.

As a journalist working at *El Mundo*, a widely circulated conservative newspaper in Spain, Figueras found herself on the frontline of a tragedy. After covering the first news of the attack, claimed by Al Qaeda, she was assigned by her editor to track potential reprisals or consequences of the attacks for the Muslim population in Madrid.

With a shadow of bitterness, she reflects that the traumatic and saddening incident was the beginning of an illuminating journey that lasted for over a decade, culminating with her embrace of Islam.

Intensely conscious that her understanding of Islam was coloured and shaped by a negative and stereotypical portrayal of Islam in the mainstream media, she set out to discover the truth on her own. She was in her twenties and started to read and research, and met and befriended several Muslims in Madrid during her journalistic assignments. Gradually, the testimonies she heard and gathered for her articles began to captivate her in an intimately intense and heartfelt way.

"I didn't ask myself transcendental questions about faith. I had no religious inclinations, nor did I reflect on such supernatural questions as what happens beyond life or why we are here on Earth. I thought that after death, everything would be darkness, and that our aim as humans was to enjoy ourselves and to do good to others," she says.

"But then I encountered Islam and I learned about the knowledge revealed to Prophet Muhammad (peace be upon him), which was such a breakthrough for me. It became so obvious that what the Quran says is true that I could no longer deny it," she affirms.

When faith appeared as a fleeting light, she knew there'd be no going back.

In a moment of solitude while her husband plays with their son, Figueras further talks about her conversion to Islam and the state of Islamophobia in Spain, the country with the greatest Arab heritage in Europe, which centuries ago was the gateway of Islam to the Old Continent.

A prominent new Muslim

When you mention *nuevos musulmanes*, which means   new Muslims in Spanish, the first name that springs to mind is Amanda Figueras. With her European physiognomy and stylish, colourful hijabs, she stands tall as the most renowned and recent case of conversion to Islam in Spain.

Kind-hearted and committed to social issues, she led a normal life void of religious fervour or attachments until faith took her by surprise, unexpectedly triggering her spiritual rebirth. Her story is compelling and evoked so much interest that she decided to pen it, and thus was born her memoir *Why Islam: My life as a woman, European and Muslim* which was published in Spanish language in 2018 to rave reviews.

Figueras was born in a village in Catalonia, in the north- west region of the country, and was raised in the working-class neighborhoods on the edge of Madrid, where her family's roots have been. After her parents' separation, she moved in with her mother and her mother's new partner, who had sons from a previous marriage, making Figueras the youngest of an extensive household.

From an early age, her parents passed on to her the values of ethics, justice and solidarity. Additionally, she attended a so-called integration school, a pioneering formula in the 1980s where discussion and understanding were encouraged, where she sat together with children from migrant families and disabled kids in the same classroom.

Faith, however, was never a topic of debate at home, and Figueras was not even baptised. Spanish families are of Christian traditions but, like many European households, religious practice is diminishing by leaps and bounds, becoming increasingly secularised, she affirms.

For this reason, Figueras does not consider herself a Muslim convert. Instead, she prefers to be labelled as a 'new Muslim', an evocative concept that dates back to the beginnings of Islam, when the first Muslims began to adopt the practices and faith preached by Prophet Muhammad (PBUH).

Prophet's influence

As Figueras writes in her book, what brought her close to Islam was her readings about the teachings and life of the Prophet. His humbleness, generosity and understanding were all traits that compelled her to affirm in a calm voice that "it was his character that made me love him."

She was particularly awed by the Prophet's capacity for forgiveness, even with his fiercest enemies. She talks about the moment when Muslims entered victorious in Makkah after being expelled from the city and the words the Prophet said to the Quraish tribe who had treated him cruelly and even tried to kill him on several occasions.

"The prophet did not take revenge, but told them: I say to you today what the prophet Jesus said to his brothers: 'Nothing will be reproached to you today. Go away because you are free!'," she says.

"No crime or aggression against him [Prophet] seemed too great for him to forgive. He was an example of complete forgiveness and kindness as mentioned in the following Quranic verse: *'Be gracious, enjoin what is right, and turn away from those who act ignorantly'.* " (Quran 7:199)

Figueras was also enamoured with the importance given to family in Islam and the relationship with parents, which has been made part of the worship of Allah.

"I found it wonderful that the main idea of Islam, the adoration of Allah, was together in the same verse with the obligation of kindness to parents. Thus, treating them well and taking care of them is also considered part of worship, if it is done with the intention of pleasing Him."

She quotes a verse from the Quran:

"And your Lord has decreed that you not worship except Him, and to parents, good treatment. Whether one or both of them reach old age (while) with you, say not to them (so much as), "uff," and do not repel them but speak to them a noble word. " (Quran 17:23)

Further on, Allah says:

And be humble with them out of mercy, and pray, "My Lord! Be merciful to them as they raised me when I was young." (Quran 17:24)

"He asks us to be aware of all the efforts our parents have made and to treat them with kindness," explains Figueras, who was always very caring to her big family, and especially, her mother. "Becoming a mother made me realise the extraordinary efforts of raising a family and parenting. Since my child was born, I appreciate so much all that my mother did for us. Suddenly, you find yourself thinking and behaving like your mother, you understand her better and make your own peace."

Figueras was also impressed by the norms of courtesy governing Muslims' behaviour. For example, she found with surprise that the Islamic greeting *Assalamu Alaikkum* is to wish each other *peace*, and the words uttered when someone sneezes also foster a spirit of peace.

"In a world where even the basic rules of politeness are often not observed, these kinds of words help to create a community of Muslims, without geographical boundaries, hierarchies or prejudices," says Figueras, adding the following verse:

*The believers are but brothers, so make settlement between your brothers. And fear Allah that you may receive mercy. (*Quran 49:10) "In my opinion, in a world where all Islamic teachings are thoroughly applied, neither prisons nor punishments would be needed except on rare occasions. The fear of Allah is enough and all Muslims are told that we must want for our brothers and sisters what we want for ourselves, and treat them as we would like to be treated. There would be no stealing, cheating, betrayal or other crimes."

In addition to her love for the Prophet, God and humanity, Figueras also felt inspired by the relationship that the Quran establishes between people and nature. A bond of respect and care that, for her, led to a path towards self-knowledge and a renewed and more intimate connection with nature.

Figueras admits it was her work as a journalist that served as her primary source of information on Islam; she met Muslims who were facing the brunt of the consequences of the Madrid blasts, some of whom became her friends, and through whom she not only gathered valuable information for her articles, but was also able to delve deep into a religion which was an unfair target of media censure. It was her realisation of the gaping difference between the negative media portrayal of Muslims and the lived reality that she experienced, in which she found Muslims to be peaceful and law-abiding, that aided her spiritual journey.

Even at the peak of her exploration, she didn't realise how much information she had garnered on Islam, but was noticed by others. One day, during a conversation with an imam of the biggest mosque in Madrid, he surprised her with a comment. She was consulting him for some information for a story she was working on when, unexpectedly, the imam asked her: "When are you going to admit yourself as a Muslim?"

"Maybe my questions were too deep, maybe he noticed my increasing interest in Islam, but what surprised me was that the imam was able to identify what was inside me before I was able to admit it myself," she confesses.

Besides her interactions with Muslims and reading of holy Quran which opened the door to holy truths, she also did other readings. An important book that influenced her was *Muhammad: Biography of the Prophet* by Karen Armstrong, which helped her to understand the historial context in which Islam was born and developed.

Absolute trust in Allah

One of the most enchanting and comforting aspects of Islam, also the most challenging for Figueras, was what she considers "being a true Muslim". It requires discipline and will and has to do with blindly trusting Allah's plans for everyone, because He has "answer for everything."

"It is about leaving everything truly in his hands and trusting that whatever happens is unquestionably in your best interest. If you are confident with that, you will accept any adversity because you know that Allah is the best planner. We often want things that are not meant for us or we try to anticipate. There is no reason to be frustrated if you believe in God," she continues.

She pauses for a while as her gaze wanders, as if she is carefully weighing her words, and then adds: "Belief in Allah bestows the same security of being in your mother's arms."

A smile invades her face as she reminisces the first time she read the Quran, which she was given as a gift. She also remembers the feeling of awe that overwhelmed her when she first listened to the Quran being recited in Arabic.

"I often play some parts of the Quran in Arabic before going to sleep. There is something that touches your heart and makes you connect with a very special and inner part of you. Faith is difficult to explain if you have never felt it," Figueras explains.

She says as a little girl, every night before falling asleep, she would be thankful for life and silently ask for good things to come. Faith gave meaning to this gratitude: "I now believe I have been harbouring faith, unaware, since childhood. It is now, as a grown woman, this gratitude has taken the shape of belief in God."

Act of bravery of saying you are a Muslim

Announcing her conversion became the most challenging part for Figueras after embracing Islam. She had an inkling of what lay in store for her from the experiences of other Muslims after the Madrid blasts – women fired from their jobs for wearing the hijab, mothers who suffered the rejection of their children, and families separated or torn apart.

Her heart sent warnings, making her hesitate and postpone the moment of publicly acknowledging herself as a Muslim, which she pondered was "an act of bravery."

"I confess I was afraid of both my family and the society," she says. After dozens of interviews with Muslim converts in Spain, she knew it was not an easy step.

As the headline in a chapter of her book shows, she calls it "The anguish of saying you are Muslim". She dreaded being the subject of discrimination and Islamophobia; after all, Spanish society remained unfamiliar with the basic tenets of Islam despite shared cultural traits and profound heritage left in the Iberian Peninsula by the presence of Islam centuries ago.

According to her, the simplest and the most essential pillar of Islam was the least known among non-Muslims and it is about confronting your fears, and committing yourself by calmly and clearly repeating the sacred oath: "I bear witness that there is no God but Allah, and I bear witness that Muhammed is His messenger."

Following that, she wore her first hijab to do the groceries, to go to work and to attend family gatherings. "Hijab helped me to develop a more intimate and conscious relationship with myself," she says. As days passed by, her relatives and friends breathed a sigh of relief; they came to the conclusion that Amanda was still Amanda, not someone else they had imagined from the negative portrayal in the media.

Another major milestone on her long road to conversion happened years later. After leaving her job at *El Mundo*, she received a call from her former boss requesting her to write a short article, as part of a story about new Muslims narrating their own experiences. The piece she wrote was so well liked by the editorial staff that it was decided to make it the lead on the front page.

It was summer of 2015. Puffing and throwing her hands in the air to signal her incredulity, she remembers how, not so long ago, she was afraid of the reaction of her family and neighbours, and all of a sudden, the entire country knew about her religious transition.

Luckily, she was in Egypt, where she wouldn't find her picture in any street shop, nor would anyone recognise her. She nevertheless turned off her phone and avoided talking to any acquaintances for a few days. "I didn't want to discuss the article. I wasn't curious about the reactions. I couldn't live - imagine yourself being on the front page of a national newspaper!" she exclaims.

Two weeks later, the phone rang again. This time it was the director of Península Publishing Company who, in the absence of first-person literature and testimonies of conversion experiences, wanted Figueras to write her personal story in greater depth for a book. Península belongs to Planeta group, one of the most influential publishing houses in the Spanish-speaking world.

Figueras recalls the feeling of nervousness and incredulity that engulfed her, and was overwhelmed by the unexpected interest her story had aroused. "Why me?" she kept repeating to herself. But her first reaction soon dissipated and she tried to find a meaning in it all.

"I finally comprehended it was an opportunity happening to me for a reason. Through my story, I could tell what I loved and discovered about Islam, issues I thought people should know. I wanted to make a book for everyone," she sighs with relief. And that is how *Why Islam: My life as a woman, European and Muslim* was born.

The book talks about the main elements of her spiritual journey and conversion. In a comprehensible and non-academic language, it informs of key features and components of Islam, dismantling myths and prejudices surrounding the Muslim community of Spain and Europe. It took no short shortcuts and avoided no controversial issues such as terrorism and Islamic feminism.

The book intellectually satisfied her. "I feel that I was helping other women who were going through the same situation as me, who wanted to take a step forward but were afraid. My intention has always been to help people who may feel lost, regardless of the book sales figures," Figueras says humbly.

The book received such a positive reception that Figueras was offered interviews in media outlets all over the world. "Islam was not what I thought it was. As a result of the media misinformation and fake news, I had a distorted and incomplete image about Muslims and their faith, which had nothing to do with what I later found in books and during my personal research," she says.

"I used these interviews and spaces to share my curiosity. If it happened to me, it can happen to anyone. My aim was to transfer to others that desire for learning, and I thought that my personal story could be useful to other people."

Today, she has become a powerful voice of the Muslim community in Spain and her testimony has inspired and helped people going through a similar process in a field notorious for its lack of first-person literature.

Now, she collaborates occasionally with media outlets and different organisations at an international level to promote inter- faith dialogue and integration through cross-cultural encounters.

Religion as a barrier

After the publication of her book, now far from the spotlight, Figueras' path as a journalist and writer over the last years has been full of ups and downs and she has intermittently collaborated with different Spanish and international media outlets, working also as a translator.

Together with her husband, she lived for a brief period in Egypt where for the first time she found the strength and confidence to live her faith in its fullness – here, her hijab was not conspicuous and she marvelled at how the whole country gathered in the streets to break the fast together during the holy month of Ramadan.

2017 was time to return home to give birth to their child and to take care of Figueras' ailing mother. Back in Madrid, she had to face the already precarious journalistic job market with a newly added layer of difficulty – her religion: "I can't directly say it's because of the hijab, but it's definitely not helping me to find a job in a newsroom."

The concept of Islamophobia and the reality of exclusion and stigmatisation experienced by many members of the Muslim population in Spain soon arise in Figueras' discourse. Her tone turns serious and weighty when denouncing the media bias that creates stereotypes and news that harm the community and the perceptions society.

"Islamophobia is a form of racism and is a systemic phenomenon, meaning that it permeates the whole of society and every aspect of our lives. It is therefore present in the newspapers, among the editors and journalists because we have been transformed this way and educated this way," she affirms dolefully.

In Spain, as in many European countries, ethnic and religious minorities are notably under-represented in the press and in social and cultural institutions. This concerns not only the Muslim population but other minorities such as the migrant community, like the Roma or, as Figueras highlights, disabled people.

"A significant part of the population is Muslim in Spain and in the world, but it is consciously or unconsciously made invisible in books and films. For example, why is it that in the image that portrays children going back to school, only white children appear, and not non-racialised children or mothers wearing a hijab? The media does not reflect society, but rather what someone thinks it should be," she affirms.

She delves into the less visible issues that often make her pessimistic: "It's not just the activism you can do outwardly, it's the day-to-day life, it's thinking about what will people say if I go swimming in my pool, if mothers will stare at me when I pick up my child from school… It's a daily burden that we carry as Muslims, especially as women, that makes you exhausted when trying to organise yourselves and fight collectively."

Islam in Spain

The presence of Islam in Spain is almost as ancient as the faith itself. The first groups of North African Muslims crossed the Strait of Gibraltar and set foot on the Iberian Peninsula in the early 700s, not long after the founding of Islam, and further progressed North towards what is now France.

The Moors erected the Emirates of Córdoba and Granada subsequently and ruled over vast parts of the territory until 1492 when, after a long agonising decline, the last ruler handed the keys to Granada over to the Catholic Monarchs closing the period known as "la Reconquista", the reconquest.

Throughout these centuries, with unprecedented periods of peace and coexistence between the three religions, Muslims established themselves as an integral part of Iberian society, leaving a prominent legacy in architecture, language, cuisine, music and art.

The imprint of this splendid civilisation flourished mostly over the Southern parts of Spain, the region of Andalucía, named after the Arabic Al Andalus, and found its zenith in the impressive Alhambra Palace in Granada, considered the finest artwork of Islamic architecture in Europe.

It is no coincidence that many new Muslims and the first Islamic public institutions are settled in this region. Among the most relevant bodies are Islamic Commission, the voice of Muslims in Spain or the Halal Institute, created just 15 years ago in order to issue certificates for permissible food for Muslims, directed by another well-known Muslim woman convert, Isabel Romero.

"Islam is for everyone, for all places and times. Living close to such a wonderful past as the Andalusian is inspiring but, in my opinion, Islam is not confined to a specific territory. When I began my journey, I quickly realised that there were many people who had embarked on a similar path to mine, from all ages, genders and from all social classes.

"For many years, as a community, we haven't organised ourselves efficiently in order to establish our priorities," she sums it up, talking of the future challenges.

Lack of resources and "an imposed agenda" prevent them from focusing on identifying their needs and sorting out their demands. "We need the voice of young people and women to be heard. I want us to be creative and aspiring, to build and find safe spaces for those who are to come, to think about our people, so that the future would be the place we dream of." She smiles.

19

Science and religion are united through the beauty, wonder and magnificence of Islam

———◆◆◆◆◆———

Dr Kari Ann Owen – American playwright, poet and horse-riding teacher

———◆◆◆◆◆———

Born into a Jewish family, Dr Kari Ann has a rare story of grit, determination and faith. Overcoming obesity, childhood trauma, and mobility limitations, she found strength through Islam, something which she thinks Western society, America included, would desperately benefit from.

PLAYWRIGHT, poet, columnist, scholar, business director, horse-riding teacher and creative movement trainer - Dr Kari Ann Owen is clearly anything but an underachiever.

And, though 73 years old, she shows no signs of letting up, either.

A widow living happily in Missoula in the US state of Montana, Kari Ann has been teaching horseback riding and creative movement classes to disabled and non-disabled students alike for over 20 years, striving to instill a sense of confidence, happiness and acceptance within them.

But where does Kari Ann get this strength from? From Allah. Because for the last 25 years, Kari Ann, who was born into a Jewish family, has been a committed Muslim, which she says has given purpose and dignity to her life, regardless of the great suffering and injustices she has had to endure.

"I love and respect Islam in so many ways. I support and deeply admire its respect for education, and for how it protects and promotes the rights of women as well as men in society. I also love and respect Islam for its modest approach to dress, and, above all, for its focus on sobriety and marriage, the two most profound foundations of my life," she affirms.

"I also find it wonderful to feel that one and a half billion people, fellow Muslims, share my faith. Society today is placed under constant pressure to sacrifice ourselves on the altars of unbridled instinct – all without respect for consequences. But Islam, in what I see as its greatest gift to society, asks us to regard ourselves as human beings, created by Allah, and with the capacity to bear responsibility in our relations with others and certainly with ourselves.

"The path of peace, through prayer and charity and a commitment to sobriety and education, allows us to follow the path of Islam, and we stand a good chance of raising children who will be free from the violence and exploitation which is robbing parents and children of safe schools and neighbourhoods, and often even of their lives."

Having overcome obesity, childhood trauma, and mobility limitations, Kari Ann is passionate about the plight of disabled children, special needs children, and also trauma survivors. As she walks in slow circuits through the soft sands of the riding track, she constantly calls out words of encouragement to the children sat upon the gentle ponies which follow her every move.

From an outsider's perspective, it is very moving. Not just for all the kindness and support she is giving to these children, but also because you start to wonder if Kari Ann is making a concerted effort to make young people feel the exact opposite of what other people made to feel as a child.

Gastric disorder and a caring elephant

Born in 1949 as Karen Iris Bogen, she and her elder sister, Judy, were raised in Brooklyn, New York, by their parents Dr Ben Bogen, a physician, and Jocelyn Bogen, his assistant.

When she was an infant, Kari Ann was already suffering from failure to thrive, a severe gastric condition which negatively affected her ability to eat at all. Soon thereafter, her body "decided" to conserve every calorie to ward off starvation. Kari Ann's weight increased beyond "normal" limits, causing her to soon become an object of ridicule by children and adults alike:

"My infantile gastric disorder caused my body to function in a state of panic, conserving every calorie. It resulted in me being overweight, which made me a subject of ridicule and torment by children and adults alike. It was so upsetting I was left not even feeling human anymore. I felt alienated from my own body."

Fortunately, Kari Ann did gain some sense of comfort, but sadly it was not from her own family. In fact, it was from an elephant.

"There was a pink elephant from Thailand which was part of the circus which appeared in New York at Madison Square Garden. I was three years old. I can't describe to you the joy she brought to my life at that meeting: I stroked and petted her, and I could tell she was responding. She probably taught me about what love really is for the first time: an experience of profoundly mutual emotions.

"She was the first friend I ever made and I loved her. I could feel her doing my soul good, so I called her my healer. Many people don't know it, but elephants have great social strength and kindness. Thai people understood this, and viewed these elephants as gifts from God. I don't want to denigrate the role of certain adults I mention in this interview, but for me the truth is that my first healers truly were animals, and my very first one was definitely this wonderful pink elephant. She probably taught me about what love really is for the first time."

Though Healer the Pink Elephant nurtured Kari Ann's soul upon that extraordinary meeting, sadly, it could not save her from the many nightmares which lay ahead. For, within just a few years, Kari Ann became the victim of horrific abuse. Worse still, it was at the hands of her very own father and sister.

"My family was violent and abusive. It termed itself Jewish, and we would light Jewish candles, and I also had to attend the synagogue and had Jewish camp counsellors and so forth. But really, there was nothing holy about my immediate family, as it practiced emotional, physical and even sexual torture on me.

"I later even found out that my father was, according to two Kaiser Permanente psychologists in the San Francisco Bay Area, guilty of genital manipulation when I was a sick infant lying in the crib."

Her intense unhappiness and feeling of alienation from her physical self, whilst also suffering abuse by certain family members and school mates and camp mates and many others, meant that at the age of just 10, Kari Ann felt suicidal.

Here, other members of her family, however, alongside certain extraordinary adults and compassionate friends and older children at camp and school, ended up saving young Kari Ann's life in different ways.

"My isolation somehow caused me to draw strength from my Jewish Aunt Rose and my cousin Frances, as they had both shown me a great example of how to live.

"Though they had very little money of their own, they still gave what they could in charity. So, although working class women, they were also philanthropists, and I was so in awe of this I found myself wanting to firmly embrace the compassionate spiritual values they had demonstrated.

"At the same time, a similar kindness and spirituality was being shown to me by other people. These included my friends' parents, and a very special teacher, Hyman Gillary, who accepted me for who I was, and treated me as a human being.

"Hyman was a Jewish science counsellor who was thrilled by my interest in science. In particular, he was fascinated by my interest in making a connection between astronomy and the Jewish dream visions in the Chumash (Torah, the Five Books of Moses)."

Inspiration from Dr. Maurice Bucaille

Many years later, Kari Ann went on to study the scientific explorations of French gastroenterologist Dr. Maurice Bucaille, a doctor and a specialist in the field of gastroenterology who was the family physician to Saudi King Faisal in 1973 and converted to Islam.

Dr Bucaille had become world-famous for his book *The Bible, The Quran and Science: The Holy Scriptures Examined in the Light of Modern Knowledge*, which relates modern science with religion, especially Islam. The book even inspired a movement – 'The Bucaillists' – who argued that the Quran is not just a work of wonder, rather it contains hard, scientifically-accurate facts.

"This revelation proved extremely comforting to me, as it basically made me realise that I had been right with all my confused thoughts when I was younger. Science and religion really are united – and they are united, of course, by the beauty, wonder and magnificence of Islam.

"I would have given all I could to meet him and tell him how much I want to see every young Muslim embrace this wonder – the union of science and religion which is present in Islam. Were I wealthy, today I would open a regional medical institute that had such values and encourage young people to further their pursuit of science, while also learning to develop love, care and respect for each other."

Kari Ann says Dr Bucaillehadadeep, immenseinfluenceonher. "The writings of Dr. Bucaille are equally moving to me, and I read them every evening. Dr. Bucaille's astonishing journey through the Quranic predictions and understanding of human biology (among other sciences) moved this brilliant and concerned French gastroenterologist to take the *Shahadah*. The humility with which he presents his convictions is another astonishment: many American doctors think they are God-like when they are merely arrogant and prejudiced, especially against the overweight (to whom few have any medical remedies or even up to date research) and against the 'mentally ill' who are generally survivors of violence in their families," she asserts.

In the preface of his book, Dr Bucaille said, "These scientific areas which Quran established to the exclusion of other Scriptures filled me with deep surprise early on, since it never struck my mind to see such a large amount of scientific issues in such a variable and accurate way that they are a mirror image of what has recently been discovered in a book which has existed for more than 13 centuries!!"

Dr Bucaille converted to Islam after he found out that the remains of salt stuck in an Egyptian Pharaoh's (Firaun in Arabic) dead body proved that he drowned, exactly like what has been stated in the Quran. Dr Bucaille puzzled over how the Quran knew about the death, as the Pharoah's dead body was just discovered in 1898.

He kept on asking: "Where did the Muslims' Quran quote these data from while the mummy was not discovered until 1898,
i.e. about 200 years only, given that the Quran has been recited by Muslims for over 1400 years, and given also that until a few decades ago the entire mankind including Muslims did not know that the ancient Egyptians had mummified their pharaohs?"

Dr Bucaille's explorations into Pharoah, the Quran and science led him to Islam. Later, attending a medical conference in Saudi Arabia, Dr Bucaille declared: "I have converted to Islam and believed in this Quran."

Tony Richardson's profound impact

Another source of comfort, inspiration, and even salvation for Kari Ann during her arduous teenage years, was the creative arts. Here, Kari Ann felt encouraged by her modern dance teacher and acting teachers to try and accept and express her physical form, even if others continued to be abusive to her.

Though she remembers this fondly, even this stage in her life was still poisoned by the ongoing abuse outside of dance class.

"My father was explosive and threatened my life with his out- of-control violence, as did my sister, who suffered from paranoia and was just filled with hatred. My mother was passive, but deeply rejecting of me, and she was not someone I could turn to or rely on for support."

Early in her life in New York, Kari Ann began attending productions and staged readings. She went to see the play "Luther", where behind the scenes she even got to hear its director, the renowned English theatre and film director, Cecil Antonio "Tony" Richardson, give notes to the cast as her teachers and directors had.

Richardson, whose accolades included everything from directing Sir Laurence Olivier to winning the Academy Award for best director, completely captivated Kari Ann. "I'll never forget, I went backstage and was just a little black-haired Jewish girl with glasses and high socks, and there I was meeting a man of such important and amazing talent.

"He was just so inspiring and so brilliant as a director. He had brought profound plays to America by various British playwrights, and these works dramatised a range of spiritual struggles. These plays inspired me so deeply that they went on to influence and inspire the spiritual struggles which I wrote about in my own plays later in life," Kari Ann says.

Little did she know, however, that Tony Richardson would come to have another profound effect on her life 24 years later, when she would embrace Islam and become a Muslim.

For the moment, however, Kari Ann was still simply trying to survive, even though the conditions around her had become even worse.

"Aged 15, my father and mother forced me to undergo a gynaecological examination performed by both of my parents. It was sexually inspired by my father's sadistic need for control, and my mother went along with his fantasy. She was not even a qualified nurse, she just dressed up in the outfit. And when a psychiatrist learned of this supposed 'examination' he deemed it an 'incestuous assault', and was documented as such. I still have the documents now," Kari Ann reminisces.

"My trauma then took various forms, and I was hospitalised after a total loss of all mental and social functioning. I had also developed a speech defect which had made an earlier appearance in childhood, and was then tormented for this by staff and residents alike.

"I was then sent for two more years to a so-called residential school for bright but disturbed kids where social cruelty by both staff and students was the sick norm, including physical assaults of students by staff."

Though traumatised, her fierce intellect, strong will and the creative arts once again helped Kari Ann stay alive. Instead of giving up, she poured all of her angst and desperation into her first play, which was then produced in 1967 at one of the Devereux Schools.

In 1968, now free of the school where she says she had been 'incarcerated', Kari Ann again drew on the powers of her intellect to flourish and thrive. In 1972 she did a Bachelor of Arts at New York University in American Literature and Creative Writing, followed by a Master of Arts in Creative Writing at San Francisco State University.

During this time, she worked on her play about domestic terrorism, *Circle of Silence*, at New York University, which was then produced in San Francisco in 1975. She also did all she could (with formidable assistance) to reject all of the crazy influences surrounding her at the time (and particularly prevalent in creative circles), including drink, drugs and sexual promiscuity. Instead, Kari Ann focused on the 12-step plan for those wishing to live an alcohol-free life and a life free from other disturbances like eating disorders to sexual addiction.

"I was set on improving my life and trying to lead a good life, so I prayed.

But at the time I was not Muslim, so it was really just me praying to a general sense of God. I was really just striving to be constructive instead of destructive and particularly self- destructive, and for me, saying no to alcohol was part of this."

At the same time, Kari Ann began her Ph.D. at the Graduate Theological Union in theodicy and tragic literature. Again, she succeeded, and three years later, she had become Dr Karen Iris Bogen.

But this name would only last for the next nine years, after which Kari Ann decided to change her official name, in an attempt to try and distance herself from her troubled past.

"In 1989, when I began performing country music in public, I chose a name encompassing my idols. These were Kari Swenson, a survivor of violent crime, and Randy Owen, lead singer of the country western group 'Alabama': It was an honest group, and he was an honest man. As my original last name, Bogen, had been mercilessly mocked throughout my childhood and adolescence, it just felt like time to leave that all behind."

In 1992, Kari Ann, now going by 'Dr Kari Ann Owen', a name she retains today, was completely devastated when she learned of the death of her childhood idol, the British play director, Mr Tony Richardson.

"His 'becoming' homosexual, moving to Los Angeles, contracting AIDS and dying was a horrifying event. He had a famous actress wife, extremely talented, and also very talented children, all excellent professionals in their own right. To my mind, he had abandoned his family, something I regard as unforgivable because of personal experience of being essentially abandoned by my own family.

"How could this brilliant and original theatre director be part of this? I deeply regret never having known Mr. Richardson personally. If I had, I would have begged him to care for his life, and also to return to his wife and children for the sake of all family members. By this I mean he should have considered their hearts and souls and their faith in one another. Family love is so very important. It is irreplaceable, and also necessary for proper, healthy functioning as a human."

Kari Ann found herself struggling to manage a conflict of emotions. On the one hand she was incredibly sad that her childhood hero had died, and on the other hand, she felt that he had been part of a destructive and dangerous lifestyle which she did not approve of.

"As a young person, I felt troubled enough, and I was in need of a philosophy that advocated human responsibility above even deeply felt emotional needs and sexual ones.

"But what I definitely did not need, and what no young person, especially highly sensitive creative young people need, is to experience the death of someone we had greatly admired, and particularly not when it is through carelessness and a philosophy of impersonal sexual consumption which had been carried without any sense of care for others. Thank you, American capitalism."

Here, however, Kari Ann found that Islam provided both clarity and compassion.

Islam's compassion

"Allah knows how much we all need help in living with love and consideration for others, no matter how problematic our sexuality. Islam, praise Allah, provides a strong system of values, because obligations to Allah and the people around us supersede our personal neediness.

"So really, my path to the *Shahadah* began on a conscious level when Tony Richardson died of AIDS. And, with his death, another part of my sense of belonging to American society also died."

Given her abusive childhood, Kari Ann had already spent years battling post-traumatic stress and clinical depression. But, with the death of a person she had revered, she now felt a sudden need to get away from a destructive society. Specifically, she wanted to escape what she saw as the profitable marketing unto death of suicidal ways of "living". For reasons of escape from economic and other privations, emotional anarchy in many forms was becoming ever-prevalent in American society, and very popular within creative and literary circles. "How could it have been otherwise with our government waging wars upon societies striving for independence and American minorities rising up from degradation"?

Kari Ann then wrote to Ellison MacMaster, a Native American medicine man who lived on the Paiute Reservation, in Schurz, Nevada.

On a quest for deeper spiritual healing, she then rode to the Paiute Reservation on her own motorcycle, which she had dubbed 'The Black Eagle'.

"Here, Medicine Man Ellison MacMaster gave me the name 'Penomee', which in the Native American Paiute language means 'she who rides the roads'. Like many great mentors of all faiths, Ellison was instrumental to my healing by providing such kindness, understanding and acceptance, and he told me to consider his family my family.

"After this, at the South Bay Islamic Association I met Imam Siddiqi, Sister Hussein Rahima and Sister Maria Abdin, who was not just a writer, but a Native American too.

"It is impossible to state all I learned from the people, but they definitely taught me the virtue of not bragging, and instead of charitableness, and of refusing to be aggressive, even when threatened or questioned.

"I was so inspired and found myself wanting to know more and more about Islam, to which I felt passionately drawn. Many things were coming together at once, in a way which is rather difficult to describe. I began visiting Islamic education centres, prayer centres and mosques in Berkley, California, and found that the call of the *muezzin* was just incredible. I found it - and still find it today - as something so incredibly beautiful, moving and powerful. For me it is as deep as the soporific sound of the sea, as the swaying of ships, as the drumming of horse hooves through the desert.

"Primarily, I read the Quran again and again, and also spent many hours on the Internet reading all I could find on Islam. Here, Allah guided my learning and found myself absorbing reams and reams of fascinating information relating to Islam over the centuries.

"My biological mother's ancestors had been Spanish Jews who lived among Muslims until the Jewish community was expelled by the Inquisition in 1492. One hundred years later, the expulsion of Muslims from Spain was to follow.

"And when I learned of the humanity of Caliph Uthman towards the Jewish refugees during the time of the expulsions of my ancestors, I was also moved by his great sense of compassion.

"I realised that my Jewish ancestors, because of expulsion and atrocity, have lived in the four corners of the world, but I just don't think the mercy of Islam is well known. The fact is that Spanish Jews, upon being expelled, were given sanctuary by Muslims. It was humbling and inspiring."

Through her studying of Islam, Kari Ann's spirit was now soaring once again. Sadly, however, she was once again suffering on a physical level. In September 1993, as the result of years of sitting in a non-ergonomic chair while writing her plays and also working for a San Francisco financial journalist, Kari Ann had developed a crippling sciatica. In 1995 the physician issued a damning diagnosis, classifying Kari Ann as 'permanently disabled'. As ever, Kari Ann refused to give in.

"I had to learn mobility from the bottom up, and trained my golden retriever, Mischa, to assist me and was marvellously assisted by a yoga teacher who was an employee of my chiropractor."

Concern for the mentally ill

During the four years preceding her *Shahadah* in 1997, Kari Ann became aware of Islam's deep concern for the medically needy. "Islamic concern for the 'mentally ill' (whatever the origins of those conflicts and conditions) go back centuries before Freud. Since I was maltreated to a horrifying degree in a mental hospital at 15 and a 'residential treatment centre' for two years after that, I was astonished by the revelation of Allah's inspiration concerning a terrifying fact which afflicts so many of us, particularly victims of violence. Certainly, I am no expert on Islamic psychology or psychiatry, but this particular revelation of love surely answers, partly, why I believe science and Islam are linked and hardly mutually exclusive," she asserts.

Kari Ann discovered that the Islamic world, in its early years, had a pioneering approach concerning mental health and psychiatry. The first psychiatric hospitals were founded in Arab countries: Baghdad 705 A.D (during the kingship of the caliph El Waleed ibn Abdel Malek), Cairo 800 A.D, and Damascus 1270 A.D, whereas the first psychiatric asylum in West Europe, the
Bethlem Hospital in London, was founded in the 13th century.
Also, under Islamic law, the therapeutic bond between a patient and a doctor is considered sacred.

"Islam has been an inspiration in its demonstration, not mere enunciation, of respect for the people and animals and four-footed and winged and leafed beings who were and remain lifelines of survival, of belief in positive as well as negative forces affecting our collective and individual present and future. The love of the Islamic sisterhood is a far cry from the female-based contempt and cruelty I experienced as a child and adolescent.

"To see love in action may well be the greatest demonstration of spirituality, in whatever community, that we see in this lifetime."

When asked why Judaism didn't satisfy her spiritual needs, she had this to say: "Very unfortunately, the Jewish community in which I grew up was hostile, particularly the hatred of both boys and adult males (including teachers) closed the door to the allegedly merciful and caring Jewish god. Children are not specialists in the abstract, particularly when human behaviour contradicts human conceit and rigidity.

"My parents' and sister's role is clear. The summer camps my parents sent me to were ostensibly Jewish, but the persecution by counsellors and campers concerning my weight included forced starvation by a 19-year-old psychopathic counsellor. My other visible disabilities (like speech rapidity under pressure of anxiety) was mocked while still on the bus to one camp. Also, Jewish education was never offered with love and respect and acceptance at Temple Beth Emeth in New York, and those experiences closed the road to Judaism. But not forever.

"I cannot state enough the magnificent role of science counsellor Hyman Gillary and later the Hillel Foundation of Berkeley, California, at helping me become an active participant in Jewish life. I cannot adequately state my affection and gratitude to the founder of the Jewish Arts Community of the East Bay (east of San Francisco), Rabbi Burt Jacobsen, whose synagogue, Kehilla, has always been and remains an emotional and spiritual refuge and place of *chesed* (loving kindness)."

She adds: "My spirituality began with an early revelation of the unity of the chambers of the emotional heart. I was nine years old.

My astonished mother was speechless. That spirituality of connectedness to all beings eventually subsumed the atmosphere of general and personal prejudice and hatred in the summer camps and Temple Beth Emeth [synagogue], and allowed my road to open."

Saying *shahadah* at Santa Clara, California

Three years later a decidedly happier Kari Ann was now to open yet another rich and beautiful chapter in her fascinating life, as she was to marry the love of her life, 6-foot-9, Mr Silas Warner. A computer genius full of love and kindness, Silas had rightly made a name for himself in 1981 when he developed Castle Wolfenstein, the world's first ever game to include digitized speech.

"My marriage was and remains the fulfilment of mutual devotion, and I hope Silas and I managed to exemplify that mutual devotion which all known spiritualities advocate."

And, a year later, came the greatest chapter of all, as Kari Ann converted to Islam.

Though more than happy to formally renounce pork, alcohol and other things un-Islamic by becoming Muslim, Kari Ann says she had really addressed all of these issues head-on many years ago. "The rigorous discipline of Islam was one I had really adapted to long before my *Shahadah*, having become clean and sober in my student years, and I had also been passionate and rigorous (I hope) in prayer since my introduction to the 12 Step anti-alcohol programs back then.

"I also had no interest in pork. My engagement to Silas Warner in Spring 1995 and our marriage in March 1996 brought an end to any dating behaviour and, Allah forgive me, any *haram* (forbidden) behaviour committed out of neediness.

"I know some coverts to Islam say that they struggled at first to overcome various stereotypes they had about Islam and the oppression of women, and terrorism. But this just was not the case with me. I was already a survivor of violence against women. And my playwrighting career had already passionately expressed what I was experiencing and observing in America on the issue of terrorism, which, to me, remains unforgiveable in all situations.

"I realised when I read the Quran that there are many examples which make it clear that Islam has nothing to do with terrorism." Here Kari Ann refers to the Quran (2:190), for example, which states that Muslims may 'Fight in the cause of Allah against those who fight against you, but do not transgress limits. Lo! Allah loves not aggressors...'.

And an even clearer example of where Islam makes clear that it does not approve of terrorism, says Kari Ann, is: 'Let there be no hostility except to those who practice oppression' (Quran 2:193). "Certain recent television broadcasts and even admissions by persons alleging themselves to be Muslim have rationalised or justified what is clearly forbidden by Allah's revelation to the Prophet Muhammad," she says.

"These individuals have stated they were taught that if they commit several forbidden acts such as slaughter, they will be given a special place at the side of Allah once they ascend to heaven.

"Yet it is clearly implied in, for example, 3:179, that it is Allah and Allah alone who chooses martyrs. 'He chooses of his apostles for the purpose whom he pleases. So, believe in Allah and His apostles: and if ye believe and do right, you have a reward without measure'."

Kari Ann took her *Shahadah* at a community and teaching centre in Santa Clara, CA in 1997.

"Young Muslims from local schools and from the various Silicon Valley industries were present. It was a very special day. My feelings were one of great relief at leaving the American sexual sewer (which I had already left long before that, praise Allah) and feeling that the choices of sobriety and spirituality and the difficult ascension toward psychological and spiritual health (the hardest struggle of all) were acceptable and praised.

"Here the values of Islam, as practiced by individual Muslims and families, gave me a sense of escape from the horrifying social pressures I was faced with, particularly in the San Francisco Bay Area. By this, I mean the pressure to drink and, within some literary and creative circles, to engage in destructive and uncaring sexual activities.

"For me it was not about having to sign up to a sense of being restricted and limited. Even though the meaning of Islam is submission, there is nothing slaving and degrading about it. Instead, the frail human will is yoked in a positive and rational sense, to a higher, more benevolent and compassionate will, and is thus deeply, lovingly connected to creation."

In 2000, Kari Ann's gastric disorder flared up yet again, and her weight rose to 107.5 kg. She required internal bypass surgery in December.

Though the surgery left her struggling with remaining mobility issues, Kari Ann just handled the situation like all the many difficulties she had faced in her life, and rose to the challenge.

Horse-riding teacher

Discovering a new lease of life teaching riding in 2001 brought her not just a renewed sense of purpose in helping children suffering with disabilities, but also gave her an opportunity for exercise which would help her build up her muscles again.

Just a year later, however, her husband, Silas lost his job. He had worked extremely hard, despite the fact that in the final four years of employment he was even on a kidney dialysis machine.

"This marvellous giant, this creative genius, this lover and husband and immensely just and honest friend of mine, had managed to support his family (wife, service dogs, two cats and a therapy horse) although on disability and unemployment benefit. "For example, when we decided to leave the San Franscisco Bay Area for a less expensive part of California where I had a mentor in therapeutic horseback riding, Silas would go out each day to find us housing while I remained at home to earn our moving expenses."

At the time, the couple's finances were so tough that the only housing Silas could find was at a Baptist mission, and Kari Ann and Silas were forced to rent housing in the home of a woman who they thought was a sincere recovering alcoholic, but soon became drunk and abusive.

After this, the couple moved to a small apartment in Chico, California, where Kari Ann was performing at a local college and also at Stanford University. Yet, tragically, it was here, on February 26, 2004, that Silas, 54, finally lost his battle with kidney disease, alongside diabetes, arthritis and hypertension for over a decade.

"I lost my husband, my love, the greatest love of mind and heart and body, and I will adore him and love him forever."

Kari Ann continued to work as a horse-riding trainer, and moved back to the San Francisco Bay Area. She taught in many locations including the beautiful Las Trampas Stables in San Ramon, next to the East Bay Regional Park District's Las Trampas Regional Wilderness Park.

Now Director of both Joy Rise Movement LLC and Wildhorse Equestrian Center, today Dr Owen lives as a widow outside the San Francisco Bay Area.

Strengthened by Islam, and by the pride she felt in having been Silas' wife, Kari Ann continues to live in a way she felt honoured him best – one of celibacy.

"Islam was a source of strength for my husband's and my own abstinence from drugs and alcohol. Also, more specifically, it gave us the strength to distance ourselves from the "suicide as self- expression" idea promoted by New York intellectuals and their audiences. This includes radical sexual groups who practice sex as a form of impersonal consumption."

Despite her horrific ordeal as a child within her family, today she wants to stress that she bears no ill-will towards Jews or Judaism.

"I would be devastated if I came across as being derogatory towards Jews or Judaism. I am not at all. Rather, I see Islam as a magnificent advancement toward the essential values of Judaism and many other faiths.

"By this I mean Islam is a shedding of aggression, and a devotion to mercy, enunciated five times daily in the Islamic prayer cycle. Islam also draws upon science as a tool of spiritual and intellectual inspiration leading us toward The One Allah; unity of the Prophetic Vision, which in Islam recognises prophets from Abraham to Jesus and to the Prophet Muhammad (may peace be upon him for eternity)."

For Kari Ann, Islam has not just provided an answer to the childhood theory she had been developing about a link between religion and science, rather it has proved a source of support and inspiration for her throughout the many struggles she has had to battle with.

"Islam's value of the centrality of female devotion and love of family, however universal the family, is compatible with my true nature and beliefs in action as well as words.

"Islam is also supportive of my long struggle toward physical and emotional health, most importantly by presenting the balanced soul as something normal and not an anomaly, which is what our hectic and selfish modern society often encourages.

"The Prophetic tradition deems Allah's universe as immortal and stretching far beyond our tormented and self-tormented planet.

Death as unity with Allah

"Therefore, death of the individual in this context is not a pessimistic event, but an affirmation of our future unity with Allah in a context of infinite growth of a universe constantly righting itself according to a unified scientific and spiritual law.

"And Islam is also deeply pertinent to my lifelong fight to avoid my original family's genetic physical and mental illnesses," she adds.

Here Kari Ann says although she had inherited an intermittent explosive disorder, through years of prayer and discipline and medical intervention, she has managed to largely overcome it.

Other scars of her troubled childhood, such as the abuse, are things which never really heal, but even here, Kari Ann says she has found strength through Islam, something which she thinks Western society, America included, would desperately benefit from.

"I really value what Islam does for addicted youth, especially our poorest youth. When I was an undergraduate at New York University, a fellow student committed suicide and two others took near-fatal overdoses. Yet there was little, if any, anti-drug and anti-alcohol education reaching out directly to the vulnerable students. The poorest communities were the hardest hit, partly because of governmental profiting from drug sales.

"Again, Islam really helps with all of this. It directly reaches out to vulnerable youth in these communities. Islam neither advocates nor practices child abuse. American society, however, from the beginning of mass media, especially Playboy in 1954, has sexualised and still continues to sexualise children. It allows overweight children to be judged as failed sexual objects by 'peers' and adults. It happened to me, and I am sure it has happened to countless other innocent children too.

"Of course, Allah knows there will be individual failures and atrocities, even with some committed by Muslims, for not everyone who declares themselves Muslim actually is Muslim based on how they live."

But at least Muslim societies do not advocate their own peoples' and societies' destruction through mass media.

"Today Islam is providing help to many young men and women in the West seeking a disciplined life of sobriety, education, sexual and moral responsibility, leading to that victory one may call oneness with Allah and others merely call responsibility, or grace. All praise to Allah.

"Islam represents a vision of the future and of harmony, young couples living in harmony and not being competitive with each other. We need more of that way of living in America for the sakes of the adults as well as the children."

20

'My first encounter with Islam was an encounter with my Sensei (master)'

Dr Qayyim Naoki Yamamoto – Japanese academic and scholar

Naoki waited eagerly at a café in Kyoto, Japan, for Professor Hassan whose wife had written a book which he had just read. Naoki had liked the book so much that he requisitioned a meeting with Prof. Hassan immediately after he had finished reading it. Prof. Hassan entered, and as soon as he saw Naoki, he started crying.

I T WAS an emotional meeting the young Naoki wasn't a wee bit prepared for, and a defining one because it changed the course of his life forever. He waited eagerly at a café in Kyoto, Japan, for Prof. Hassan whose wife had written a book which he had just read. Naoki had liked the book so much that he requisitioned a meeting with Prof. Hassan immediately after he had finished reading it. "Prof. Hassan entered, and as soon as he saw me, he started crying. I was stunned," says Naoki, remnants of that surprise still writ large upon his face.

At the time, Naoki was an undergraduate student at Doshisha University in Kyoto. "I acquired this insatiable interest in all religions. I was studying Christianity in the Faculty of Theology," he says, "yet I read books about Buddhism. I also read books about Taoism, Confucianism, Protestants, or any religion for that matter."

During this intensive exploration, Naoki came across a book in the university library. Titled *A Brief Introduction to God*, the book introduced and elaborated the idea that God is the one and only. The book was in fact an introduction to the God of Islam, Allah. Yet, Naoki was not then aware of that, because the author did not use any specific Islamic terminology, mentioning neither the name of Allah nor that of the Prophet of Islam. "This book had a deep impact on me," recalls Naoki, and adds, "I was really amazed how the author expressed otherwise sophisticated and abstract concepts in plain Japanese."

Coincidentally, and surprisingly, the author of the book, Khawla Kaori, turned out to be the wife of Hassan Ko Nakata, a professor of theology at Doshisha University, the very university Naoki was studying at then. Naoki recalls that he thought "this was rather a call" to him. He sent an email to Professor Hassan right away, writing to him that he developed a strong interest in Islam thanks to his wife's book and asked him whether he could study Islam with her. Prof. Hassan immediately replied and asked Naoki to meet him in a café in the neighbourhood of the university.

"I was already in the café when Prof. Hassan arrived. As soon as he saw me, he began to weep." Prof. Hassan explained to Naoki that he unfortunately lost his wife a year ago due to cancer and was still struggling with his loss. He also told Naoki that, while reading his email, he recalled what the Prophet Muhammad (PBUH) once stated: "When a person dies, all their good deeds end, except for three of them: charity (*sadaqa jariya*), beneficial knowledge, and a virtuous offspring."

This Prophetic statement, Prof. Hassan told him, made him realize that his wife's good legacy was alive in Naoki's heart in the form of knowledge. To keep his wife's legacy alive, Prof. Hassan wanted to become his teacher.

"This was my first encounter with Islam," he sums it up. In other words, his first encounter with Islam was an encounter with his master (Sensei).

Dr Qayyim Naoki Yamamoto was born in 1989, and it was 13 years ago, in 2009, that he made that big decision and converted to Islam, when he was an undergraduate student. He is now an assistant professor of Turkic Studies at Marmara University, one of Turkey's most prestigious public universities.

Gateman's hospitality

Naoki befriended Prof. Hasan and a year later, in the summer of his second year, he took a trip to Cairo to study standard Arabic. It was the holy month of Ramadan. He was not yet a Muslim and therefore not fasting. But he still could not buy any drink or food because all restaurants were closed during daylight. "I was so stressed," he recalls. Later in the day, as the sun set and he went back to his apartment, he saw the gateman of the apartment having his *iftar* dinner on the floor at the entrance to the apartment. Naoki even recalls that the gateman was eating cucumber. He had nothing else.

"I stared at him. He stared at me and immediately uttered '*tafaddal*', a phrase of invitation in Arabic. I was so surprised because this was the first time I met him and I did not know anything about him. Yet, he offered his food to me even though I was nobody to him."

Naoki found himself amazed by the gateman's behaviour. The gateman's salary was most likely very low. That cucumber might even be the only food he had for his *iftar*. Yet he did not hesitate to offer it to a foreign guest. "That behaviour deeply influenced me," Naoki recalls. Back in Japan, however, things were different. There were many homeless people in Tokyo and other big cities; many others died of hunger during the winter and were ashamed to ask for help. Naoki saw homeless people in Egypt as well, but they could at least ask for, and were receiving, help.

Naoki later realised that the gateman's behaviour was not a unique act, exceptional to him. It was part and reflection of a broader culture. He later experienced that the Turks also have the same culture, and even have a name for it, '*ikram kültürü*'. "I do not think that the word 'ikram' has an exact translation in English. Serving others, maybe. But, I think, 'ikram' has richer and broader connotations." Naoki believes that this culture of giving, or unrequited offering, deeply influenced his decision to embrace Islam.

Naoki's formal embrace of Islam, or utterance of the Shahadah, came during his stay in Cairo. Prof. Hassan was also in the city. One day, he introduced Naoki to a professor of Al- Azhar University and the three engaged in a long conversation. In the middle of it, Prof. Hassan suggested to Naoki that he become a Muslim. There were already two Muslims in the room and they could serve as his witnesses. Why miss this opportunity? "I thought," Naoki recalls, "there's no strong reason to decline this suggestion, so I said, 'Yeah I can be a Muslim'."

If anyone presumes that a person who makes such a major decision in life must be undergoing some truly dramatic, or even traumatic, experience, that is not the case, Naoki says. His conversion at that particular moment in his life did not require much of an emotional or intellectual journey. By then, he'd already had his own 'road to Damascus' moment. That moment came when he encountered and read that short book on *tawhid* (oneness of God) by Khawla Kaori. Uttering the *Shahadah* was just a symbolic act, a formal declaration. Naoki believes that he already had the faith of a Muslim by then.

Muslims as uncivilised people

Naoki says he in fact had quite negative ideas about Islam in the beginning. When he thought of Islam then, he imagined uncivilised people who lived in the desert and spoke a language that he did not understand a word of. He also thought that it was a religion of people who hijacked planes and bombed places when stressed.

"I believe," he says, "many others shared this negative image of Islam in Japan." He was 12 years old when the 9/11 attacks happened. The Western media, particularly in America, was quite negative and biased in its portrayal of Islam and the Japanese media adopted almost the same narrative. Khawla Kauri's book helped Naoki notice that there was an Islamic tradition in Japan as well and that Japanese Muslim intellectuals in that tradition could have better explained Islam and the Islamic concepts in the local language.

Naoki's family was Christian. He was not a pious person at all. Yet, in Christianity, he argues, being pious does not require much: going to church regularly, respecting the pastor, reading the Bible. He did all these. But, were these enough to be pious? Christianity, he believes, does not set clear standards of piety. "So, I am not sure if I was pious." But, he recalls, even before embracing Islam, he had already nurtured a belief in the oneness of God thanks to that short book he read. But he simply did not know what that belief required morally and ritually.

His grandmother was a kimono merchant and was well- versed in traditional Japanese culture, including the tea ceremony. "On the other hand, my family was open to foreign cultures and allowed me to experience various cultures, including a homestay in the U.S. when I was nine. My parents told me we must train our spirit to learn balance. There are no absolutes in human-made things, and we have no right to judge others. Culture is the same; I was taught to absorb different cultures and build that balance within ourselves."

How does it feel for a person immersed in Japanese culture to embrace Islam? Does he find anything difficult to grasp? He frankly accepts that he has to, in fact, grapple with many theological and doctrinal questions. He argues that any Japanese will find it difficult to understand monotheism. The second is prophethood. In the first place, the idea of monotheism, or believing in only one God, is not present in Japan. Japanese people are not exclusively Buddhists or Shintoists, but rather follow several religions in a syncretistic manner.

There is also no concept of prophecy or prophets in Japanese religion. People who convey God's message to the masses on behalf of the masses are imagined in Japanese society as leaders of new religious cults, and the Japanese have a negative image of them. The Japanese are skeptical of religious leaders and religions, especially since Buddhist cults committed terrorist acts in Japan in the late 80s and 90s.

Therefore, he suggests, one has to start with explaining the idea of *tawhid* to spread the message of Islam in Japan, not the idea of prophethood. That concept might literally "freak the Japanese out." Because the Japanese will find some theological concepts difficult to understand, they might keep a distance to Islam and even to Muslims.

"That's why," Naoki remarks, "I'm encouraging myself and others to try to first introduce the practical aspect of the Islamic spirituality in Japan. Understandably, some people express their worry that if we only introduce the practical aspects of Islam, the Japanese might never understand and embrace *tawhid* or prophethood, until the end of their lives. I agree. There is such a risk, but still, I believe, not pushing the Japanese away must be the first priority."

He further elaborates. "When I first embraced Islam, I cannot claim that I really had this strong faith in Allah or the Prophet. Let me use a metaphor. As I see it, acquiring faith is like cooking. By embracing Islam, you just start to cook a meal. And it is a process. It takes time. You still have unresolved questions. You still have prior beliefs. When you embrace Islam, you just start to believe in Islam. It is not yet a completed process."

Naoki claims that this is the nature of things. Historically, Islam has not spread like a wildfire. It has taken time for the societies to digest its message and embrace Islam in numbers. "In some societies," Naoki claims, "it takes at least three generations for the majority of the society to embrace Islam. In some others it takes at least 300 or 400 years."

Prayer is not difficult

Is practicing Islam difficult? "Praying five times a day or fasting... it has never been difficult for me. Prayer just takes five minutes of your time. All you have to do is to find the right place and time. And then you just do it. That's it."

Yet, this is not the point Naoki wants to make. He takes another perspective to the question and declares: "We must acknowledge that this is a private matter. I see people asking Muslim converts how many times they pray a day or whether they wear hijab. If they are not wearing hijab, they ask why they are not wearing hijab. But, this whole thing is a private matter. Faith or *iman* is not just about how many rituals one undertakes. It is a private journey towards Allah, the content of which is unknown to others."

Naoki continues: "We never know a person's future or their final state in faith. Look at Malcolm X. The person who was instrumental in guiding Malcolm X into Islam was not even a Sunni Muslim. Yes, he was Elijah Muhammad, a highly controversial figure, who guided Malcolm X into Islam and even shaped his life in his last few years."

Naoki says, "In almost 80 per cent of his whole life, Malcolm X lived like a radical Black American activist. But in the last few years of his life, he totally changed: he made pilgrimage and became the Muslim he was."

From Malcolm X's life, Naoki derives a valuable life lesson. "You cannot judge one's life by just looking at their one moment, or one action." What really matters is that how one ends their life and that end can only be known by Allah. So, he advises all Muslims to do their best in rituals and sincerely repent if they make any mistake or commit any sin. But, he insists, "we should not pass judgment on others and also we should not let others pass judgments on others."

Naoki speaks of another challenge Muslim converts face. He says Muslims expect converts to become Muslims as fast as possible. But that is against the nature of human beings. "I have been Muslim for 13 years now," he sighs, "you know what, I am still digesting the Islamic creed. And if I were living somewhere else, not in Turkey, I am sure it would take longer to totally digest it, maybe 20 years or 30 years."

What really matters is the state of your faith in the end of your life. Naoki cites a verse from the Quran in Arabic. *Wa la tamutunna illa wa antum muslimoun* (Al-i Imran, 3:102); "Do not die unless you are a Muslim." Trying to live like a Muslim is certainly vital, Naoki believes, but trying to die as a Muslim is even more important. He interprets that this verse is essentially asking Muslims to try to digest the message of Islam until the end of their lives. "And if you can digest it then you're fortunate. If you cannot digest it then Allah is to make the judgment."

He adds, "I'm still trying to understand Allah, I'm trying to still understand life of the Prophet, peace be upon him. I confess. There are times that I don't understand this verse in the Quran or that *hadith* (prophet's saying). But this is part of the process of digesting the message of Islam. I give my best to understand Islam. I read books or consult with others, with more knowledgeable people on the matter. Still, I often feel I do not have my answers. So, I think, I just need more time. What I am trying to say is that, we must not rush in our own spiritual journey. Patience. Having patience not only toward others but also yourself. One has to be patient with his/her own self."

He read the Quran before becoming a Muslim. "I understood the themes, but I am more interested in how the scriptures were understood and attempted to be applied to society by those who historically existed," he says.

"Prophet Muhammad (PBUH) lived in the same era as Prince Shotoku. Although Japanese people remember the ethical example set by Prince Shotoku, no one thinks of putting it into practice. However, Muslims still regard the Prophet Muhammad as an ethical role model, and his life lives on in the hearts of Muslims as a vivid experience. This is remarkable," he says.

Keeping the faith is very important

Speaking about the challenges of a convert, Naoki has a different view. According to him, embracing Islam is really the easiest step, but keeping one's faith is harder and the most important task. Before conversion, he was worried if it was possible for him to become a good Muslim.

"I told Prof. Hassan that I saw many good Muslims and I fear that I can't be one." He also recalls saying, "I was also really worried if I can become happy if I embrace Islam." Prof. Hassan's response was rather unusual. He told Naoki: "Of course, you will never be happy if you become Muslim. Quite the opposite," he added, "you will face the most difficult time of your life if you accept Islam. You will suffer and you will make mistakes. I have also made many mistakes, and regret and repentance have become my best friends. You can just be a flawed, weak and sinful Muslim like me, and that will be enough. Then Allah will guide us to what He wants us to be."

In retrospect, Naoki thinks, Prof. Hassan's response proved to be wise and insightful. Naoki has often faced disrespectful behaviour of his co-religionists for simply being an East Asian. He does not say racist. But that is what he most likely means. "Once I was in Cairo," he remembers, "I tried to enter a masjid to pray. But, the people in the masjid told me 'No Chinese'."

Prof. Hassan told him that, by becoming a Muslim, one is not becoming a perfect human being, nor, by accepting Islam, is one plunging into a perfect, happy life. That person is just another human being, one with the same flaws.

"By embracing Islam," Professor Hassan told him, one also "accepts the difficult path that extends ahead." Accepting Islam is easy. Leaving Islam is also easy. It is so because living as a Muslim is not easy. A Muslim has to be constantly vigilant in figuring out ways to keep his/her faith alive.

This is a more serious challenge than many comprehend, Naoki believes. He conjectures that converts enjoy their happiest moments when they embrace Islam. This is because many other Muslims come to celebrate them and utter statements of joy, such as *mabrouk* (congratulations) or *alhamdallah* (thanks to Allah). New converts come to believe that they acquire new brothers and sisters and that all of their previous sins are forgiven by God. But soon the celebratory atmosphere dissipates. This happens, Naoki claims, because with no tradition of Islam of their own, new converts simply get lost in their paths and receive no help or guidance from other Muslims who previously claimed brotherhood or sisterhood in religion.

Feeling of estrangement

As to his own post-conversion problem, Naoki speaks of a feeling of estrangement. "When I first became Muslim, I tried to be like a good Muslim. I tried to wear Egyptian clothes like Arabs. I also tried to wear Indonesian clothes, and I studied Arabic. I tried to mix Arabic vocabulary when I spoke in Japanese. But it didn't work." Soon, Naoki began to feel estranged in his own native country. "I started to feel that I am not Japanese anymore. But I was not an Arab Muslim neither, nor Indonesian Muslim, nor Turkish Muslim." Naoki uses the Turkish idiom, "arada kalmak," to describe the feeling he felt. 'Arada kalmak' literally means 'to be stuck in between'. "I was somewhere between being a Japanese and being a foreigner. As a result," Naoki adds, "I started to lose my confidence."

But he was able to resolve this problem of estrangement. Naoki recalls a public lecture he attended in the university. The lecture was about the Ottoman Empire and delivered by a Turkish professor. Naoki remembers the professor describing Islamic civilisation as an open civilisation. The professor meant, Naoki explains, the Islamic civilisation has the flexibility to embrace other cultures and to transform those cultures into their Islamic versions. Naoki recalls, "I was so impressed because I had thought that by embracing Islam one undergoes some sort of Arabisation or Indonesianisation, or Pakistanisation or Turkification." That speech suggested otherwise. For Naoki, there was the possibility that "I can be like a firm Japanese Muslim."

Naoki introduced himself to that Turkish professor and asked for his advice on how to study more about the history of Islam. The Turkish professor encouraged him to study in Turkey, in Istanbul. After this advice, Naoki travelled to Turkey in his final year of the university and stayed in Istanbul for nine months. In Istanbul, he learned Turkish and studied some Islamic history while also deepening his knowledge of classical Arabic. "Living in Istanbul helped me a lot," Naoki recalls, because "Istanbul is the best example of this openness of the Islamic civilisation. Istanbul has the spiritual power to encourage me to live as a Japanese while also practicing Islam."

Japanese tea ceremony in Istanbul

It would be a great mistake to think of Naoki Yamamoto as a scholar only, who shuts himself up in the ivory towers of academia. He is also very much socially active. He holds regular Japanese- style tea ceremonies, during which he meets with and talks to Istanbulites from various socio-economic and age groups. He argues that holding a traditional Japanese tea ceremony teaches and trains its participants one chief virtue Islam preaches - patience.

In other words, Naoki fascinates Turks in an unusual way.

Speaking perfect Turkish, Naoki is also active on Twitter and is regularly interviewed by the media, sharing his reflections on various themes and issues that concern Japan and Japanese culture and bringing to light those similarities between the Turkish and Japanese cultures that only meet his eye.

What changed in him by embracing Islam? "Did you watch the Squid Game?" he asks. "It is the South Korean drama, which became Netflix's most watched series, attracting more than 142 million viewers from 94 different countries. "You know," Naoki continues, "that drama is not just for entertainment. It is also a really good depiction of the modern society especially in East Asia. It is not just the Korean society, it is also about the Japanese society."

The series is about some 400 players, all of whom have serious financial problems, risk their lives and play a series of deadly games. "Characters play a game right? And if they fail, they die. And this is exactly how the contemporary society is. People are competitive and don't trust each other. And if they make just one mistake, that is the end of their lives." If Squid Game is indeed a realistic depiction of the contemporary society, Naoki holds, Muslims' primary task is "to fight against that kind of society." Then he recalls the Egyptian gateman. His attitude, Naoki believes, "is what exactly we need… in the modern society people never give their own cucumber to other people. They do not even let you do that." Naoki declares, "I strongly believe that this is not the nature Allah has given to human beings. The nature that Allah put in us is compassion towards others." This is what changed in Naoki after embracing Islam. "If there is any spiritual change in my life, that is, I realised the importance of compassion and patience."

Naoki sees himself as being on a religious mission in Turkey.

He gets in touch with new converts to Islam in Japan and helps them come to Turkey and expand their knowledge and deepen their understanding of Islam. One day, he dreams of going back to his own country and spreading the message of Islam there. Yet, he already serves that latter mission, not in his own country, but in Turkey, a country of Muslims by birth. He offers such fresh perspectives about Islam that Muslims by birth fail to consider and see due to their already settled notions and beliefs about Islam. An inquiry into this man's inner world will surely make you reflect on your own deeply held religious notions and beliefs, whether you be a Muslim or not.

21

'I didn't want to be alive – I was going to end it all. But Islam saved me'

Weldon Angelos –American music producer turned criminal justice reform advocate

For Weldon Angelos, hearing the Quran being recited for the first time gave him goosebumps - despite not knowing the meaning of what he heard. Later, amid serving what he thought would be a 55-year prison sentence, he turned to the verses of Allah for comfort and solace. For him, it made prison that much more bearable - he held onto the words of Allah and knew he was not alone.

O N 22 December, 2020, it was announced that former President of
the United States, Donald J. Trump, had granted full pardons to 15
individuals convicted of committing offences[1]. Among those granted
presidential clemency included a music producer whose portfolio spans
working alongside the likes of Tupac Shakur, Mutah 'Napoleon' Beale,
Snoop Dogg, hip hop duo The Dogg Pound – just to name but a few.

In 2004, said music mogul found himself indicted for the sale of
marijuana while allegedly in possession of a firearm – a crime he committed
before his conversion to Islam. He was subsequently sentenced to 55 years
imprisonment – a case that, from the very beginning, was embroiled in
controversy.

"I was indicted for peddling $900 worth of marijuana. I gave $300 worth
to a friend three times. I didn't know he was working as a confidential
informant and the police were on a witch hunt to get rappers. Their thinking
was," said Weldon Angelos, "if they could bring me down, then they could
get all these other famous rappers afterwards."

Despite him having no prior convictions and his being a low-level
drug offence, as per Title 18, Section 924(c) of America's federal code, he
was dealt a harsh sentence. "I think the original motivations for wanting a
heavy sentence against him – hip hop played a large role. The government
was trying to make Weldon look like a *gang member*[2]," concluded Jerome
Mooney – Weldon's attorney.

"Initially," said Weldon, "the federal government had charged me

---

1   The White House, 2020. Statement from the Press Secretary Regarding Executive Grants of
     Clemency. [online] Available at: <https://trumpwhitehouse.archives.gov/ briefings-
     statements/statement-press-secretary-regarding-executive-grants-clemen- cy-122220/>
2   HBO Max, 2021. Weldon Angelos Documentary TRAILER. [video] Available at:
     <https://youtu.be/fuJLNyfL2XI>

with 105 years. I was facing going to prison for a century for merely $900 worth of marijuana. The fact that they were doing this to me just really made me want to seek out a better understanding of God, our world and how I ended up in my situation."

Weldon recounted this period of time being marked by him searching for answers as to how all he had worked hard to achieve seemed, at that point, to be in vain. "Losing my freedom was a very traumatic life event," he sighed. "At the time, I had just signed a major record deal. I was making really good money – I was putting out records with Mac Dre, Snoop and had so many other projects on the way. Then all of a sudden, everything was taken away from me."

He further recounted battling with the need to know why he had to go through such hardship, and concurrently seeking counsel from long-term friend, Mutah 'Napoleon' Beale.

"Even prior to me facing jail time, Mutah had been speaking to me about his then new-found Islamic faith for about a year – maybe even more to be honest!" he said. "I initially wouldn't pay much attention to him when he would start talking about Islam," he confessed, "I'd say to Mutah, 'Oh yeah, great – that's cool!' and try to change the subject. Looking back, I guess I just didn't have the time of day for religion. I didn't really care for it either!" Mutah, however, did not relent and continued telling Weldon all he came to discover about Islam as a new Muslim.

"Over time, I became more and more curious about what Mutah had to say. Now that I think about it, some of what he did tell me early on may have been a little bit inaccurate," he chuckled, "but he was young and just a new Muslim at the time – but there were no major mistakes that he made and a lot of what he said just struck a chord with me. Especially what he had to say about the concept of Jesus in Islam."

'You get exactly what you give'

"I grew up in a single-parent household," began Weldon as he reminisced on his childhood. "My father raised us by himself, even though he was disabled." He continued further, recounting his younger days blighted by poverty.

"We grew up really, really poor and living off the system – dad couldn't work," he said. "So, we were always worried about getting our next meal and surviving. Religion didn't really have an impact on our lives growing up." And yet, Weldon remembered childhood church visits and odd bouts of discussions he and his father would have concerning belief.

"We did go to a few churches a couple of times, but that was mainly because a lot of churches do provide support for people that are destitute. So, it wasn't until I was in my teens that I started learning more about the Christian story." He continued: "But before that, I wouldn't have been taught a faith system that was structured."

Weldon's father sought belief within a plethora of traditions – believing in karma, reincarnation and voodoo. According to Weldon, a lot of his father's beliefs would in fact contradict one another most of the time. "I'm not even sure whether Dad really knew what he believed, but somewhere within that mix was Jesus!" He continued to explain his father's wholehearted belief in Jesus: "But," he said chiming in, "Dad never believed that Jesus was God."

"It's really weird," he said, "and I'm not even sure where he would have gotten this from, but dad would always say to me, 'Jesus was a man, but he was a special man – a very wise man!'" He continued: "This in many ways shaped my personal belief system growing up and stuck with me until I eventually became Muslim."

Although there was an absence of what he referred to as a "structured belief system", devoid of religious practice and scripture, his father yet stood as a figure who helped him to discern between right and wrong. "In many ways, even though I didn't subscribe to a particular religion at the time, my dad taught me his understanding of karma, and how in life, you get exactly what you give." Therefore, despite becoming involved in Salt Lake City's world of gangdom, Weldon recounted an inner voice that inhibited him from overstepping the bounds of morality.

"I joined a gang at around 14 or 15; not something I really wanted to do. It was sort of forced upon me, I didn't have much of a choice at the time – I was looking for a way to survive. But even though I was out on the streets and I would get caught up in fights, shootings and gang wars – I still felt like there were some things I couldn't do because it's absolutely wrong." He continued: "I was someone who sold marijuana when I was young and I was, at times, met with situations where I had to defend myself, but I never robbed anyone or hurt women. You know, fighting with gang members is one thing, but harming innocent members of society is another – so I wouldn't do it."

He also spoke of always having the belief in there being 'something' out there. "I did believe in God; I just didn't have an understanding of who God was or if any religion was accurate. But because I knew God existed, I knew we weren't just here by accident and that life had meaning."

As he grew older, Weldon found his knowledge of world religion being shaped by those around him and what he saw in the media. "One thing my dad was really good at was talking to people and engaging in debates – I think I picked up on that very early on. So, growing up I would always look for ways to spark conversations with my peers about what they believed in –

I truly wanted to know more." However, Weldon found himself at odds with what he was told by the Christian majority.

"Remember, it was instilled in me that Jesus was a wise man of the people. So, when I would be told that he died for our sins, I couldn't accept it. And, the more I began knowing more in-depth about Christian belief, the more I became confused."

Despite embarking upon gaining a better understanding of God and his purpose as a created being, said journey was, temporarily, forestalled by distancing himself from life on the streets.

'Who Do Ya Turn To?'

"I became really busy working on my music career," he said. "Within a month of starting high school, I got kicked out and just focused on making money – growing up poor meant we didn't have enough to buy new clothes. In fact, all of my clothes would have been hand-me-downs. Even getting a decent haircut was a luxury we just couldn't afford."

Prior to honing in on his musical talents, a disenfranchised Weldon worked at a local restaurant and hustled drugs on the side. "Even though I was living the life of a drug dealer," he recollected, "I was also conscious of when I was doing something and what the higher power, or God, would think of my actions. Remember, this would have been at a stage in my life when I didn't know who the higher power was, yet, I still had that sense of God-consciousness within me."

Despite the unsavoury path he was initially walking, Weldon further recollected his younger self having a constant awareness that his was a destiny for greatness – he just did not know it at the time. "I truly felt I had a special purpose in life that I needed to fulfil and when I was younger, I did feel like I was being guided on a path by God – even though I was doing things that were not right or good. But I knew God was leading me to my proper calling." Said calling would later prove to be music.

"When Dr Dre and Snoop Dogg first began taking the rap scene by storm," chimed Weldon, "I was a huge fan of theirs and all the music that was coming from Death Row Records. Then later, Tupac's music grew more and more influential. From there, I knew for sure a career in music was definitely what I wanted! I wanted to be a beatmaker and producer and, possibly, a recording artist myself!"

Weldon began trying to make inroads in the Utah music scene, starting off as a beatmaker and learning as he went along. "But my ultimate goal was to become an executive and someday have my own record label." Locally, however, the quality of recording equipment just was not up to scratch and he found himself in Los Angelos for a better shot at catching his big break. Thereafter, he recalled his career becoming a whirl of excitement.

"I was in a studio in Long Beach, California, and this was in '95 I think – I ran into one of Snoop Dogg's group members; Daz Dillinger! He and I hit it off and became friends – we started talking and making music together for a bunch of different projects. From there, I started travelling to the Bay Area and eventually met Tupac, Mutah and so many other people in music – everything really happened so fast!" he said. Weldon and Mutah would go on to forge a very strong bond, with the two remaining good friends to this day

"My friendship with Mutah is so important to my story of embracing Islam," said Weldon. "For instance, I'll say when 9/11 happened, it raised my curiosity about Islam as a religion. The coverage of the attack didn't lead me to develop a negative impression of Islam," he asserted, "however, I did want to know what would make somebody feel the urge to commit such an act in the name of the religion." He also highlighted the notable changes in Mutah's character, as well as the conversations they would have, serving as a counterweight to the stereotypical rhetoric surrounding Islam and its adherents at the time.

"I knew 9/11 wasn't representative of all Muslims – fortunately, I had Mutah to tell me that. I could also physically see how Islam changed him completely as a person compared to the younger Mutah who was wild. To be honest, he was pretty bad!" he laughed, reminiscing on his friend's days as an 'Outlaw'. "But after he became Muslim," he continued, "Mutah just had this glow about him, and that's what made me progressively more and more inclined to listen to what he was trying to tell me – I wanted to hear more as I saw him develop into his religion."

He further remembered Mutah as being the one who gifted him a translation of the holy Quran. "When I first began reading it, I didn't read it cover to cover," said Weldon. "Instead, one of the first things I did was to search for 'Jesus' in the index. I grew up believing that Jesus was a special man – but I could never find anywhere to back up what my dad was saying about this." Weldon found himself resonating with the depiction of Jesus as a man sent to his people with the mission of Prophethood juxtaposed with the Quranic message of Almighty God being One, with no partners.

"When I first started reading the Quran, I suddenly felt like I understood what's true. This is what I was missing in my life all those years prior," he recollected. "The Quran described God as the All-Knowing, not having any kids or demi-gods below Him, before or after Him – all this just felt real to me!" His conviction in Islam was to eventually become solidified during a studio recording session with Mutah.

"Napoleon came to Salt Lake City – I was working on an album project with him. This would have been before he started working on 'Have Mercy' – we didn't even have a name for the project we were working on," said

Weldon. He further recounted how rappers such as Snoop Dogg, Nas and Eminem were planned to feature on Mutah's project. "It was gonna be big!" he said. He further detailed how a project that immense required a dedicated work ethic to see it to fruition.

"When he came to Utah, Mutah stayed and worked in the studio for two days straight." Over the course of the two days, their conversations about Islam took a more in-depth turn; serving as a much needed follow up to a series of conversations they had had prior. "Then in an instant," recounted Weldon, "everything changed after Mutah recorded 'Who Do Ya Turn To?'"

Weldon remembered the power of Mutah's lyrics being such that sparked a debate in the studio. "Aside from me and Mutah, the room was full of gang members! There were, I think, two different gangs – both trying to do music with Mutah. But when he began speaking about Islam, everyone fell silent!" Weldon continued to describe the scene of pin-drop silence and gang members covered in goosebumps with their jaws to the ground.

"We would film each session," he explained, "a documentary was in the works, so I'm happy that I got all this on film." Weldon smiled. "Sometimes I watch it over and I'm just amazed at how well Mutah captivated all of us that day – the way he was breaking down everything about the religion really touched me, and everyone in the room."

Mutah explained the Islamic notion of *tawheed*, as well as the seal of the Prophets – Muhammad (PBUH). "He told the story of how he (PBUH) would have to tie rocks to his stomach out of hunger – this touched me, especially since, in many ways, it mirrored my experiences growing up poor," said Weldon.

"Honestly," he narrated, "when Mutah was speaking, everyone just shut up – the way he spoke was so powerful, that I, alongside two gang members in the studio that day, took our *shahadah* during the recording session with Napoleon.

"We all concluded that what he was saying made sense," said Weldon. "Mutah looked at me and said, 'Do you believe this? Do you believe the words that I'm saying – that Islam is the religion of truth, the religion of Jesus, Moses, Abraham?' I said, 'Absolutely! Everything you have said makes sense to me! This sounds real!'" Weldon further explained how all that he had come to know about Islam in the moments leading up to that fateful studio session answered a lot of the existential questions he once had as a boy and filled the unexplainable void in his life. "At that point, everything just seemed to fall into place," he said.

Mutah asked Weldon if he would be willing to say the Islamic declaration of faith and become a Muslim. "I said, 'yes!'" said Weldon chiming in. "So, me and two other individuals took our *shahada* right then and there – on camera and in a recording studio." He went on to speak about an immediate sense of being renewed, knowing he was now on the path of truth. "It felt like Islam was going to fill that hole that was once in my life. And that's what it did for Mutah, too! He told me that – so it was life changing for both of us.

"So, in many ways," concluded Weldon, "Death Row and Mutah – this is where my story of embracing Islam begins. Not to mention, at the time I had just become Muslim, I was going through the trauma of losing my freedom. It was this combination of factors that led me to take my *shahadah*."

Search for meaning in one's struggle

When asked how he took the news of losing his court case, Weldon retorted, "I found myself hoping to find purpose in what was happening to me – why I had to suffer so badly." This proved to be a very trying time for Weldon, leading to his suffering from depression as a result.

"Even before being incarcerated," he said, "depression was something I started battling with when I was around 18 or 19 years old. From then onwards, it was just something I never seemed to be able to shake fully. Like I said, there was just something missing in my life – I wouldn't have known at the time, but what was missing was Islam."

During the pre-trial phase of his would be sentencing, Weldon was not detained but was left pondering how things in life took such a devastating turn. "The thing was, I really didn't need to sell the marijuana!" he asserted. "I thought I was doing a favour for someone who was my friend. A friend who turned out to be an informant."

Upon sentencing, Paul G. Cassell – the judge in case – adjudicated, without recourse to discretion, Weldon was to serve a 55-year sentence. "My religion was even snuck in during trial by prosecutors to prejudice the jury," he recollected. "I remember saying in a press interview during the trial that I was Muslim. I said, 'Whatever Allah has written for me will come to pass'. Not too long after that, this was presented as evidence under the false pretence of me being less than an upstanding citizen." He continued: "Remember, this would have been around the time when President Bush junior's global war on terror was in full swing."

He further went on to explain the many ways in which this traumatic experience served to affirm his belief in Islam being the truth. "As crazy as it might sound, my sentencing cemented my faith in Islam," said Weldon. "Judge Cassell's hands were tied – he wasn't able to use his discretion and show any leniency when he sentenced as the prosecutors had framed the charges to elicit maximum punishment. Yet, despite him being a Bush appointee known for his hard stance on the law, he stood up for me and said that my punishment was cruel, unjust and irrational." Judge Cassell further went on to call upon former President Bush to commute Weldon's sentencing and penned a 67-page letter to Congress as to why the case ought to be overturned.

"When I lost my trial, I gave Mutah a call," recollected Weldon. "I told Mutah I was facing 55 years and he could hear it in my voice that I was low. But then he said something to me that comforted me immediately. He said, 'Allah must really love you because He only tests those He loves.' It made me tear up when he told me that." For Weldon, this helped him to understand that there is meaning in times of hardship. "Not only that," he said, "but I feel like this experience showed me suffering can purify a person. It was a test, but I held onto my faith every step of the way. I'm hopeful my perseverance will erase all the wrong that I've done in the past."

He continued: "Without Islam, I don't think I could've handled having to go through this. I probably would've ended it because I didn't want to be alive, you know? But I had Islam – so, I knew Allah does not give a person a test beyond what they can bear."

During his time in prison, Weldon was able to further build upon the basic knowledge of Islam he had. "When I got to prison, I wasn't the most educated. But I quickly began learning from the older Muslims who were there. They really took me under their wing and taught me about Islam in-depth."

Further, he said, "To be honest, in prison, I was able to practise my religion with no trouble – they let you access the most important aspects of Islam, and this really saved me. For instance," he continued, "at the chapel, there were tapes and CDs with Quranic recitations – I would just sit back and listen to the Quran, and it truly did comfort me and took away all my anxieties."

Weldon recollected how, despite not initially understanding Arabic, the first times he heard the Quran being recited left him with goosebumps. "I can't explain why hearing the Quran for the first time just gave me chills. What I do know for sure was that hearing it felt amazing. I won't lie, prison is tough, but thankfully I had fellow Muslims around me, and I was able to listen to the Quran. This made prison that much more bearable – I didn't feel so alone."

Life after lock-up

After a 13-year prison stretch, Weldon was finally exonerated in 2020. His release was ushered by a wave of support and campaigning from personalities such as Mutah, Snoop Dogg, Alicia Keys and senators such as Corey Booker. "When I got out people didn't even recognise me – my character had completely changed! I wasn't cussing anymore – everything was just so different; people couldn't recognise me at all," he said while laughing.

He further spoke of how welcoming his peers were to his embracing of Islam. "The reaction of those around me was very positive – in fact, there are a lot of Muslims within the hip hop community. I think for many in the industry, it's easy for them to identify and see themselves within Islamic traditions as opposed to Christianity which, historically, has proven to be exclusionary of those who hail from the Black, Hispanic and ethnic minority communities." This memory of warm welcome upon his release, however, was juxtaposed by the difficulty he had to endure, and the sense of time and opportunities lost as a result.

"I went through such hardship. I lost my career, I missed out on my sons growing up - they went from being five and six-year- old boys to grown men with facial hair, and I didn't get to see any of that." Despite this, Weldon maintained this was all part of a divinely preordained plan. "Who knows?" he pondered. "Maybe if I wasn't incarcerated, I wouldn't have taken the time out of my schedule to learn more about Islam. Not just that," he continued, "in my suffering, I was and still am able to help so many others through my advocacy.

"A new law was passed because of my case!" he exclaimed. "After I was released, I was able to work alongside Senators like Mike Lee and Corey Booker – even President Trump, to change the way prosecutors indict people like they did me. Today, prosecutors can't just give someone 55 years for what I did. That law is now gone!"

While on a more personal level, Weldon happily remembered how this experience prompted the rekindling of his relationship with his father. "During this time," he explained, "we bonded in a way we never seemed to be able when I was still growing up. But that changed when I went to prison." He further remembered how, despite all the support he had garnered from celebrities and politicians, his dad was the one who stood out for him the most in lending him the backing he needed at the time.

"'I'm here for you', is what he would say to me. He really sacrificed so much for me during this time. He didn't have a lot, yet he would still put money aside for me – even if it was just
$50, $60 or $75 a month – he always would." Weldon further recounted how, in their reconnecting, they began talking to one another a lot more.

"We would talk over the phone a lot," he said, "and during those conversations, I would do my best to tell Dad about Islam." He continued: "I'd like to believe that my dad died as a Muslim." He further lamented, "As Dad got older, he suffered from dementia. But I know in my heart, when I talked to him about Islam, he somehow did understand and connected with Islam's teaching. For years and years, I would talk to him about Islam, and eventually, I asked him if he would want to take his *shahadah* and he said yes! I just hope it wasn't too late for him to do so."

Towards the end of the discussion, Weldon talked about no longer being as active as he once was in the music industry – "A lot of my work now is more centred around activism and getting people that I used to work with involved in doing things for the community and bettering our justice system."

In circling back to where his story all began at the height of hip hop's golden era, Weldon expressed gratitude for being able to give back to a person who was key to his big break. "My story has come full circle," he smiled, "Michael 'Harry-O' Harris was one of the founders of Death Row. It was his company that impacted me so much by giving me the chance to make it in music." In 1988, however, Harris found himself on the receiving end of a 40-year drug charge and imprisoned.

"'Harry-O' is now Muslim," said Angelos. "When I got pardoned by President Trump, I took it upon myself to help as many people as I could before the end of his presidency." He continued: "It was Harry-O who helped me all those years ago in the 90s, then, a couple decades later [sic], I had the opportunity to free this man from prison. Snoop, Ivanka (Trump) and I went to work on Harris' case and within three weeks, he was freed

. "He may not have made it to the end of his sentence," sighed Weldon. "So, helping to free the man who was indirectly responsible for my introduction into the music industry – I'm just so proud that this was something I was able to do."

22

'I was on a spiritual path that I didn't even realise I was on'

————◆◆◆◆◆————

Jonathan Yousef Abdilla – Canadian writer, film director and producer

————◆◆◆◆◆————

Without clear answers to his burning existential questions, Jonathan Abdilla's life took a dark turn. Convinced there was no religious truth and life had no purpose, a spiritual void blighted his teenage years. However, amid the shockwaves that reverber- ated worldwide following 9/11, thoughts of his own mortality plagued his mind – leading Jonathan to discover a people, a religion and a holy book he once had no knowledge of.

AT THE crux of Jonathan Yousef Abdilla's road to embracing Islam was his inquisitive mind. His inquisitive nature not only saw Christian doctrine fall from favour in his subconscious but, eventually, even as an atheist, cosmological models explaining the origins of the universe also proved to be unsavoury for him to accept.

"There just always seemed to be this missing link," he began to explain. "Later, when I started reading the Quran, little by little, it would tick the boxes and gave me clarifications I just couldn't find in science or Christianity. I eventually came to realise that Islam was the true religion and was then confronted with a choice – if I know this to be the truth, am I now willing to accept it?"

However, looking back on his childhood, he remembered his first interaction with religious practice being during a trip to Sunday school. This memory especially stood out in his mind as it coincided with his younger cousin's baptism and his first introduction to the concept of the trinity as a child. He recounted his teacher drawing a triangle on the chalkboard and dividing it thrice – illustrating the Christian principle of God existing in three divine persons.

"That didn't compute with me," he said. "Even in my infant mind, when I thought of God, I instinctively thought of an Omnipotent being. Why would He need to exist as three entities?" his younger self pondered. This was a doubt that lingered and ultimately led to him adopting an agnostic outlook as he grew older.

"The Trinity was so central to what I was taught at Sunday school, but it just didn't sit well with me. So, it got to a point where, while I would have believed in God, I didn't believe in Christianity." His agnosticism, however, was to be dismantled one evening after school, when his dormant uncertainties resurfaced – steering him to an atheistic impasse. However, he remembered his prior endeavour of thinking deeply about Christianity to better understand its doctrine.

"Outside the four walls of Sunday school," he explained, "there wouldn't have been anywhere to discuss religion. At the time, Canadian culture was geared towards keeping matters of politics and religion private. Religion just wasn't something we'd talk about publicly." Therefore, in the home setting, Jonathan would voice his theological unease to his mother.

"I remember The Simpsons' Reverend Lovejoy, of all people, triggering a conversation between Mom and I about religion," he chuckled. "The reverend's character would always make me laugh but, in many ways, his apathy personified the sentiments of most people in the West who grow to become disinterested in religion." While listening to one of Lovejoy's 'sermons', Jonathan remembered quizzing his mother one night. "If he's worshipping Jesus and we do the same thing at Church – then where does God come into all this?" Rather than a cognisant explanation, Jonathan's innocent inquiry was instead met with a shrugged shoulder. "The conversation didn't go any further from there," he said.

"I couldn't get the answers to my questions about God in Sunday school, wider society or at home. So, in that moment, I concluded that there was no religious truth and lived my life accordingly; I became a hardcore atheist."

The awareness that eluded him

Jonathan, who studied Cinema and Media Arts at Toronto's York University, described the media as a "tool – it can either build or destroy". As such, when asked of the perception that was built in his mind as a youngster, he remembered hearing soundbites mentioning Islam being concurrently presented alongside imagery of soldiers marching, parades of military tanks and panoramas of the Red Sea.

"I just always assumed Islam was an island somewhere in the Middle East," he said, laughing. "Coverage of Palestine almost always overlapped with discussions about Islam and, over time, I came to associate Islam as being its own country with a newsworthy military." Aside from news media coverage, he further remembered the role of 'terrorist' being cast exclusively to individuals portrayed as Muslims in films. This only further fed into his ignorance – "I thought Muslim terrorists were part of international cells for the *country's army*," he motioned in inverted commas.

Despite growing up in a city as diverse as Toronto, he further confessed to not only having no awareness of Islam being a part of the Abrahamic tradition, but he also did not know that a Muslim was one who follows Islam. Although the 1990s were an era that saw a sharp rise in immigration into Canada from the Middle East and Southeast Asia[1], Jonathan described his newly arrived Muslim peers as being more concerned with trying to fit in, rather than, as he put it, "wearing Islam on their sleeves". As such, his knowledge of Muslims was limited to knowing nothing beyond them abstaining from food and drink during what they called *Ramadan*, not eating pork and women donning the veil – "I wouldn't have even known at the time they believed in God!" he exclaimed. "I thought that, just like Buddhists, Muslims live according to a set of principles, such as not drinking alcohol, and their way of life didn't feature a Creator."

When asked whether he thus turned to scientific explanations for solace as an atheist, Jonathan instead depicted yet another barrier to his understanding of the universe. "I hated science growing up!" he exclaimed, recollecting his younger self sat in the classroom being told how phenomena

---

1   Statistics Canada, 2011. Foreign-born population in Canada, by selected regions of birth, 1951 to 2011. Chart 4.

occur, but always finding the explanation of *why* wanting. For Jonathan, his was a mind that necessitated a thoroughly holistic approach – taking into consideration all factors, to be able to understand and process new knowledge. This may go a long way in explaining how he gravitated to computer programming at the young age of ten.

"Programming is so systematic – I was able to grasp it right away and had a knack for making websites!" This pastime equipped him with the realisation that order cannot be achieved through disorder. A mere misstep in the HTML script or the omission of just one character in the code are both classic recipes for disaster in the programming field. In due course, it was this very understanding that would later prove instrumental in easing his reorientation from rejecting faith, to embracing Islam wholeheartedly.

"Explanations of The Big Bang cosmology that I was given never sat well with how my mind was wired as a programmer; knowing all the intricacies involved in getting an app, software or even the computer itself to work!" he said. He recalled his younger self feeling there was more to the picture of the universe's origins that science could not seem to answer – namely, what triggered The Big Bang and what came before it.

"So, when a Muslim friend of mine asked me one day, 'How do you think all this stuff – our solar system, our planet, the nature you see all around us – how do you think everything came to be?' I began searching for the *Master Programmer*. In many ways, I was on a spiritual path that I didn't even realise I was on."

An atheist's prayer

"It's one thing to not think about purpose, but it's another thing to think that you have no purpose, right?" Jonathan retorted while remembering the void in his yesteryears as an atheist. Aimlessly wandering through life as a teenager, his academic attainment began to decline apace and, instead, he became more engaged in activities that were detrimental – both to his physical and mental health. With the observable changes in his personality and behaviour, Jonathan's friends advised him to curb his substance abuse.

"'Give me a good reason and I'll stop all this today!' is what I would say in anger to them." But he could never get an answer convincing enough for him to leave the only thing that made him feel alive in those fleeting moments. This was a lifestyle, however, that could only endure for so long – "In life, things have a funny way of eventually catching up with you," he said, chiming in.

On the hollowness of his living a fast life, fraught with recklessness, he spoke of an emptiness deep inside him becoming increasingly apparent. "Instinctively, I felt that I *needed* to do something! My psyche just suddenly became overpowered by this awareness that the path I was going down wasn't the right one, and I needed to change." Jonathan found himself ruminating about the purpose of life and his own mortality – a period he described as a personal low point where things did not seem quite right. In a desperate bid for relief from his inner grapples, an atheist Jonathan briefly spoke to God.

"They call it the *atheist's prayer*," he said. As antithetical as it may seem, The Guardian's Religion Correspondent, Harriet Sherwood, penned how at times of crisis, prayer is often used for recourse to feel less lonely or gain comfort – even for those who do not necessarily believe in God[2]. "I remember exactly what I said when I prayed." He continued: "I said, 'God, if You're real and You exist, please help me.'"

---

2   Sherwood, H., 2018. Non-believers turn to prayer in a crisis, poll finds. The Ob- server, [online] Available at: <https://www.theguardian.com/world/2018/jan/14/ half-of-non-believers-pray-says-poll>

In his mind, thoughts of there being more to life beyond what he knew were steadily creeping to the foreground. Then, "When 9/11 happened, I was forced to act – I couldn't let those thoughts remain passive any longer."

For Jonathan's 16-year-old conscience, the scenes of the lives of so many cut short in an instant served as a wake-up call. "I can remember the image of the man who jumped from the tower – it's an image that will remain permanently etched in my memory forever." He was especially struck by the thought of how those were real people who had lives, families and hopes for their futures. Then, in a matter of moments, all of that was taken away. On that fateful Tuesday, he and his friends met up after school to hang out. And naturally, the attack was at the centre of their conversations.

He recounted his Muslim friends and their religion now being brought to the fore and how they had to vehemently defend themselves amid an onslaught of criticism. Hurls of insults, such as 'Islam is a stupid religion' were flung into the Muslims' corner from his aggrieved non-Muslim friends. "Wait!" his 16-year-old self-exclaimed in thought, "Islam is a religion?" A perplexed Jonathan, formerly convinced that Islam was a distant island   in the Middle East, sat in awe as his ignorance began to unravel before his very eyes.

"I had so many questions racing through my mind, but the first question I asked simply was – 'What is Islam?'" Much to his surprise, he was told that Islam upholds a monotheistic belief system whereby God – Allah – created the heavens and the earth and is worshipped with no partners. "This was so foreign to me" he said. And yet, he described a subtle pull towards the religion that he was only just beginning to discover. "I was told that Islam teaches belief in one God and it clicked for me! The reason why I rejected Christianity in the first place was because I believed in one God and could not align myself with worshipping Jesus." Curiosity now piqued, Jonathan went to work to find out more.

Jonathan anew

"I was still *very* sceptical in the early days," said Jonathan about the start of his four month voyage to becoming a Muslim. "I became very close to one of my friends who actually converted two years before I did - Basil. I would always ask him questions and, now that I think about it, some of what he did tell me wasn't correct," he said, chuckling. "But on the positive side, it proved to be a learning process for both me and him." Alongside seeking counsel from his then newly converted friend, Jonathan also found himself becoming fascinated by Islam's holy Book.

"The Quran is such that it presents a series of challenges and tasks to the reader," he began to explain. For instance, in chapter *Hūd*, the Book encourages the reader in doubt of its veracity to:

"[…] *Produce ten fabricated sûrahs (chapters) like it and seek help from whomever you can – other than Allah – if what you say is true!*" (Quran, 11:13)

What especially caught his attention was the Quran declaring itself as a book, confirming the scripture that came before it[3]. Jonathan, who borrowed his grandmother's copy of the holy Bible and was eventually gifted with an English translation of the Quran, embarked on a two-month period of comparative religion self-study.

"My grandmother used to work as a Sunday school teacher before I was born," he revealed. However, it was not until he began studying Islam that the two discussed religion in depth. "Grandma too became very disillusioned with religion at one point – even stopped going to church!" he continued, retelling how his grandmother's story mirrored his.

---

3   See Quran 3:3 and Quran 6:92 for examples.

"She grappled a lot with what she perceived as inconstancies in the Bible," he said. "And there was this one day when a famous travelling evangelist was in town, and she thought he would be the best person to quell her worries." Much to her incredulity, the travelling preacher instead retorted to her, "Well, the thing with the Bible is, it's probably best to take it for what it's worth, if ya catch my drift [sic]" – insinuating the questionable nature of the Bible's contents.

"That brief conversation sat with Grandma for many years," he said. "So, when I began talking to her about the mismatches I found in the Bible, she was open to having those talks with me. Truly," he continued, "I fondly remember this time talking about the Quran and Bible with her – I wasn't alone on this journey; we both learned a lot together and I think we became closer because of that."

For Jonathan, the concept of Jesus in Islam proved to be a determining element in whether the Quran truly was a Book aligning with the scriptures that came before it. Isa in the Quran is described as one of the mightiest messengers of God, to whom the *Injīl*[4] was revealed. This especially struck a chord for Jonathan since not only did the Quran assert that he was not God, but, as he discovered, the Bible did not do so either. In fact, when he stumbled across Matthew 26:39, he was caught by surprise reading an instance where Jesus fell to the ground in prostration and prayed to God.

"Not only was Jesus praying the same way Muslims prayed," he said, "but he was praying for God to spare him from those who plotted to kill him!" For Jonathan, this Biblical verse simultaneously coincided with the Quranic notion that Jesus was a Muslim, and further shattered a fundamental Christian doctrine.

---

4   In Islam, the *Injīl* is believed to be the scripture revealed to Prophet Isa [Jesus].

"Jesus' entire purpose in Christianity was to die on the cross. This mere fact that he didn't want to do so and prayed for God to stop it from happening was really key in solidifying my conviction in Islam."

He also told of how the Quran provided him with the much needed *why* behind the occurrence of scientific phenomena. One such gripe he had as a youngster was in relation to hydrology – "And this is something the Quran very clearly addresses," he interposed. "The Quran says that Allah sends down rain from the skies, bringing to life the earth's vegetation. Then, after some time, He reduces it to dry remnants as a sign and reminder for people of reason[5]." For Jonathan, overwhelmingly, this was the missing *why* to the lone *how* that science was able to answer. "I found myself thinking, 'the answers to my questions are all in Islam's holy Book'- that's just how real it felt to me." Yet, the more the Quran erased his doubts, the more internally conflicted he found himself becoming.

"How can I be a Muslim?" his younger self pondered. "I'm a White guy – Islam is an ethnic religion!" In search of guidance for his unsettled mind, he beseeched God once more.

This was a method for achieving clarity he would use throughout his journey to becoming a Muslim. At times when his conviction would falter, he found himself asking God to show him that Islam was true and, more often than not, he would find the answers he was looking for in the Quran. Notwithstanding, prayer further became entrenched in routine as per the advice given to him by Basil. "Talk to God; pray to Him however you know and however you can," is what Jonathan was told.

See Quran 39:21.

"Interestingly enough," he revealed, "the more I would pray – and it would just be for simple things, the more I would get little signs that said to me, 'God is near'."

By December 2001, he concluded that not only did Islam *feel* real, but it was also the truth and he therefore wanted to become a Muslim. "It honestly was a little nerve wracking," he confessed. "My decision to become Muslim wasn't necessarily easy but, after four months of studying the Quran, I felt compelled to pursue the path of Islam – it was just the obvious thing to do." He continued: "There would have been a few *da'wah* tapes I listened to here and there, such as Khalid Yasin's[6] 'The Purpose of Life', before converting. But, truly, what really changed my mindset were the words of Allah."

Jonathan told his Muslim friends the news he wanted to embrace their religion and become a Muslim, too. It was then settled that he would take his *shahada* on the Friday of that week to coincide with *jumaah* prayer – December 28th, 2001; the day of Jonathan's 17th birthday.

He was taken to a local mosque by a friend, and later joined by the rest of his buddies thereat. "It was hard not to miss me at the *masjid*," he said, laughing. "It was predominantly Somali – I was the only White person there. But I felt embraced by them; they all made me feel welcome."

In the immediate moments after having taken shahada, Jonathan, who dubbed this as a defining moment, remembered feeling as though he was on cloud nine. "The act of taking my *shahadah* happened so fast," he said. "But, that night, after the brothers from the *masjid* took me out to eat, I had the best sleep I have ever had in my life. The dream I had that night? It was complete bliss! I was now a new person."

---

5   Khalid Yasin is a Christian convert to Islam.

As a 'new person', one of the first things Jonathan did was buy his beloved grandmother a copy of the Quran. "To be honest, I think Grandma had a better understanding of Islam than me!" he chuckled, then smiled as he remembered her embracing Islam shortly after he did. "Her becoming Muslim was actually a bit of a secret. Let's face it, the aftermath of 9/11 left Islam with a *really* bad PR problem, so I can understand why she didn't want the rest of the family to know," he continued, fondly remembering their time exploring the Quran together prior. "After she died, I kept the copy of the Quran I gave her – I still have it to this day. She got up to *surah al Nissa*." Jonathan's grandmother was not the only person in his family to follow suit and embrace Islam after him.

"Just like with Grandma, I started gradually having more in- depth conversations with my dad about inconsistencies I found in the Bible," he said. Jonathan and his father would talk about *tawhid*, the chain of Prophets and Messengers – each armed with revelation to the people they were sent to; Islam at its very core. "I was talking to Dad about my faith as a Muslim – he just didn't realise it at the time. I was introducing him to my new faith subtly and it resonated with him that God is one and cannot be man."

He continued: "Islam clicked with him so much so that when I eventually told him I became a Muslim, it was no big deal; he understood it!" Eventually, after bouts of long conversations with his father, he soon discovered where his own inquisitive nature had come from.

"Dad said he wanted a copy of the Quran, but insisted he wouldn't be converting anytime soon – he just wanted to take a look." However, within a matter of weeks, his father picked up the phone to tell him the news that he wanted to embrace Islam and become a Muslim, too. At this time, Jonathan spoke fondly of Islam's heritage within his Maltese roots.

On his father's side, his family hails from Malta – a Mediterranean archipelago sandwiched between Italy and the North African coast. From the 8th to the 10th centuries, Malta was under Muslim rule following the Aghlabid dynasty's successful conquest. A lasting remnant from that now-bygone era is to be seen in the Maltese language. "When my dad and I would go to the *masjid* together, it was easy for him to follow along, even if the *khutbah* was in Arabic – there's so much overlap between the two languages that Maltese can be described as an Arabic dialect," he said. He further highlighted how, despite Islam often being charged as a religion spread by the sword, in his estimation, the Maltese context proves the antithesis of that argument.

"Christians were able to live in peace under Muslim rule, whereas under Christian rule everybody was forced to adopt Christianity," he said. Today, only 2% of the Maltese populous are adherents to Islam. "And it's ironic," he said, interposing. "You can go back generations into my family and will find a long lineage of Catholics, and yet, we bear a very Muslim-sounding name – *Abdilla*."

Finding one's footing

Regarding his early years as a convert to Islam, the phrase "isolating experience" instantly sprang to his mind. On multiple fronts, Jonathan found himself feeling like a guest or an outsider. "There weren't a lot of my Muslim friends who were practising at the time, and this was difficult for me to reconcile as someone who was trying to practice the best I could as a new Muslim," he sighed. However, he and Basil forged a strong bond over learning more about their religion and giving *da'wah* to their peers – eventually becoming successful in guiding some to reexplore their Islamic roots and encouraging others to convert.

"However," he sighed, "being a new Muslim could prove testing at times. My first Eid for example? It was probably the loneliest day of my life." Despite being embraced by his new community of Muslims, Jonathan soon discovered the harsh reality of being a convert during Islam's major religious festivals. "Everybody else was busy with their own family and doing their own thing. In the early days, I did feel sidelined during Ramadan and Eid but, gradually, I began to meet more people. This helped me to grow socially within the Islamic setting."

Part of what helped Jonathan enrich his network was venturing into creating an outlet for entertainment geared towards a Muslim audience. His portfolio spans producing feature films such as 'Righteous Sinner', comedy e-series 'Guess Who's Muslim' as well as Mutah Beale's biographical documentary; 'Napoleon: Life of an Outlaw'. "My goal from the very beginning was not only creating quality content for Muslims to watch, but to also play an active role in enhancing the authentic representation of Muslims on-screen." He concluded the discussion of his story with a few words of encouragement for the next generation of Muslims to hold on to their faith, even amid times of tribulations. "Faith is not always easy to maintain in a secular environment," he said. "At the same time, it isn't something worth gambling. If the gamble ends up going horribly wrong, you stand to lose everything for eternity. So, it's not a small decision at all." If in doubt, he continued, "Allah tells us He always answers those who call upon Him. So, call upon Him with sincerity to guide you to the truth, and be open to that truth."

Lastly, he remarked 'growth' as being the keyword he thought of when asked about the future of Islam in the West. "I think with Islam and science – that's a ripe territory to build a solid foundation between us and the wider community. Allah has given us the gift of the Quran – the miracle of all miracles that discusses science at great depth. All we have to do now, is share it."

23

'My mind is clear, and I feel I have more purpose in life now'

**Christian Betzmann –
German travel vlogger**

Christian's extensive travel and interactions with various cultures had a positive impact on him. Visiting a Muslim country, he would see lots of mosques and people praying. He says it was lovely to see everyone so happy, and "after that they are all having chai [tea] and food together, so it's really nice."

FEW would ever consider suddenly selling all of their possessions and bravely stepping out into the unknown. But this is exactly what one young German did - 21-year-old Christian Betzmann.

Betzmann left Germany and went on to have a weird and wonderful range of exciting experiences across the world. He now has 1.3 million followers across Instagram and YouTube, where his fans are captivated by his stunning photos and fast-paced video clips.

Here, for example, you can see this six-foot, four-inch tall German posing in front of everything from elephants to helicopters, or watch as he is propelled high into the air via an ocean water jet. Sometimes, he is charming snakes in India, or rafting, sailing and jumping cliffs in Turkey.

Other videos show him paddling on rafts next to Indonesian waterfalls, standing on top of jeeps in the Pakistani desert, or swimming with sharks in the Bahamas, or quad biking in the deserts of Karachi. You can also find about how he skydived out of a plane at13,000 feet over Dubai, or taught Thai policemen and monks how to speak English.

But the most unexpected of all his adventures was his conversion to Islam.

"[Some people] have said it is a little funny that I am Muslim but my name is Christian, but the thing is, despite my name, I was never actually raised as a Christian within my family," he says, explaining the coincidence of carrying the name of a religion he doesn't now believe in, and not having the name of a religion he believes in.

"Some people have commented on me not having a Muslim name since I converted, but I really just don't think it is necessary. In Pakistan, many Muslim friends of mine have told me that all this is more of an old-fashioned practice which you don't have to follow as a Muslim, and I met plenty of Muslims who have not done this."

Turkish influence

Born on 18th June, 1991 in Dieburg, in the western German federal state of Hessen, Christian Betzmann was one of two boys. Unlike most German children, he did not receive a strictly Christian upbringing.

"Growing up in Germany where I did, most people were Christian, so you would have a Christian upbringing at school and so forth. But my family was not really religious at all. My mother had been raised in a very religious family, but her parents died when she was 18, and because of that she lost all of her faith in God. She just didn't focus on God, and instead when it happened, she just put all of her energy into taking care of her brothers.

"So even though at school I was exposed to more of a Christian environment, you could say I did the bare minimum. I really only went to church, for example, at Christmas. I was also never really a believer of all the stories in the Bible about Jesus or Moses. I did believe in God, but was just never really a complete follower of all of the books.

"Also, many of my closest friends at school when I was a child were Muslim. This is because Germany, and particularly the region I lived in, has a very large Turkish community. Germany actually has the largest Turkish population outside of Turkey, so I was really exposed to cultural diversity at a very early age. I guess it is possible that indirectly and subconsciously some of the cultural influence of the Muslim friends was rubbing off on me, but I was really too young to be aware of it, and I really liked them and felt comfortable with them and was glad to know them."

At the grammar school Christian attended for 13 years, he was an extremely happy and social boy who loved sports, geography, meeting new people, travelling and also photography. Little did he know, however, that one day he would find a career which ended up combining all of these elements.

"As a young boy, in a way, life was all about football every day. I was also very extroverted, and into sports and arts. I was always very creative, and loved taking photographs with my mobile phone. I also loved meeting friends and going out. So really, I was very pro-active, and not really into subjects like politics and history. I was more a 'people person' than an academic, I guess, more into practice than theory.

"As a flight attendant, my mother would always tell me of the various places across the world which she had flown to, and it all sounded so exciting and intriguing and I longed to see it for myself. So I guess I got my passion for travelling from her, and I began travelling when I was 13. Here I really enjoyed taking photos all the time, and also making short videos where I would be documenting everything."

With a policeman as a father, Christian had always thought that he would follow in his footsteps, as the idea of helping people and caring for those in need really appealed to him.

"Since I was young, I always wanted to do something good for the people, and as my father had been a policeman, it seemed like a natural step. This is fascinating really though, as now I would not consider working for the government or for anyone else.

"Originally, I wanted to go to the police, as it was a pretty good career in Germany. Stable and well paid, and quite prestigious. Competition is very tough, though, and you have to study really hard and complete lots of fitness tests, so it makes sense to apply not just in the federal state you live in, to increase your chances of making it. So, I when we later moved to North Rhine Westphalia, I applied not just there but also to Lower Saxony. I did really well and passed all the tests, and was one of nine people who made it out of around 6,500 candidates."

But life in Germany for him had become dull and stagnant. And though the sense of a secure job with the police was very appealing, he was now bitten by the travel bug.

Though he tried to focus on other things, and managed to study and graduate from a college in media marketing, he felt an ever-growing, irrepressible desire to simply leave the country and go out and explore, while also continuing his photography and amateur film making.

"I was just really fed up with the repetitive cycle of everything. I wanted change. I just felt I wanted new sights and smells and new experiences. So, extreme as it may sound, in 2012 one day I simply decided to 'just do it', and I went ahead and sold all my belongings and then used this money to buy a one-way ticket to Australia.

"The plan was just to be there for one year. Clearly, however, it certainly did not work out that way at all. I've now been on the road for the last ten years!"

Betzmann's planned one year in Australia turned into three. In 2015, he then spent six months living in London, followed by a year in Thailand and then a year in Pakistan, something which, again, would change his life forever.

Life in Pakistan

It was in pakistan that Betzmann met Zoya Nasir, a Muslim actress and daughter of renowned script- and songwriter Nasir Adib, who holds the current world record for writing the maximum number of film scripts.

Their friendship and Betzmann's interactions with other Pakistanis, his observation of their religious practices and culture resulted in his own exploration of Islam, and finally, his acceptance of the religion as one that gave him peace.

Revelling in each other's company, Zoya and Christian made a range of entertaining clips, encouraging followers to play games, have fun and generally stay positive despite the Covid-19 lockdown restrictions imposed in those days. Their ever-expanding fan base lapped up their new videos, ever hungry for more of these fun-packed mini-clips and never knowing what they would be handed next.

But suddenly, Betzmann posted a video which no one had been expecting – certainly not his family back home – it was a clip declaring to the world that he was about to embrace Islam.

"It all started in Pakistan, when I was travelling around the north, and the plan was to travel just for one month, then move to India and Sri Lanka. But things changed. When I teamed up with Shahveer Jafry, a Pakistani social media star who had been raised in Canada, the number of followers on my YouTube channel suddenly went through the roof, so I didn't want to just suddenly move on from Pakistan.

"And then the [Covid-19] lockdown happened, so there was no way of leaving, and it meant I was now fully exposed to the life and culture and ways of my Muslim friends in Pakistan. I found it fascinating. I was exposed also to a lot of Jafry's Muslim friends and attended many Muslim weddings and I really liked what I witnessed.

"It became very clear to me that Islam is a religion of peace. I felt like it was a beautiful community. I met so many kind and really incredible people and learned a lot about Islam and also about cultural life as a Muslim.

"As a German, as I received my information through the media, the idea of Islam was always connected with negativity, war, terrorism, which is of course just wrong.

"The problem, as I see it, is what the media does with the religion, and also some people are doing with it in terms of how they interpret it. These are the ones who bring Islam into a bad light, and then the Western media focuses on these bad examples, and this then creates the impression that the whole religion is like that, which it definitely is not. So really, I guess Islam is as peaceful as you experience it, I would say."

Prayers give peace

When the lockdown was lifted, Christian and Zoya travelled to the USA for two months, where they visited Zoya's brother in Miami, and here he had a lot of discussions and kind of mentoring sessions with Zoya's brother about Islam. "I also read the Quran, and I felt very connected to all of this," he says.

Christian says there was a certain pressure on him to convert as he and Zoya were so much in the public eye because of the social media work they did, but his conversion wasn't the result of this pressure.

"This pressure was not coming directly from her family, indirectly perhaps, but there was definitely a certain social pressure for us from social media to get married and also for me to convert to Islam, as these things in Pakistan are interconnected really.

"Initially, I was not willing to do that [convert] as I am not a person who just wants to accept something I don't believe in, but, over time, I realised that I had lots and lots of questions about Islam; it had really awakened my curiosity, I genuinely wanted to know and I was really enjoying finding out so much about it. I just got the feeling that it was not just something new which I wanted to experience, but that it was really the right step for me." Christian says he had a lot of specific questions when he started studying Islam. But they were not really academic questions, rather more practical things. "So, I wanted to know, for example, how often did I have to pray, and how exactly would I have to pray. I did also read different parts of the Quran and I liked what I read. I like, for example, this verse: *"So, verily, with the hardship, there is a relief. Verily, with the hardship, there is relief"* (Quran 94:5-6)" Another favourite verse is: *"Do what is beautiful. Allah loves those who do what is beautiful"* (Quran 2:195). Christian loved this verse because it helped him appreciate how beautiful life is, and how it should be valued, and how lucky he was to be travelling around the world, learning so much by experiencing how different people live their lives. It also helped him remember, as much as is possible, to be a good person.

Zoya's brother urged him to read more about the Quran and try to experience it. "So, I did really like some parts of the Quran, and read a little background material but the bulk of my research was definitely more practical and took place simply by asking questions at every opportunity I got."

For his research, he spoke to friends whenever he had questions. "As I am a very curious person who loves travelling to new places and meeting new people and finding out about new countries and cultures and religions, I question literally anything which is new to me.

"So, I was of course constantly filled with questions, and here people answered in a very natural way. So, every time I went to an event or gathering or Muslim wedding, I gained a lot of knowledge - just by talking to friends, my girlfriend's family, to people I met, so there was no real book or article which helped me, it was really people who helped me."

So, what ideological aspects of Islam appealed to him?

"The prayers in Islam, I think, give you peace; it is like an internal manifestation of goals and dreams, and I like that you pray for your family, or your loved ones, or for the victims of natural catastrophes for example.

"I did not delve too much into studying the life of the Prophet as this is too much into history and what happened hundreds of years ago. I was not too interested in that, it is more for me the messages you can take from Islam about approaches to life, and about living a good and spiritual life, that appeals to me.

"I feel like everyone can do what feels right for them, it's everyone's life so they can decide if they want to follow any religion 100 per cent or not. I was never a super religious Christian, of course, I went to church at Christmas and things like that, so I can't directly compare Christianity and Islam, but I would say there are definitely fundamental similarities in terms of focusing on being good and being a better person.

"But now, with Islam, I have to say it felt really good becoming a Muslim, it felt like there is someone taking care of you, and watching over you, and you give your energy to that person.

"Zoya's brother was particularly helpful when it came to dealing with certain small excerpts from the Quran which would perhaps sound a bit alarming at first. By this I mean reference to killing people who were not Muslim and so forth. But here the historical and cultural context was pointed out to me, and it then became much easier to understand. And, of course, if you looked at the Bible or other religious texts then you can always find certain passages which can seem a little odd or even frightening if you take them out of context.

"So really my conversion was more of a process than an event, so it is hard to put a fixed time reference on it in terms of how long it took, but it would be I guess four to six months."

Christian's extensive travel and interactions with various cultures also had a positive impact on him. Visiting a Muslim country, he would see lots of mosques and people praying. "The impact was that it is a nice community with nice gestures, sharing the same house of God, it was nice to see this kind of community, and then the call to prayer, it was lovely to see everyone so happy, and after that they are all having chai [tea] and food together afterwards, so it's really nice."

Shahadah in Miami

Betzmann converted at The Islamic School of Miami, USA, posting a video of him saying his *Shahadah* on YouTube, as well as using social media to post his certificate of acceptance.

What were the reactions from his family and fans after the important decision?

"When I started my channel, all of my subscribers were from Pakistan so they all really loved it when I converted, it was really amazing, and it was really positive for me to see their reactions. It made me feel really good."

"Also, when I said my *Shahadah* that was almost incredible.
There were so many people who congratulated me, came up to me, shook my hand or hugged me, wished me the best. It was like you had just joined a huge loving family. I received many thousands of DMs [Direct Messages via social media] congratulating and welcoming me."

But when Christian broke the news to his family, however, he didn't quite get the same response.

"I was a little nervous about telling them at first, so I waited a while. My friends and family were really confused to begin with. Though my friends came to terms with it fairly quickly, for a while my family were just really taken aback. They just couldn't understand why I would do it, and what would ever attract me to Islam.

"I understand this though. The picture you tend to get in the media in the West just ends up making you see Islam more as something to feel nervous about, rather than something which you feel positive about and attracted to," he says.

"In Germany, Islam has been given a very bad reputation because of the media, especially with old people. What they read they don't question. But the youth is more open, because there are many Turkish people in Germany, but overall, Islam still has a bad reputation in Germany, which should be fixed.

"So even though my family are very open minded, they were just confused, they were not upset but just curious. They didn't understand it. After their initial shock and confusion, though, I have to say that my friends and family were wonderful. They just saw that this was important to me, and they decided to get behind me and accept my choice, and stand by me, and I was very grateful for that and love them for that."

So, how has his faith helped him to navigate life?

"Since I converted spiritually, I definitely feel my life has become more enlightened, I feel like I am on the right path and being guarded by Allah, and this is a wonderful thing. I feel very peaceful within myself, and that my mind is clear, and I feel I have more purpose in life now.

"I am about travelling, meeting people, experiencing life, and I am so incredibly thankful for being able to see the world and to document these beautiful new experiences. The world is a fascinating place and full of adventures.

"After all, one of my favourite parts of the Quran is: Do what is beautiful. Allah loves those who do what is beautiful. (Quran 2: 195)."

24

'I met my true self in Islam, and saw Allah's magnificence'

---◆◆◆◆---

Ilhaam Stoloff – South African artist

---◆◆◆◆---

Born to Jewish parents in South Africa, Lisa Stoloff had succumbed to the Western propaganda that Islam was dangerous, but a meeting with Rukea Akoojee changed her life. Rukea was an enlightening and inspiring presence; they spoke about difficult topics - about death, religion, politics, the purpose of life and one's relationship with God.

SOUTH African artist Ilhaam Stoloff's journey from Judaism to Islam is a story about both passion and reason. Ilhaam was born in 1969, in a small town in South Africa called Springs. Born to Jewish parents, they named her Lisa. She is one of three children, each born two years apart, neatly sandwiched between two brothers. Her father was a lawyer and her mother was a full-time homemaker. Their life was good. As she herself says: "I can't complain about my childhood."

The Stoloffs were deeply steeped in the Jewish community and Lisa and her brothers grew up in a rich tradition. Shabbat was commemorated every Friday and they went to synagogue on Saturday morning.

Lisa was always an arty child. "Ever since I can remember I was an 'artist'," she says. "I was fixated with the structures of things and forms. I wanted to capture them, represent them. I was always a seeker, a risk-taker, an explorer. I had an active imagination and I daydreamed a lot."

Once, when she was about five, they visited Kruger National Park, South Africa's most famous nature reserve and, at almost 20,000 km2, one of the biggest in Africa. "I remember there was a striking moment that I've never forgotten: We were sitting in my dad's Valiant and watching a troop of baboons and suddenly I found myself looking at my father and my mother and my brothers and feeling like there was no separation between us and the baboons outside the Valiant. I'll never forget that moment; I felt connected to them and quite foreign to my family and I remember thinking, 'What is the point of this and why are we here?' It was quite an existential moment. I wanted to know, but nobody wanted to have those conversations take place."

Lisa's family wasn't one for discussing such deeply challenging questions, she says.

No exposure to Muslims

In 1970s South Africa, it was the height of apartheid and deeply discriminatory policies and segregated areas. Lisa's Jewish community lived like most other white South Africans, not challenging the status quo, not contesting the state of affairs that privileged them and not living or mixing with other races. They were never exposed to Muslims, says Lisa. "We were really living in a different paradigm and Islam was very unknown."

Lisa and the other kids in her group, including her best friend Nicci, were all from the same background: Wealthy, white, privileged and sheltered. They all attended synagogue and *Khaida*, the Jewish equivalent of Sunday school or *madrasa*. "I saw it as a kind of punishment, that I was being forced to do it. I knew I was being taught to read Hebrew, but it seemed very disassociated from meaning."

Retrospectively, she says, what stands out for her is that the Jewish teachings seemed more about satisfying parents' needs – the need for the children to succeed at the Bar or Bat Mitzvahs, to read the ultimate Torah portion – than an actual connection with God. "I can't remember my parents ever sitting me down and having a conversation with me about God, an intimate conversation, like who is God to you and how do you experience God?" she says.

Most of the kids also belonged to Maginim, a Zionist youth movement launched in South Africa in 1977. Today it's known as Netzer. It was part of a broader international Zionist movement that was based in Jerusalem. Children from across South Africa, from the ages of 10 to 17, were part of it and attended the summer camps, which were about three weeks long.

Although Maginim was also progressive, the narrative was definitely a 'single story' that "we, as Jews, were or are the chosen people," says Lisa.

The message was that "Jews have been given the land of Israel by God and it is the land of milk and honey, and our homeland. And what was also very integral to the message is that we should aspire to go live in Israel, make Aliyah [it's the law of return where Israel permits Jews to automatically emigrate]," she says. "Throughout my upbringing and my exposure to Maginim, I was not aware of the Palestinians and Muslims in Israel. I was only aware that there were Jews in Israel."

In all of this – Maginim, great family events, the Jewish community – there was great togetherness, love and laughter, it was all well intended, says Lisa. But, she says, subconsciously things felt out of kilter for her, and that might have had to do with the growing disconnect between the religious messaging about a "whole" world, and what she saw – a very segregated world where Black people were obviously at a great disadvantage. She also struggled with puberty. These disconnects played out in her body, physically.

"When I was still living in Durban, I stopped eating. I think I didn't want to grow up. I didn't want the responsibilities of adulthood and didn't want my body to change. Puberty was a difficult experience for me, I wanted to continue being a child, so I think it was involuntary and I was trying to prevent my body from developing."

A life-changing accident

Lisa was registered at the University of Witwatersrand as an art student, and had started doing a post-graduate degree, a Higher Diploma in Fine Art. There, she excelled. In Grahamstown she presented a body of work in which she explored the rituals and concepts and lore of Judaism. She was already searching for something back then.

One painting was inspired by a *mikveh,* a body of water in which a woman immerses and cleanses herself. "I wanted to have the experience and I was allowed to immerse myself in this holy water. Then I did a painting, it was quite an abstract piece." Another piece was of a giant hog running across a landscape, which was titled *Forbidden*. All the paintings explored what is and isn't allowed in Judaism, a theme that is present throughout her life story. One of the paintings won an award.

In a November, the university closed for holidays and Lisa, one of her brothers and his girlfriend travelled to Knoetzie, one of the most beautiful coastal wilderness areas along South Africa's Garden Route. Life was good and had been pretty smooth up to this point, she acknowledges. But that was about to change.

On their way back to Johannesburg, they decided to visit one of South Africa's most famous art sites, the magical house of eccentric artist Helen Martins, the Owl House Museum. Her brother was driving, and then the moment that separated Lisa's life into "before" and "after" occurred.

The car hit a pothole. It spun out of control and launched off the road, flipping head over tail a number of times before landing by the side of the road. Lisa was in such extreme discomfort; she heard strange, strangulated, animal-like sounds coming from somewhere. Then she realized she was making them.

The two girls lay side by side, unable to move, in severe pain. It was midday – in summer, temperatures in Karoo can reach 40°C. "Sam was pouring with blood and I didn't know what I was," says Lisa, "I just know that I wished I was dead. We were unable to move and we were actually cooking in the heat. Birds of prey began circling above us."

Help arrived what felt like two hours later, says Lisa. Her brother came with an ambulance from Graaff Reinet, a small town about 50km away. The critically injured women were loaded into the back with the medic, while her brother climbed into the front with the driver.

"The back was shielded from the driver and my brother. We weren't strapped down properly – we were literally lying on hard planks and the road was bumpy and our broken bodies were bouncing up and down. We were in severe pain, and then the medic started sexually molesting us."

For the sake of brevity, what followed was traumatic in itself: Three operations, surgeries where rods were inserted into Lisa's spine, then removed, then put back in. She was in a brace and couldn't paint large canvases any longer, nor could she work for long. "The agony, the anger, the torment and sorrow were unbearable," she says.

Lisa grew obsessed with Frida Kahlo, the Mexican artist who had had a similar accident and also lived with rods in her spine, in constant pain. But Lisa's life had changed so quickly, so drastically, and she was in constant, unrelenting pain, and she felt it was too difficult. She no longer wanted to live. Still, she completed her post-graduate degree and, after that, decided to try to leave the trauma behind her. She packed her bags and left for London.

"I wanted to go away, somewhere where I could disappear. And I did disappear." From 1995 to 1997, Lisa lived in squat houses in London and joined the underground rave scene. She took lots of painkillers, ecstasy and speed, smoked hash, and was completely outrageous and out of control.

"The euphoria I felt on drugs was addictive. I didn't want to come down. I just wanted to be completely euphoric and as far away from my reality as possible. I was having ecstasy for breakfast, lunch and supper. I was also in a very intense relationship." It ended, and Lisa hit rock bottom – and had a moment of sanity.

"I realised I was either going to remain in London and be pulled out from a gutter, or I was going to leave London and try to save myself. There was a moment where I couldn't have been more hopeless or helpless, and yet there was still a candle burning inside me that was leading me towards healing." That light was leading her towards Cape Town.

A transformational course

Lisa arrived in the city in 1998, and it was here that she met Rukea Akoojee, the woman who was to change her life. She had reluctantly agreed to sign up for a transformational course – she had hated every therapy experience she'd ever had. She describes their first meeting.

"When I walked through the door of the training room, there was this woman who was very visible. She was dressed in a beautiful, flowing, white cotton hijab, and she had a long, grey plait down her back, and she was really fat," Lisa giggles. "She had such an interesting face, with a nose that came almost directly from her forehead. When I first laid eyes on her I thought, 'I really don't want to be here'."

Lisa still held prejudices against Muslims, she admits. Although there are many Muslims in London, Cape Town was the first place where she had experienced Muslims in bigger numbers. "I think I had succumbed to the Western propaganda that Islam was dangerous, that Muslim men were misogynistic, that Muslim women were oppressed."

It was with this mindset that she met Rukea and thought, "What can she possibly teach me?" That was until Rukea opened her mouth and began the training. "This was a huge turning point for me," says Lisa. "She demonstrated such power, enlightenment, humour and strength, and everything that I had thought that Muslim women were not, and it made me sit back and start questioning my positionality. It made me realise the degree to which I had been constructed socially, and how I had just bought into this construction."

Although she didn't know it, Lisa had been craving release from her pain, to feel innocent and natural again, to experience her true nature without all the complications and excesses of her past. Rukea recognised this, states Lisa. "Rukea later said that when she saw me walk into the training room, she could see I was in such pain that my eyes were bleeding, they were bleeding spiritually. She pushed her thumbs into the beds of my eyes hard and the physical pain was unbearable, but she kept on until the screams turned into more screams and more screams, and until that layer of pain had been unravelled from me. And then the cries started. I found that something so radical had happened to me. I didn't understand it, but it was unmistakable." After that, she just wanted to be near the woman who had created this shift in her.

"It was me, really, that gate-crashed Rukea's life, because … she helped me release a lot of my physical and emotional pain, and the shame of the choices I had made that really took me down a very dark road. I felt that she helped me take the cork off the pressure that was actually in my body, and for the first time I could actually experience my breath again… I felt innocent again."

Lisa took more courses, each time releasing more of her past trauma. The sessions were a deeply collaborative healing space, she says, in which Rukea helped each participant understand themselves and facilitated a deeper self-knowledge.

Long conversations about life

Lisa became part of Rukea's family, often seeking her guidance. "The more time I spent with her, the more my heart started becoming more absorbent and just open to this thing that I didn't understand previously, this thing called Islam." They used to have long conversations. "We spoke about the difficult things, the disturbing conversations. We spoke about our death deeply. We had long conversations about religion, about sex, about politics, and about the purpose and point of our lives as individuals, as a group of people, as humanity. We spoke in depth about our relationship with God, and about our relationship with ourselves, like, who are we in all of this?"

Lisa loved Rukea's open home and the warmth and spirit of the community she lived in, the humour and straightforwardness. "I'd never experienced anything like it. The way they expressed themselves was so refreshing. It was so honest and authentic, in such a relieving way. It relieved me that I could be real… and that made me want even more of it."

She felt this was in stark contrast to her own family and the Jewish community, where there was a pretence that everything was alright. Things there were swept under the carpet and confrontation was avoided.

"I think that the pretence became us," she says. "The family, my particular context within my family structure, was very 'there's things we don't talk about, we don't discuss death and we don't discuss the way you get on my nerves because it hurts me. And we don't discuss apartheid and we don't discuss sex, religion and politics'."

One night, Rukea invited Lisa to a prayer meeting. "I walked in and she gave me hijab because that's what I needed to wear. There were a few circles of people sitting down wearing hijab, men and women … It incorporates Allah's 99 names, and so you say it in a repetitive style. And through repetition and breathing and through the oneness of the group that you are making *dhikr* with, there is an experience of such connectedness with one another, and with Allah. I felt like I'd come home.

"When I heard the Arabic, the sound of Allah's words over and over and over again, and with such meaning and connection, it awakened something inside of me I had never heard: It was God being uttered with such praise and love and connectedness and exaltation and depth of meaning that Allah became for me the only God. It just went right through me and I just couldn't think of God in any other way after that, as than Allah."

When Lisa made *Salaah* before becoming Muslim, she joined the Jama'ah (group prayer). What moved her about the prayers was the act, supplicating and putting her head on the *mussalah* (the prayer mat). She loved the idea of being able to connect directly with Allah wherever one is. "The method of praying appealed to me, the act of *sujud* [touching the forehead on the ground] had a 'rightness' – it made me feel like I was humbling myself and that felt very, very appropriate."

Learning to face death

In her journey to Islam, she also learnt to face death. She accompanied Rukea to wash the bodies of a few deceased women. "It was the first time I was exposed to the dead. This had an enormous impact on me. I was struck by the dignified way in which the body was washed and wrapped in cotton and prepared with camphor and rose petals. The fact that the body was in their own home when being prepared for burial, with family present, praying for them to be granted a high place in paradise [Jannah]. The realness of it, the tangibility of the experience. I felt like this experience demystified the notion of death for me and I became less afraid of it."

One day, Lisa accompanied Rukea to Gatesville, a shopping centre in Rylands, a suburb in Cape Town with a big Muslim community. They walked into a shop selling Islamic paraphernalia, everything from hijabs to fragrant *attars* and, inexplicably, the shop keeper gave Lisa a copy of Quran. Later that day, she opened the holy book for the first time in her life, and had what can only be described as a vision.

"I just remember I was reading a verse about the Quraysh, a tribe in Makkah, and my whole body just went completely weak… There was a very, very strong voice in my mind, body and soul that said, 'Go to the mirror'. So I walked to the mirror and when I looked at myself, the mirror disintegrated and I was standing in front of my true self. I was not an illusion in the mirror, I was me. In that moment, I met myself for the first time, my true self, and I was completely overwhelmed and awestruck by my own beauty and my innocence and my purity and the miracle that I was. I was just touching myself all over my face and crying like a baby, and that's when I knew I was Muslim."

She began reading books Rukea gave her. There were two more mystical experiences that moved her closer to conversion. One night after the mirror vision, she was falling asleep when she became aware of an internal chanting: *"Bismillah Hir Rahman nir rahin"* [In the name of Allah, the most gracious and the most merciful]. She fell asleep to the rhythm of the chant, and when she woke up it was still going. Then she had a dream.

"I was swimming underneath and through the sweetest, sweetest milk and I was swimming to Allah," she says. It was so profound that she cried, non-stop, for ten days "…because I was experiencing the honey. The closeness that I was experiencing with Allah, the connectedness, was very, very deep, it was overwhelming. I was in a state of ecstasy. Rumi even refers to being drunk with Allah's love – it can make you go mad," she explains. "I really felt like I was seeing things for the first time, like veils had been removed from my eyes, and it was so painful because it was so majestic and exquisite."

There was no going back. Lisa felt she couldn't undo what had happened, it was too powerful. About ten days after meeting herself as a Muslim, in the year 2000, she said her *Shahadah* and took the name Ilhaam, meaning inspiration or intuition. Rukea's husband, Abd Abdul Samad, was her *Wakeel* (witness), and Rukea's brother, whom everyone called uncle Archie, was also present.

"He was singing 'Happy birthday' to me very loudly, because it's believed that when you say your Shahadah you are like a new- born baby. I'll just never forget his joyfulness and happiness."

'I will never see or speak to you again'

Her family were appalled. She had let her brothers and parents know beforehand. Her father begged her not to do it, to try to find what she was looking for in Judaism. But she explained to him that she had done that, she had even gone for Kabbalah classes, but she simply couldn't find herself there. There were weeks of emails between family members, between Lisa and her mother in particular, talking about the decision and how it would change them as a family. A cousin, a female rabbi based in Jerusalem, called her and said, "I don't know why you've done what you've done, I don't understand it. Know that I will always love you, but I will never see or speak to you again."

It was very painful, says Lisa. Her family couldn't recognise her, and she recognises that that was because, in her first ten years of Islam, she was very staunch, fanatical even. She was all passion. "I needed to immerse myself in every aspect of it, which I did. And I think I was unrecognisable," she says. "I think that when it became apparent to me that there was another truth, that, for me, was very massive."

She saw herself in Islam, and she felt that she had a direct connection with Allah's greatness through the religion. "The more I could connect with myself, the more magnificent He became. From my smallness, I was experiencing Allah's greatness." It made sense to her.

Ilhaam performed Hajj in 2004, which was "completely life changing and I do believe that it changed me and instilled in me a gratitude that I could never imagine I could feel. I feel I walk with gratitude every single day and I feel I found my purpose in Hajj. I feel that as a Muslim, as a person that submits to God's will, I live that every day because I'm committed to serving humanity. My purpose is to inspire people to connect with who they truly are, to help people connect with themselves, because I believe that once you connect with yourself, it's hard not to find God there. That's where your God-connection is."

Respect for women in Islam

Now her journey with Islam is changing, still growing. She is beginning to explore reason more. For example, how does she reconcile many Islamic practices with being a feminist? "The way I see Islam regarding women," she says, "is to hold women in extremely high regard. Even the Prophet Muhammad, peace be upon him, had such enormous love and respect for Khadija, his first wife, who was a successful businesswoman. He did not direct her to stop being a businesswoman."

The thing that she explored about Judaism in her art as a young woman, what is permissible and what is not, she struggles with in Islam, too. For Ilhaam, there is a distinction between culture and religion. Many of these aspects – many with regard to women – are cultural. "I struggle with cultural colonisation, cultural codes, the concept of 'the way things are done', the expectations that are all ascribed within a culture that one doesn't or cannot question. There can be alternatives. Even just being able to have a conversation about culture and religion – they do overlap, but they can be separated and one has to be quite discerning to see where the separation is."

Take the hijab, for instance. "I'm very aware that the hijab is probably the most contested item of clothing in this world. It's unbelievable actually." She points out that women wear the hijab for many different reasons.

"I wear the hijab … because of the way it makes me feel: Protected from my own *an-nafs al'-ammarah*, my own lower self – knowing where I've come from, knowing my trauma response, knowing how dark my road was after my accident. It makes me feel in balance, it reminds me of the presence of Allah. But," she adds, "nowhere in the Quran does it say that a woman must wear a hijab – it says that they must cover their bosom and lower their gaze. If you look at all the Biblical women they were all wearing scarves, Mary, Sarah, the Jewish and Christian women, yet it doesn't say that in the holy books. It's a cultural law that has become enmeshed in the religion."

She is exploring new schools of thought about Islam, mostly from women who are academics and activists such as Blair Imani and Irshad Manji, who argue for a reformist interpretation of Islam and the right to engage honestly and critically on issues without polarisation. They argue for the right to reason, the balance to passion. Ilhaam doesn't believe in violating human rights on any level, and that freedom of choice is vital.

Firm belief

Ilhaam will never leave Islam, she says. It is the truth that is "my way to the water, and Islam does provide a method to guide me to the water. I relate to the method that Islam provides, the five pillars of Islam, the *Shahadah*, daily prayer, charity, fasting and Hajj." She sees herself here.

The Surahs she loves include the very first, Surah Fatiha (1:2): "The first one I had to learn off by heart as soon as I became Muslim." Another is Surah Ar-Rahman. "It's very powerful to me
… because I see Allah in everything, and nature especially, and that's when I feel very, very connected," including in her relationships.

But her favourite Surah is suitably visual for an artist, Surah Luqman (Quran 31:27):

"If all the trees on earth were pens and the ocean were ink, refilled by seven other oceans, the words of Allah would not be exhausted."

"For me, I connect so deeply with this verse not only because it's such a visual image – I can imagine every human on this planet taking a tree and dipping it into one of the seven oceans and praising Allah with words, and it's still not enough to praise Him – that's how much He ought to be praised."

Her faith in Allah, in His wondrous creation of nature and everything on earth, is deep and passionate. But the right to have challenging conversations, the right to freedom of choice, are also important. Ilhaam has always believed this. As Khalil Gibran once wrote: Both passion and reason are fundamental to balance.